Louis Prima

Music in American Life

A list of books in the series appears at the end of this book.

Louis Prima

GARRY BOULARD

University of Illinois Press
Urbana and Chicago

P76543

∞ This book is printed on acid-free paper.

Unless otherwise noted, all illustrations are from the author's collection.

Library of Congress Cataloging-in-Publication Data

Boulard, Garry.
Louis Prima / by Garry Boulard.
p. cm. — (Music in American life)
Originally published: "Just a gigolo": the life and times of Louis Prima.
Lafayette, La. : Center for Louisiana Studies, University of Southwestern
Louisiana, 1989.
Includes bibliographical references.
ISBN 978-0-252-07090-7 (pbk. : alk. paper)
1. Prima, Louis, 1910–1978.
2. Jazz musicians—United States—Biography.
I. Title.
II. Series.
ML419.P72B7   2002
784.4'165'092—dc21   2002018013

Printed and bound in Great Britain by
Marston Book Services Limited, Didcot

In memory of my father
John R. Boulard
1919-77

Contents

Illustrations follow page 140

Preface to the Illinois Paperback

A blue-tinged light slices through a fog of smoke above slender tables topped with formica. The crowd is thick with salesmen, tourists, con artists, and celebrities.

It is past midnight in the middle of the desert, an unforgiving spot made distinctive by its yellowish-brown sage and the mostly barren soil that somehow gives it life.

Just weeks before the official beginning of the Eisenhower era, in late 1952, Milton Prell, a balding, bespectacled man given to shiny suits, unveils his dream: the 276-room Sahara Hotel, a modernistic wonder fronted by tall plastic camels posing as sentinels and a handsome tan-brick pylon bearing the inn's name.[1]

Without irony, Prell, a Los Angeles jeweler, proclaims his new hotel a "Jewel of the Desert."[2]

But his publicists, working overtime, do him one better: "Come to the Garden of Allah at the Hotel Sahara," a company pamphlet entices. "Embraced by twenty acres of velvet lawns and myriad blossoms, surpassing in beauty all that the warmest imagination can anticipate. . . . Indulge your whims as you wish."[3]

Plopped down near the county line, on the almost vacant Las Vegas Strip, the Sahara is in many ways little different from the other Vegas clubs of the 1950s, each with a name that suggests whimsy and illusion in the desert city: the Flamingo, the Thunderbird, the Desert Inn, and the Tropicana.

It boasts a sea of green-carpeted gambling tables, constantly churning roulette wheels, ringing slot machines, and restaurants and lounges busy with conventioneers, cowboys, and comedians twenty-four hours a day. Like other casinos, the Sahara has an Olympic-sized outdoor pool, this one edged by two wings of rooms set off with sleek metal balconies and shaded patios.[4]

The Sahara attracts celebrities: Ray Bolger dances, John Wayne gambles, and Jimmy Durante plays golf there. Guests include—the Sahara's publicists are only too eager to reveal—Grace Kelly and solid World War II–era stars like Cary Grant and Spencer Tracy.[5]

The Sahara also provides a good view of the glow from the atomic bombs that the federal government is testing at nearby Frenchmen's Flat, explosions that Wilbur Clark of the Desert Inn—just down the Strip from the Sahara—is convinced are good for business: "I don't know exactly how much the bomb had to do with it, but around shot time the play in our casino seemed to go upward and the drinking got heavier," he later remarks.[6]

Beginning in the late fall of 1954, the Sahara proudly boasts one attraction that none of the other clubs in the city—or anywhere else for that matter—can equal: Louis Prima, a middle-aged Italian-American entertainer, adored in equal parts for his musicianship as well as his broad comic style; and Keely Smith, his young Cherokee wife, whose untrained voice, even critics who loathe Vegas admit, is a jazz natural.

At midnight, Prima and Smith—soon joined by Sam Butera, a darkly brilliant New Orleans saxophonist who handles all of the duo's scores—climb to the top of a small stage in the Sahara's Casbar Lounge.

From their elevated vantage point, Prima, Smith, Butera, and the Witnesses—Butera's backup group—can touch the lounge's pitted white tile ceiling. They gaze out on a hazy scene contained between aqua walls bearing African masks. A crowd of rowdies demands to be entertained.

The Casbar, recalled Smith, who was only twenty-five years old when she first appeared there, had a "low ceiling, poor ventilation, one spotlight, one microphone, and an upright piano—there wasn't room for a baby grand. And there was a service bar right in front of us!"[7]

But it also offered the kind of music that could not be heard anywhere else: an odd eclecticism that dared to mix rock 'n' roll with Dixieland, jazz, and swing. Some listeners were certain that Prima, Smith, and Butera were the direct descendants of Benny Goodman or even the Original Dixieland Jazz Band; others would swear they heard a little bit of Louis Armstrong in the group's style. Showing how the group confused virtually everyone, still others compared them to Little Richard and Jerry Lee Lewis.

"It was something I came up with," Butera would later bluntly declare when asked how his unique sound with Prima came to be.[8]

"Let's do a shuffle," was all Prima told him when the two men first contemplated the kind of sound they wanted to create.[9] Butera, who had enthusiastically followed Prima's career for years—he was still a schoolboy in New Orleans when Prima was already a national figure—readily agreed.

But he could not leave it there. The sounds and rhythms of too many other artists filled his head: "Dizzy Gillespie, Charlie Parker, Charlie Ventura, Vito Musso, Coleman Hawkins," Butera would later roll out the list when asked who he listened to. "I love them all. . . . But I couldn't make no money playing bebop."[10]

Now, however, Prima was promising his young charge that he would soon be making plenty of money. Prima paternalistically told Butera he should only worry about writing good scores. And with the desert sun as his constant companion, Butera suddenly saw a way to make money off of bebop, and other kinds of music too. "I took what I liked and added my own thing to it," he explained.[11]

For her part, Smith, dark-skinned and compelling beneath a pageboy haircut that would soon be a national sensation, was interesting to fans primarily because she seemed so uninterested; gazing indifferently from the stage, she could have been casually flipping through a movie magazine in a hair salon.

Women singers—think Ethel Merman and Martha Raye and Judy Garland—were expected to be up to the challenge, "belting" a blues or swing song above ferocious horns, sending music out into the middle of an audience that might be too drunk or preoccupied with the money just lost at craps to care.

But Smith did not seem to care, transforming studied cool into an "in" joke that only her devotees appreciated.

"I used to stand in front of the piano, lean up against it, fold my arms and stand there for half an hour," Smith later said.[12] As Prima, one of the last of the great cavorters in the business, gyrated his remarkably supple frame, and Butera and the Witnesses jumped and hopped—if the boys had been paid sweat equity they'd all be millionaires—Smith would continue staring until Prima, as she put it, "would come over and pull on my skirt and break my concentration."[13]

Later, in a voice that never seemed forced—indeed, the one thing critics did not like about Smith was that she never seemed to try hard enough—she would plunge into a standard, perhaps "Embraceable You," or her signature tune, "I Wish You Love," and achieve the impossible by quieting the noisy Casbar Lounge.

Five shows a night. From midnight until dawn.

"I've always lived with music; listening, playing," Prima later reflected. "And I mean all the time."[14] Prima was schooled in the same kind of trumpet that Armstrong played in New Orleans half a century before, and when he played, he could be excused if the very music that transported his audience did the same to him too.

His clean sound would greet the pink Las Vegas sky as the night turned to morning, but Louis Prima, a man with a million memories, could have been anywhere else: back in the dismal, cheap clubs he and Keely played in the late 1940s when no one cared; back in the big baroque theaters of Washington and New York during World War II when his big band had suddenly become the rage and he delighted thousands of dark-skinned, dark-haired girls, competing with an equally young Frank Sinatra for the same audience—who howled for his funny Italian novelty tunes.

But Prima went back even farther: to Fifty-second Street—Swing Street—in midtown Manhattan in 1935. He was only twenty-four years old and virtually an overnight sensation. The *New Yorker* and *Esquire* assured their erudite readership that Prima and his gang, neighborhood pals from New Orleans, were playing legitimate jazz. But the women who packed the tiny Famous Door—the same club that cut Billie Holiday—were more interested in this wavy-haired creature up from the Deep South who looked and sounded like a black man, and danced that way too.

"I grew up in a hard-working, tough, mixed New Orleans block," Prima would later reveal of the slice of city that gave life to some of the nation's most talented jazz greats, black and white. "My father worked two jobs to keep us eating. No matter who anyone was, we called them 'Mr.' and 'Ma'am'—my mother swapped food and friendship with the colored families, and I chased the parade bands and funeral processions."[15]

In the New Orleans of Prima's youth, jazz was everywhere, not the Disneyland version that tourism officials would concoct many decades later, but music with a real-life, unbordered, uncontrollable energy and sound that shot through old rotting wood-frame halls and mud-crusted tough inner-city streets where sheep, goats, and dogs wandered.

Jazz took in dozens of young men—Sharkey Bonano, with his trumpet and brown derby; Danny Barker, with his banjo and big stories; Red Allen, who was Armstrong's musical twin. These were men who would spend the rest of their lives playing music, sometimes in forgotten bars in the corner of the city, other times in stately concert halls—depending upon the whim of fortune—during most of the twentieth century.

Theirs was a generation accustomed to upheaval. Louis Nelson, who played trombone for the Sidney Desvignes Orchestra, recalled the schedule his group was forced to endure: "Every Monday we was on at the Pythian Temple, they call it the Roof Garden; and every Tuesday the Bulls Aid and Pleasure Club, and the rest of the week was for white [playing in white clubs]."[16]

Drummer Earl Palmer, landing a traveling job that kept him on the road for weeks at a time with Dave Bartholomew's big band in the late 1940s, was astonished one day to hear his wife tell him he should abandon the music business and "get a real job." "What's a real job?" Palmer wondered. "In a good week with Dave I made sixty-five, seventy dollars. That was good pay." When Bartholomew himself later told Palmer he wanted to move on to something else, Palmer spoke for hundreds of out-of-work New Orleans musicians when he remarked: "Bullshit. This my only job!"[17]

For some musicians, the constant pressure to find a good-paying gig was too much. George Guesnon angrily put down his banjo in 1960 upon hearing of the lucrative contracts enjoyed by Al Hirt and Pete Fountain. "All this while the true creators of this art are playing for nickels and dimes," he complained.[18]

It was no wonder that Prima, almost from the time he organized his first group—Prima's Kid Band, in 1920—wanted not just to be in the business, but to *survive* in it as well. As Satchmo himself knew too well, frequently that meant being not only a good musician but a funny one too.

In the early 1930s at the Beverly Gardens, a suburban New Orleans club, Prima arranged for the black Earl Palmer, then only five or six years old and already a tap dancer, to interrupt him while he was talking to the whites-only audience between songs.

When Palmer did, Prima would exclaim: "Go away, boy, you're bothering me. I'm trying to talk."

But Palmer would continue to tug on his sleeve, until Prima finally would ask: "What do you want?"

Then Palmer would deliver the punch line: "Daddy, Mama wants you on the telephone!"

This was daring enough for Southern audiences weaned on warnings against race-mixing, but Prima would take things one step further when he introduced Palmer's dance troupe as "Hats, Coats, and Pants." Then, pointing to Palmer, he'd add: "And this is my son Buttons!"[19]

"We learned about music and jazz and show business," Prima would say. "Right along with learning how to get along with people."[20]

That approach—happily mixing jazz and show business—worked for Prima over the lifetime of his career. "We play the way we feel," he admitted decades later. "With good-time music and improvisation. They're as much jazz as the blues, and my audience wouldn't sit still for a full show of the heavy stuff."[21]

One day in 1974, more than a half century after Prima's Kid Band, and a long thirteen years since his split from Keely, Prima was relaxing in a New Orleans lounge the afternoon before a show and observed that teenagers—during a time when acid rock was everywhere—were listening to his music, noting that they were "getting caught up in the nostalgic thing."[22] Prima seemed bemused by those who were hearing his old Capitol records with Keely Smith and Sam Butera for the first time—or listening to the even more ancient jazz swing records on Brunswick and Vocalion from the 1930s. He pointed out: "Well, you see, we kept those old numbers in our act all along."[23] The kids who were suddenly excited about Louis Prima, he added, "were just returning to our way of thinking."[24] Though prescient about many things, even Prima could not have foreseen the enormous popularity his music would enjoy yet one more time with the *children* of the rockers, beginning in the late 1990s.

Prima died in 1978, three years after lapsing into a coma while undergoing surgery to remove a brain tumor. During the course of the next two decades, the public's memory of him and his legacy grew ever fainter. His music virtually disappeared from the national airwaves, now crammed with post-Prima sounds: disco, country, rock, rap, and hip-hop.

Jazz scholars for the most part ignored him, and even his greatest albums—the Capitol recordings he and Keely made with Sam Butera and the Witnesses—were relegated to the discount bins in used record stores.

Then, beginning in 1996, an amazing thing happened.

Young swing bands—Big Bad Voodoo Daddy, the Cherry Poppin' Daddies, the Royal Crown Review—began to rediscover Prima, performing his music in tribute on new, handsomely packaged CDs. That same year the film *Big Night,* in which a fictionalized Prima is part of the plot and soundtrack, was released.[25]

In 1998, a spark was lit when the Gap clothing store chain unveiled a slickly produced national TV spot, using the actual "Jump, Jive, and Wail" recording that Prima, Smith, and Butera made for Capitol in 1956.

"People remember him fooling around on stage, his comedy," remarked the director Joe Lauro in 1999 at the time of the release of his award-winning documentary *Louis Prima—The Wildest!* "They fail to see him as a great jazz man. But the evaluation of him was done in the 60s and 70s, when he was past his prime. People finally woke up and realized how completely cool a lot of these older guys are and always were."[26]

Between 1997 and 2001 virtually all of Prima's music over the breadth of his career would find its way to a new generation of fans via a series of fast-selling CD collections.

This unlikely Prima comeback naturally sparked a new wave of interest in Keely Smith as well as Sam Butera, both of whom had continued to work and perform in the years after Prima's death. In the spring of 1999, after playing to a packed house of worshipful Prima fans at Bimbo's nightclub in San Francisco, Butera remarked: "You should see the kids at Bimbo's, they come in with their zoot suits and all of that stuff. I think it's great."[27] When Smith, who released a series of well-received CDs in the wake of the Prima revival, appeared at the House of Blues in Los Angeles one year later, more than fourteen hundred fans crammed into the club. "They knew who I was," she remarked to a reporter for the *Las Vegas Review-Journal,* "and you know what? They sang my songs with me. I'm so thrilled," Smith continued. "It's almost like it's happening to someone else—not me."[28]

In one of the most comprehensive surveys of Prima's career, David Kamp, writing in *Vanity Fair* in 1999, took note of Prima's return to national prominence and observed that the new Prima vogue "has a poignancy to it—a belated reckoning by kids reared on rock 'n' roll that they missed out on something."[29]

That yearning has proved remarkably strong: writing about the sweeping new interest in Prima, Jerry Fink, a columnist for the *Las Vegas Sun,* has concluded: "As long as we can jump and jive, Louis Prima will stay alive."[30]

The New Orleans, New York, and Las Vegas of Prima's era, of course, have gradually become invisible, chipped away by years of upheaval and neglect. Many of the haunts of Prima's youth in New Orleans are gone, as is Swing Street itself in New York. Meanwhile, the once open horizon of the Vegas Strip has thickened with high-rise hotels, condos, and casino complexes. The desert town of lonely hearts and broken dreams is now Anywhere USA.

Yet somehow, beyond the earthly measurements of progress and time, the spirit of Louis Prima endures, electrifying a new generation at the crest of a new century, proof that truly good things can never go away forever.

Notes

1. Eugene P. Moehring, *Resort City in the Sunbelt—Las Vegas, 1930–2000* (Reno: University of Nevada Press, 2000), 75–76.

2. History of the Sahara Hotel, <www.lvstriphistory.com>, accessed June 28, 2001.

3. Sean O'Faolain, "The Coarse and Lovely History of Las Vegas," *Holiday,* September 1956, 59.

4. For more on the history of the Sahara Hotel, see the Sahara Hotel Collection, Lied Library, Special Collections, University of Nevada at Las Vegas.

5. Moehring, *Resort City,* 76.

6. Barbara Land and Myrick Land, *A Short History of Las Vegas* (Reno: University of Nevada Press, 1999), 112.

7. David Kamp, "They Made Las Vegas Swing," *Vanity Fair,* December 1999, 373.

8. Mark Meister, "Backtalk with Sam Butera," *OffBeat,* April 1999, 100.

9. Ibid.

10. Ibid.

11. ibid.

12. Mark Meister, "Backtalk with Keely Smith," *OffBeat,* June 2000, 85.

13. Ibid.

14. Philip Elwood, "Prima's Prime Memories," *San Francisco Examiner,* September 7, 1968.

15. Ibid.

16. Frank Driggs and Harris Lewine, *Black Beauty, White Heat—A Pictorial History of Classic Jazz, 1920–1950* (New York: Morrow, 1982), 36.

17. Tony Scherman, *Backbeat—Earl Palmer's Story* (Washington, D.C.: Smithsonian Institution Press, 1999), 75.

18. Driggs and Lewine, *Black Beauty, White Heat,* 35.

19. Scherman, *Backbeat,* 17.

20. Elwood, "Prima's Prime Memories."

21. Ibid.

22. Newton E. Renfro, "Move to N.O. Considered by Band Leader Prima," *Times-Picayune,* March 11, 1974.

23. Ibid.

24. Ibid.

25. Kamp, "They Made Las Vegas Swing."

26. Jerry Fink, "CineVegas to Show Documentary on the Legendary Louis Prima," *Las Vegas Sun,* December 6, 1999.

27. Meister, "Backtalk with Sam Butera."

28. Norm Clarke, "Diva of Swing Keely Smith Thrilled to be Hip with the 'Kids,' " *Las Vegas Review-Journal,* May 1, 2000.

29. Kamp, "They Made Las Vegas Swing."

30. Fink, "CineVegas to Show Documentary on the Legendary Louis Prima."

Preface

This book is the result of a love of Dixieland, swing, Big Band and rock n' roll music. In his nearly fifty years as a performer, Louis Prima, embodied all of these musical influences. A New Orleans musician who won national acclaim in New York in the mid-1930s, Prima has been criticized frequently by jazz scholars who believe he wandered too far astray from his hometown's musical roots. Because of this critical objection to Prima's career direction, there are relatively few scholarly articles or critiques of his work. This lack of critical information on Prima makes any profile of his career and life a difficult task.

To fill in the gaps, I have attempted to make this book more of a "pure biography" rather than a critical biography which analyzes a subject in a scholarly fashion. My goal has been to humanize history by narrating a life story; in this case, the story of Louis Prima.

Although Prima was not written about with any great regularity throughout his career, I have found much information concerning his whereabouts in such music magazines as *Variety, The Billboard, Down Beat,* and *Metronome.* I have also relied upon a number of biographical profiles of Prima and interviews with him in a number of metropolitan newspapers. In obtaining access to these articles I am indebted to Lori Pike with the *Los Angeles Times;* Bernadine Aubert, *Detroit Free Press;* Mary Jo Crowley, *Philadelphia Inquirer;* Gay Nemit, *Miami Herald;* Linda McMullen, *Las Vegas Sun;* Glenda Harris, *Las Vegas Review-Journal;* Lucy Morey, *San Francisco Chronicle* and *San Francisco Examiner;* and Elmaria Keslo, *New York Post.*

In search of documented material, I sought information in files and old scrapbooks of libraries, special collections, and music archives. Among those who helped me, special thanks goes to Don Marquis, curator, New Orleans Jazz Museum; Don Morgenstern, director, Rutgers University's Institute of Jazz Studies; Richard Allen, curator, William Ransom Hogan Archive of Jazz, Tulane University; Wilbur "Bill" Meneray, director, Rare Books and Manuscripts in the Special Collections Division of Tulane's Howard-Tilton Memorial Library; Dorothy Swerdlove, curator, Billy Rose Theatre Collection, New York Public Library; Paula M. Sigman, assistant archivist, Walt Disney Archives, Burbank, California; Lorraine Accardo, director, American-Italian Renaissance Foundation in New Orleans; Wayne Everard, archivist, Louisiana Collection, New Orleans Public Library; and D. Clive Hardy, director, Special Collections, Earl K. Long Library, University of New Orleans.

I was also given valuable background information on Italian-American culture and life in New Orleans by Evans Casso of the *Italian-American*

Digest and Bruno A. Arcudi, editor, *Italian Americana,* SUNY at Buffalo. Assisting me in reviewing secondary source material was Mary Elizabeth Yordy, Tulane University Microfilm Department, Howard-Tilton Memorial Library and Banny Rucker, director, Interlibrary Loans, Las Vegas City Library.

The real spirit of this book, though, comes in the memories, observations, criticisms, and scrapbooks of Prima's friends, relatives, associates, sidemen, and critics. A word of thanks for their kind assistance and information must be given to the late Leon Prima and his wife Madelyn; Frank Federico, Louise Pollizi; Louis Masinter; film historian David Chartok; Alma Ross; Gia Maione; Ralph Cooper of the Apollo Theatre; Bob Pepitone; Barbara Belle; Keely Smith; Lou Sino, Jr.; Joseph Segreto; Joyce Prima; Jimmy Vincent; Keith Rush; Arnold Shaw; John Bentley of radio station WWIW-AM in New Orleans; and D. Pierce of WYES-12, New Orleans' PBS affiliate.

For his time and generous interest in editing and reviewing my manuscript, I also thank Michael Enright, a reporter with the *Frederick News-Post* in Frederick, Maryland. And, of course, this list of acknowledgements would not be complete until I mentioned my wife, Anne Compliment, who listened with me to dozens of Prima songs on record, edited parts of this manuscript, and was always there when I needed support or advice. She now knows more about Louis Prima than I believe she ever thought possible in a lifetime. And despite all of this, she is still talking to me!

I have tried to make *Just A Gigolo* a pure biography. Of course, the question remains, how can anyone make a figure like Louis Prima more lively than he already was? Prima was a wild man, and today all we have are his albums of recorded tunes and old film clips of his movie shorts and television appearances. Based upon the recollections of his friends and associates, as well as through observing him in action in various film settings, I soon concluded that Prima was also something of an enigma. Even his closest friends admitted that they never really "knew" Louis. This makes the task of humanizing a man who has been dead for more than ten years all the more difficult. I don't know how close I have come to capturing the real Louie on paper, but I do know that his music, which tends to grow on you, is sometimes highly autobiographical. Because of this I suggest the perfect accompaniment to this biography might be a Prima album or two—reissues from Capitol originally recorded in the late 1950s are still available—and that the reader starts with such Prima classics as "Zooma Zooma," "Jump, Jive, an' Wail," "That Old Black Magic," and, of course, "Just A Gigolo."

Chapter I

"You Had to Play Trumpet"

Three themes dominated a Louis Prima performance. First was his tremendous musical showmanship, wherein he presented his artistic wares in a dizzying maze of jazz, rock, and swing rhythms. Then there was Louie's broad comic genius which exhibited itself through a slyly suggestive wit as well as through overtly slapstick humor. Finally, there was Prima's ethnic origins which came to the fore in a series of fun, nonsensical Italian novelty tunes going by such unlikely titles as "Felicia No Capricia," "Please No Squeeza Da Banana," and "Zooma Zooma."

All of these themes could be traced back to New Orleans, the home of American jazz, and, on December 7, 1910, the birthplace of Louis Leo Prima. Nineteen ten is a good year to start. In that year New Orleans was a teeming, wide-open, fun-loving town with a sanctioned neighborhood of bordellos. Live, uninhibited jazz was played in the streets. More people of Italian and Sicilian descent lived within the city's borders than in any other city in the United States. By 1910, there were more than 150,000 Italian residents calling Louisiana their home. The immigrants arrived by the thousands, sometimes on a weekly basis. Observing one such "immigrant-freighted vessel," a writer for the New Orleans *Daily Picayune* reported:

> As it gradually came closer and closer to the shore and recognition was possible from ship to landing, and terra firma to the floating mass, there arose a chorus of excited yells, queries, exclamations, and calls in a high-pitched vernacular, that was positively deafening. And the gyrations of arms, heads and the bodily contortions which, strangely, seemed to be indispensable with the exchanges of greeting among some of the Latin races, were enough to cause any sedate and practical onlooker to fear that a limb or two of the most vehement of the excited performers would suddenly be severed and fly off.[1]

---

[1]Luciano K. Iorizzo and Salvatore Mondello, *The Italian Americans* (Boston, 1980), p. 140; Evans Casso, *Staying In Step: A Continuing Italian Renaissance* (New Orleans, 1984), p. 26; New Orleans *Daily Picayune*, October 25, 1898.

In retrospect, New Orleans was a likely destination for the arriving Italians. The city had a Mediterranean culture and love of gambling, feasts, and music—all staples of life in the old country. In addition, the weather was perfect: "In longitudinal terms, barely a few degrees separate the two sections," one author noted of New Orleans and Sicily. "Both were relaxed by soft trade winds from nearby seas. Similarities like this spurred resettlement." Almost a century later a writer noted the family names printed in large letters and set in tile fronting some French Quarter residences: "They're names like Giacomo, Paterno, and Palermo . . . They're clearly and unmistakably Italian."[2]

The Italians settled in an industrious, crowded section of the French Quarter dubbed "Little Palermo." The streets here were muddy and livestock ran loose. Fruit vendors, door-to-door salesmen, and organ grinders filled the city air with their calls. It was here also that the Italians and Sicilians owned or managed countless corner grocery stores, were employed in hundreds of menial labor slots, and took over a number of inner-city Catholic churches and schools.

Although their rise to positions of status in New Orleans was steady and slow, the Italians did meet with a measurable amount of hatred from those who represented the city's ruling elite. One critic in the years before Louis Prima's birth said Little Palermo was

> an area of gin, cheap wine, and dope. . . . There were scenes that duplicated Naples and Palermo—long lines of family wash hanging out on once-lovely iron lacework balconies . . . half-naked children . . . old, dark, fat men and women sleeping on their stoops . . . the odor of garlic and rotten fruit everywhere.[3]

When Louis Prima's parents, Anthony Prima and Angelina Caravella—both second-generation Italian-Americans whose families had immigrated from Sicily in the 1870s—first met one another, New Orleans was in the throes of a nasty anti-Italian campaign. Reactionary sentiments had sprung forth in the spring of 1890 when the New Orleans chief of police was murdered on a New Orleans street. His reported final words—"The dagos did

---

[2]Ronald L. Morris, *Wait Until Dark—Jazz and the Underworld, 1880-1940* (Bowling Green, Ohio, 1980), p. 84; New Orleans *Times-Picayune*, March 17, 1979.

[3]Robert Tallant, *The Romantic New Orleanians* (New York, 1950), pp. 308-309.

it"—set off a vicious vendetta resulting in the death of ten Sicilian murder suspects by an angry crowd of New Orleans uptown whites determined to keep the new immigrants in their place.

Even the popular journals of the day encouraged such acts of violence. The *New York Times* was perhaps typical when it called the New Orleans Sicilians "Sneaky and cowardly . . . the descendents of bandits and assassins who transported to this country the lawless passions and cut-throat practices" of their native land.[4]

The white gentry was perhaps further angered by the unwillingness of many Italians to join in the effort to suppress black Louisianians. While native-born white New Orleanians quickly and enthusiastically answered the calls of racial hatred, many Italians ignored such pleas, creating what one historian would call a "hindrance to white solidarity in Louisiana." Noting that many Italians were willing to work in the state's sugarcane fields—a demanding task usually relegated to blacks—the historian added: "Apparently the new-comers were not so sensitive about their work that they could not begin at the bottom and work up. Their comparative lack of prejudice and their economic status fitted them for Populism, which was proposing that both whites and Negroes look with less prejudice at their mutual problem of making a living." Another scholar, this time in the *Italian Americana*, observed that "Italians, not schooled in the racial prejudice of the South, associated freely with the blacks, going against the accepted social order."[5]

In the middle of this churning mixture of ethnic pride and hatred were the Primas and Caravellas, two of the many first-generation Italian-American families in New Orleans who settled in or near the dense French Quarter. First appearing in New Orleans' city directory in 1884, various members of the Prima clan worked as fruit vendors, drivers, salesmen, and even in a macaroni factory. Louis' father, Anthony, was born in New Orleans in 1887, married before he was twenty, and in 1913 became a city-wide distributor for Jumbo Soda Pop, the most popular beverage produced by the World Bottling Company. Anthony, a massive man with a passive disposition, was also a workhorse and a thoroughly dependable employee.

---

[4] Iorizzo and Mondello, *The Italian Americans*, pp. 83-88.

[5] George Cunningham, "The Italian, A Hindrance to White Solidarity in Louisiana, 1890-1893," *Journal of Negro History*, (1965), 24-25; Paolo Girodana, "Italian Immigration to the State of Louisiana: Its Causes, Effects, and Results," *Italian Americana*, (1977), 172.

His sons would grow to be wealthy and nationally known, but Anthony stayed on the job at the World Bottling Company until his retirement in the early 1950s. Louis' mother, Angelina Caravella, was the loquacious daughter of Louis Caravella, a barber who worked outside of the French Quarter. Like the Primas, the Caravellas were vibrant embodiments of the work ethic: cousins Bernard and John Caravella sold oysters in the late 1880s until Bernard became a shoemaker in 1891. Another Caravella, Dominick, worked as an "oyster opener" throughout the 1890s.[6]

The daughter of a barber and the son of a fruit vendor, Anthony Prima and Angelina Caravella were married near the turn of the century and settled in a wood-frame house at 1812 St. Peter Street in a neighborhood populated with fellow Italians, Arabs, Jews, and blacks.

In the early years of Anthony and Angelina's marriage, social life centered around religious holidays celebrated at St. Ann's Catholic Church between North Roman and North Prieur streets, four blocks from the Prima household on St. Peter Street. A large, ornate white stucco building, St. Ann's was the home of colorful religious celebrations, not the least of which was the annual St. Joseph's Day festivities in the spring. Every year the congregation at St. Ann's took note of the holiday by constructing elaborate altars in their homes laden with a large amount of Italian candies and foodstuffs. The Prima household, and dozens of other Italian homes, hung a freshly cut evergreen branch outside their front door to announce the presence of the altar and invite fellow Italian Catholics to visit, enjoy a sampling of the baked delicacies, and remember St. Joseph, honored for centuries because he was said to have provided food for starving Sicilians in the Middle Ages.[7]

The energy and preparation that went into St. Joseph's Day symbolized the role that religion played in the New Orleans Italian community. All of the Prima children were baptized at St. Ann's—Leon, their first boy, in 1907; Louis in 1910; and two daughters, Elizabeth and Marguerite, in the

---

[6]*Soards' New Orleans City Directory* (New Orleans, 1884), p. 619. Joseph Prima is listed as a "macaroni manufacturer" in 1890. *Ibid.*, p. 726. Anthony and Leonardo were fruit vendors in 1892. *Ibid.*, p. 659. Anthony is listed as a driver for the World Bottling Company beginning in 1913 and continuing until 1949. *Ibid.*, 1913, p. 927; 1949, p. 1001. See also the *Times-Picayune*, April 18, 1961; and the New Orleans *States-Item*, April 17, 1961. Bernard and John Caravella are listed as selling oysters in 1890. *Ibid.*, p. 222. In 1891 Bernard is listed as a shoemaker. *Ibid.*, p. 214. Louis is listed as a barber in 1892. *Ibid.*, p. 209. And Dominick Caravella is an "oyster opener" in 1901. *Ibid.*, p. 181. See also the *Times-Picayune*, January 8, 1965; and the *States-Item*, January 8, 1965.

[7]*New Orleans Magazine*, March 1986.

years shortly before the beginning of World War I in 1917. Youngest daughter Marguerite died at the age of three.

Despite the tragedy of Marguerite's death, the Prima family home was generally remembered as a happy place. There were regular family dinners, music, laughter, and lavish Italian meals prepared with great care by Angelina, whose kitchen was usually packed with stuffed meats, Italian cheese, jars of herbs and seasonings, large cans of tomatoes, and a variety of hand made pastas. The dominant personality in the Prima household, Angelina reveled in her reputation as a great cook and considerate hostess. Almost nightly, neighbors and relatives came by for a sampling of her dishes. "I cook by ear," Angelina joked when asked for a particular recipe. She said she didn't bother with recipes and that she never prepared a meal for fewer than fifteen people at one time: "I'm used to big families," she proudly noted.[8]

During these meals in which families and friends would sit shoulder-to-shoulder at a long table in the Prima dining room, all matters of finance and fortune would be thoroughly discussed and settled. Papa Anthony, sitting like a reigning monarch at the end of the table, teased his guests and gloried in Angelina's attentions. "Kid," Anthony called out to Angelina, "Give me the left-overs." Angelina piled the final spaghetti helping on the plate of her three-hundred pound husband as Anthony turned to a visitor and winked: "The closest I ever got to Kid is when she hung her underwear next to mine on the wash line."[9]

Anthony's quiet bearing served him well in the labor and merchant environment of Little Palermo where fights were quick to begin and sometimes bloodily concluded. One night, sitting alone in a neighborhood tavern, Anthony was taunted by a drunken, punchy sailor. "Who needs all of these loud-mouthed wops?" the man yelled. Anthony listened for awhile, finished his beer, and then walked over to the man and picked him up in one forceful bear hug. He plopped the surprised sailor down on a faraway stool, quickly quieting the jester and sending the rest of the tavern patrons into delighted laughter.[10]

---

[8]*New Orleans Item*, undated clipping, ca. 1950.

[9]Madelyn Prima interview, July 1986.

[10]Leon Prima interview, May 1984.

But such displays of machismo were rare for Anthony. Papa Prima was sedentary and patient. Friends thought him quiet, but friendly, the sort of neighbor who would smile and wave to both friends and strangers alike. "Papa was a kind man," Louis remembered. "He always tried to help people. If there was a raffle for a widow with eight kids, Papa took 40 cents of chances. Mama would say 'Tony Prima, why waste your money? You never win.' But one day Papa won a raffle. He won a goat, a live goat. He brought it home on the streetcar. Mama saw Papa coming with the goat and she said, 'Tony Prima, don't you dare bring that goat in my house.' So Papa gave the goat to the Arabs down the street and the Arabs ate the goat."[11]

At the other end of the emotional scale stood Angelina, volatile and emotionally explosive. A slender woman with a pronounced Roman nose, Angelina handled all of the family fortunes, gave Anthony a pocketful of coins to get through the week, and freely dispensed advice to those who sought such wisdom and even those who did not.

Years later two New Orleans sociologists noted the role women like Angelina played regarding their daughters in Little Palermo: "Be careful about spoiling the child," the Angelinas of this tightly woven world warned. "Stay away from boys, they are only after one thing," she might say to her daughter. This was Angelina—anxious, curious, energetic, and verbose. The matriarch of St. Peter Street. She hovered over her children, fretting about their likely prospects for success in America, worrying about their health. To ward off the dangers of disease—in 1900 New Orleans was reportedly the only major city in the western world without a sewer system—Angelina concocted homemade remedies designed to keep her offspring healthy and resilient.[12]

Outside of her role as the nominal head of the Prima family, Angelina spent an extraordinary amount of time at St. Ann's organizing special religious entertainment programs and feasts. She was expansive and willing to take on a dozen voluntary church chores. In time, the Catholic church played such a strong role in the Prima family that daughter Elizabeth joined a local convent in the late 1920s.

[11]*Philadelphia Inquirer*, June 20, 1974.

[12]Anthony Margavio and Jerome Salomone, *Perspectives on Ethnicity in New Orleans* (New Orleans, 1981), p. 79; William Ivy Hair, *Carnival of Fury: Robert Charles and the New Orleans Race Riot of 1900* (Baton Rouge, 1976), pp. 69-70.

For Louis—the baby boy of the family and the center of Angelina's attentions—the church held an attraction of a different sort. It was at St. Ann's that Angelina showed Louis the fundamentals of show business with her suggestive musical act that she lovingly called "Sadie Green, the Vamp of New Orleans." Her voice ringing out in a pretty, if somewhat jarring, contralto, Angelina gave spirit to her songs. She danced and mugged for the audience and little Louis sat near the stage mesmerized. Angelina even had her own formula for show business success: "Always smile," she told her children. "People want to see that you're having a good time."[13]

But even if Angelina's dominance and the influence of St. Ann's were stabilizing forces in Louis' life, they were the exception. Throughout Little Palermo were murders, marriages, fights, death, and the departure of family members who might seek out a better life working in the sugarcane fields of southern Louisiana. The outbreak of war in 1917 proved to be only one more cataclysmic event for the Italians of New Orleans. Many young men left their families to fight in the conflict, while some young women lost employment opportunities when the federal government closed the infamous red-light district of Storyville. New Orleans was a port town, the feds argued, and too many embarking and departing soldiers would be tempted to visit and take part in the attractions offered by the large neighborhood of bordellos.[14]

It was also in 1917 that Angelina plotted her own upheavals. Already she had broken with one early Sicilian tradition that required sons and daughters to help the family economically even at the expense of formal schooling. Angelina demanded instead that her children attend the public schools and was further bolstered in her convictions by her own interest in education. "She taught herself to read and write English," Louis later proudly noted. One evening Angelina pushed what she hoped would be her offspring's immersion into the culture of the new country by announcing that Leon, Louis, and Elizabeth were going to take music lessons and become musicians. They would perform in threesomes, she told them, at St. Ann's festivals, and they should learn the classic, symphony pieces that Americans seemed to enjoy. Soon Leon and Elizabeth were playing piano,

---

[13]"Louis Prima—The Chief," *WYES-TV*, Channel 12, New Orleans, Louisiana. Written by John Byer. Originally broadcast in 1983, Leon Prima interview, May 1984.

[14]John V. Baiamonte, Jr., *Spirit of Vengeance—Nativism and Louisiana Justice, 1921-1924* (Baton Rouge, 1986), pp. 12-15.

while Angelina selected Louis as the family violinist. "We never did anything real hard," brother Leon said. "But we played for Mama. And we learned a lot, after awhile. Especially with chord progressions."[15]

Within a month after Louis started violin lessons he constructed his own version of the string instrument by tying a discarded mandolin string to a wooden cigar box. But Louis disliked both his creation and the more traditional version of the violin almost instantly, later joking that he wished he had made a cigar box out of a violin "instead of a fiddle out of a cigar box." Louis said he played the violin "Because my mother done 'tole' me," revealing his lack of enthusiasm for the instrument.[16]

Both boys, in fact, were growing increasingly restive until Leon, within a year of Angelina's order to begin musical lessons, declared one day he was quitting piano and taking up the cornet. If Angelina accepted Leon's decision, she adamantly drew the line when Louis proposed the same idea several weeks later. "Just stay with it." Louis acquiesced to his mother's wishes, but playing the violin during his adolescences was an exercise in frustration. "I wasn't making it with the violin because I was playing all of that 'long hair' stuff," Louis recalled. When his classmates at Jesuit Junior High School selected him as leader of the class band, largely because he was one of the few students to own his own instrument, Louis grew even more despondent. Even worse, Louis won, in 1921, first prize in an amateur fiddle contest, receiving $10.00 for his efforts.[17]

But none of this seemed to matter. There was a newer and more lively sound being played in New Orleans. Some called it "jazz," and Louis, liking the music instantly, wanted to be part of it. In 1923, when he was sixteen, brother Leon began to land jobs playing his cornet in French Quarter jazz pubs. Louis was ecstatic. He listened to Leon practice in the day and play professionally at night. This, at long last, was the music he yearned to play. Louis became obsessed with Leon's prowess on the horn. "I followed Leon and the boys in his jazz band around," Louis remembered, referring to a small group of young musicians Leon played with. "Leon got me started pretty young," said Louis in explaining his lifelong addiction to jazz. "I used to hear clarinetist Leon Roppolo, Jack Teagarden, Sid

[15]*Philadelphia Inquirer*, June 20, 1974; Leon Prima interview, May 1984.

[16]*The New York Times Autobiographical Service*, August 1978; story by syndicated journalist Betty Brown, 1945, uncited clipping.

[17]Leon Prima interview, May 1984; *Schnectady Gazette*, July 24, 1974.

Arodin—can't begin to tell you the great music I heard in afternoon living room sessions. And standing outside the clubs . . . when I was too young to get in."[18]

The problem with this new musical expression was that it challenged Louisiana's rigid racial laws. Not only were blacks prohibited from sharing restaurants, hotels, hospitals, and schools with whites, they were also forbidden to perform with whites in public. "We couldn't play publicly together," Louis said. "But the white and colored musicians listened to one another and played sessions."[19]

Yet Louis and Leon were able to blur the color lines, primarily because of their ethnic origins. As Italians in New Orleans, the Primas worked, lived, and associated freely with blacks. And it was in large part because of their ethnic origins that the Primas felt natural in viewing black musicians and entertainers as their friends. This was a part of their cultural assimilation. While the Italians and blacks in New Orleans shared economic, social, and political values, they also embodied similar entertainment rituals. One author later listed the similarities: Both the Italians and the blacks played music in gambling halls, both groups financially supported "itinerant musicians" who travelled from town to town, both enjoyed and participated in music played at funerals as well as weddings, and, finally, both groups shared a vision of what music represented: "Sicilians were much like black people in seeing music as a highly personalized affair, a reflection of an individual's feelings, although born of a collective experience."[20]

In addition, the number of Italian jazz clubs in New Orleans during Prima's boyhood almost equalled the many smaller and lesser-known bars and pubs in the black sections of the city that also featured jazz. Such clubs as Matranga's, Joe Segretta's, Tonti's Social Club, and Lala's Big 25, were owned and operated by Italians, but featured both black and Italian musicians. It was a direct violation of the segregationist mores of the day, but both black and Italian musicians regularly performed together in many of these same clubs—although such combos were usually spontaneous in nature and never advertised. Author Ronald Morris put it this way: "Long

[18]*San Francisco Examiner*, September 7, 1968.

[19]*Ibid.*

[20]Morris, *Wait Until Dark*, p. 94.

before the jazz upsurge of the 1920s, blacks and Sicilians gathered together in New Orleans for the performance and promotion of jazz," he said, adding

> For both, their arrival was the direct result of conditions bordering on economic chaos. Depressions, wartime dislocations and endemic corruption and long-standing vice ruined aristocratic operators, simultaneously presenting Italians with opportunities which aided blacks, themselves pushed off the land and into the cities.[21]

By the 1920s, Sicilians such as Sharkey Bonano and Leon Roppolo were at least as well known to music lovers in New Orleans as their black musical counterparts "Satchmo" Armstrong, "Jelly Roll" Morton, and "King" Oliver. It was a dream world for an enterprising and eager-to-learn jazz fan like Prima. Everywhere he turned the sound of music filled the hazy New Orleans air.[22]

Jazz guitarist Danny Barker recalled those sounds:

> A bunch of us kids, playing, would suddenly hear sounds. The sounds of men playing would be so clear, but we wouldn't be sure where they were coming from. So we'd start running, start trotting—'It's this way!' 'It's that way!'—and sometimes, after running for awhile, you'd be nowhere near that music. But the music could come on you any time like that. The city was full of the sounds of music.[23]

It was only natural, then, that Louis felt compelled to play jazz, particularly a wind instrument such as a trumpet. His brother was becoming known as a jazz cornetist, his family raved over such music at weddings and other festive occasions, and all around him young musicians—black and white—were breaking new ground in jazz expression. In the early 1920s Leon purchased an old horn for $5.00, wrapping a towel around it to

---

[21]*Ibid.*, pp. 98-99.

[22]Paul A. Giordano, "The Italians of Louisiana: Their Cultural Background" (Ph. D. dissertation, Indiana University, 1978), pp. 103-110.

[23]Nat Shapiro and Nat Hentoff, *Hear Me Talkin' To Ya* (New York, 1966), p. 3.

conceal a hole among the horn's many dents. By 1924, Leon was able to buy a new $75.00 trumpet, which he played at a growing number of clubs while still in high school. Louis, to Angelina's great dismay, regularly snuck out of the house after dinner and skipped across tree-lined Claiborne Avenue to the French Quarter. There he'd listen to Leon and a host of other greats. "You had to play trumpet," Louis said longingly.[24]

One of those musicians Prima particularly liked was a stocky young black with a thick chest and an enchanting sound on the horn. Prima was Louis Armstrong's biggest fan in Little Palermo. He liked everything about him—his timing, phrasing, and legendary control. Years later when asked to list his favorite New Orleans, musicians, Prima didn't hesitate: "Buddy Petit, Louis Dumaine, Punch Miller," Louis said. "And, of course, Louis Armstrong."[25] The great Satchmo had, by the early 1920s, left a permanent musical legacy in the Crescent City. Although not the world-wide entertainment giant that millions would later come to recognize, Armstrong during his final years in New Orleans had already shown the promise of genius. Armstrong's biographer noted

> By 1922 Armstrong had acquired that *sine qua non* of the great artist, an individual voice. Just as we recognize the voices of family and friends from a phrase or two, so we know from a page of prose or bit of canvas, that we are in the presence of Dickens or Faulkner, Titian or van Gogh. In the same way, anybody who has listened to much Armstrong can identify him instantly from a few notes . . .[26]

By the summer of 1924 Louis' curiosity with the cornet overwhelmed him. With both Leon and Angelina out of town, he began to experiment with an old horn Leon left behind on St. Peter Street. "I got smart," Louis said. "I decided that a trumpet player eats better than a violinist and has a lot more fun." He was fourteen years old.[27] While his brother played in a

[24]*Schnectady Gazette*, July 24, 1974.

[25]*San Francisco Examiner*, September 7, 1968.

[26]James Lincoln Collier, *Louis Armstrong: An American Genius* (New York, 1983), pp. 83-84.

[27]*New Orleans Tribune*, August 25, 1938.

summer-long engagement with Leon Roppolo in Texas, Louis blew the cornet for hours at a time. "I picked it up one day to see how hard I could blow," he later wrote. "Well, my mother was with Leon in Texas, and there was no one at home to tell me to stop making so much noise. That's how I got started."[28]

In the summer the Prima children were expected to work. Angelina had set up a snowball shop, specializing in the finely shaved ice flavored with syrup that so many New Orleanians favored during the hot months. Both boys, as well as Elizabeth, were expected to work in the shop. On other days, Leon and Louis helped Papa Anthony with his horse-drawn Jumbo Soda Pop route. During the summer of 1924, Louis honored all of his family chores, but his mind was on that old worn cornet left behind by Leon. Louis later said he couldn't wait to get home in the early evening and fumble with the cornet. Marching around his bedroom, horn in one hand, snapping his free fingers in the air, Louis said he had the time of his life.

It took only days for Louis to tell his friends of his discovery. He picked out young contemporaries who he knew to be particularly talented and asked if they wanted to form a small band. Not only was his enthusiasm contagious, but young Louis also displayed the sort of leadership talents that would someday make him a national figure. Louis Prima's Kid Band was the result. Twelve-year-old Irving Fazola was on clarinet and eleven-year-old Johnny Viviano was on drums. Looking tall, lean, and hungry, Louis posed with members of the band that summer. Imitating the slick matinee idols of the day, Prima parted his thick, kinky hair down the middle and dressed, as did the other members of the seven-piece band, in white bowties with large shiny cumberbunds.[29]

It was an energetic leap from practicing Leon's horn to forming a small band, but Louis was greatly assisted in his efforts by the spectacle of cornet and trumpet players who practiced their craft throughout the city. How Louis developed his fingering techniques or learned how to blow properly and form a correct embouchure came initially by simply watching some of the masters who could be found almost anywhere in the city. It was a musical education of perhaps the best kind—watching and listening to polished musicians who played on a daily basis. The example of their

---

[28]*Ibid.*

[29]Al Rose and Edmond Souchon, *New Orleans Jazz: A Family Album* (Baton Rouge, 1984), p. 314.

talents and skill was quickly absorbed by Louis who made up for what he lacked in know-how through sheer enthusiasm.

A transformation took place that summer. Known by family and friends as a quiet boy who sat silently by himself during family gatherings and usually answered Angelina's frequent directives with a monosyllabic affirmation, Louis was now a whirlwind of activity: dancing, singing, and laughing with his fellow Kid Band members before audiences on street corners. Everything went well for more than two months until Angelina returned home. "When she found out I was playing the cornet she nearly threw a fit," Louis said. "She couldn't understand why I'd stopped playing the violin . . . my mother was peeved that I'd broken up the family's musical tiro." Leon's reaction was different: Watching Louis fastidiously tying on a colorful vest and pretending that he was about to go onstage, Leon laughed. But several days later Leon saw his little brother performing on a street corner and was amazed. "Everybody kept telling me how good he was," Leon said. "So the next time he played, I went to see him, and, I gotta tell you, he was good. He was jumping all over and the audience loved it."[30]

Louis, who attended high school at Jesuit before transferring to Warren Easton High in the fall of 1926, also sought more exposure by performing with a band called the "Eastonites." The band was weighted toward the Italians, with Prima now playing both a cornet and a trumpet, Jacabo Sciambra on clarinet and John Viviano on drums. There are no recordings of either the Eastonites or Prima's Kid Band, but if Louis was truly as adept as his contemporaries suggest in emulating the rhythms of the day, it can be assumed that both bands specialized in jive street jazz, a sort of raw Dixieland emphasizing Mediterranean and African melody lines that were already incorporated into some of the most popular sounds in New Orleans. In addition, Prima admittedly emulated those cornetists in the city who most impressed him, and, inevitably, Armstrong became his greatest influence. "I sounded like Louie in those early days," Prima later said. "Who didn't?" But, Prima continued:

> Honestagod, from the first time I heard Armstrong I felt
> such a close understanding of his phrasing, his handling of a tune,

---

that it was impossible for me to do some tunes without being like
him.[31]

In his high school years, Prima developed a lifelong interest in athletic
competition, playing sandlot baseball and football with neighborhood
chums and even stepping into the boxing ring at the Gayosa Gym to go a
few rounds. The new-found interest in boxing, coupled with Louis'
continued interest in the cornet, presented Angelina with a dilemma. By the
fall of 1924 her youngest son was a fireball of energy whose activities
dazzled the entire family. Angelina was troubled over Louis' boxing
matches, still outraged that he had abandoned the violin, and worried about
his interest in playing the cornet in French Quarter pubs that might be filled
with danger for her youngest son.

After winning a boxing match one evening at the Gayosa Gym, Louis
was confronted by his mother and a united front of relatives determined to
prohibit future boxing dates. "I whipped the guy in the ring," Prima
recalled. "But when I got downstairs I got the surprise of my life. My
mother and all of my relatives were on hand to skin me. That finished my
fighting career." It also effectively gave approval to his burgeoning jazz
career. While his class records at Warren Easton showed no real distinction
in any particular subject, Prima was busily organizing the Eastonites for
weekend club dates and festival appearances. The names and faces in the
young band changed with the seasons, but Prima continued to hustle from
one musical engagement to the next.[32]

By his junior year in high school in the spring of 1927, Prima and
school guitarist pal Frank Federico were playing in a run-down French
Quarter club called The Whip. Audience response was good, and more
importantly, local word had it that both Prima and Federico were tireless
performers willing to play with almost any combination of musicians,
hoping to be heard, waiting to be seen. From the start, Prima and Federico
were natural allies. Shy and retiring, Federico was the perfect foil for
Prima's wit, and because of his energy and adaptability, the best sideman an
ambitious musician like Louis could ask for. "We played wherever we
could," Federico remembered. "Louie and I would go somewhere at the drop

---

[31]*The Second Line*, Summer 1986; *San Francisco Examiner*, September 7, 1968.

[32]*New Orleans Tribune*, August 25, 1938.

of a hat." They jumped from The Whip to the Studio Club on Bourbon Street where they played until the sun came up. It was exhilarating, even though after two weeks the club abruptly closed with no paychecks for the boys.[33]

In the spring of 1928, Louis left Warren Easton for good without the benefit of a diploma and began to consider himself a professional musician. Several months later his application for membership into the Musician's Mutual Protective Union, Local 174, was approved. In 1928 also, New Orleans was in the throes of yet another musical upheaval. The old greats like Armstrong, Jelly Roll Morton, and King Oliver had long since left the city. Their absence coupled with national musical trends, prompted an evolution that drastically altered the fortunes of Dixieland. Larger organizations, such as New York's Paul Whiteman Orchestra, were fashioning the public's musical tastes. The New Orleans groups who expected to survive had to do so by increasing their size, using written music, and adding three or four saxophones. The consistent New Orleans front line of cornet or trumpet, trombone and clarinet was no longer in the local demand it once enjoyed. Additionally, the memberships of many of the smaller Dixieland combos were dwindling, depleted by musicians who left to join larger orchestras in Chicago or New York.

Now there was a lure for instant stardom—stories of overnight discoveries. With the hook-up of the major radio networks—NBC in 1927 and CBS in 1928—the potential for national audiences and instant professional success were heady prospects for scrambling musicians everywhere. Within a period of five years, previous unknowns such as singers Bing Crosby and Russ Columbo were vying for the nation's attentions with hit songs and regular network radio show appearances. None of this was lost on Prima, who, although he disliked listening to radio, was dreaming that his name would also be known someday nationally, that he'd land a radio spot, or record a hit song and rise from New Orleans to fame and adulation elsewhere.

Joining the short-lived Ellis Stratakos Orchestra in 1929, Prima, Federico, and saxophonist Dave Winstein one night found themselves on their way to Tampa, Florida, for what was supposed to be a "long engagement" at a local night club there.

[33]Frank Federico interview, April 1985.

Sixteen people showed up the first night the orchestra appeared—and then things got worse. No one bothered to come to the next shows, and after several nights of this, the club simply closed its doors. Not surprisingly, the boys in the rented tuxedos went unpaid, and the car they drove to the Sunshine State almost ran out of gas.

Stratakos had relatives in another city near the central part of the state and the orchestra members opted to pay a surprise visit to that family. En route, the musicians ate oranges, grapefruit, and mandarins found on the side of the roads. "It was the best part of the whole trip," Federico later said. A free meal and a tank of gas from Stratakos' cousins was their eventual reward.

Such were the fortunes of many neophyte groups of the period. After the Florida fiasco, Louis returned to club work in New Orleans and eventually landed in the fall of 1929 what he thought was a good position with the Joseph Cherniavsky Orchestra at a gambling house in Jefferson Parish, a suburb of New Orleans. Cherniavsky's gig was what might be called a "novelty act." He played the sweet dance numbers, but would also get himself and his orchestra members involved in various stage productions.

Cherniavsky was looking for someone who could play "legit," with difficult triple-tonguing techniques and an emphasis on semi-classical numbers. Prima, who by now was regularly practicing jazz improvisation, was out of his league. But he loved to perform and mug, making people laugh as well as tap their feet. Whether Cherniavsky could see the natural conflict between the orchestra's style and Prima's method, or whether he was actually jealous of Prima's increasing showmanship abilities is a debatable point. In any event, he shortly fired Prima and the young trumpeteer was stunned.

Driving home with Dave Winstein, Prima sat silently, trying not to cry in front of his friend. Several times he muttered something under his breath, but then dropped it. Finally as they neared Prima's St. Peter Street home, Louis declared: "One of these days this guy is going to feel sorry . . . I'm going to make it. He fired me, but he's gonna be sorry he fired me because I'll be bigger than he is."[34]

In 1929, Prima also secured a temporary job playing on the *Steamship Capital*, which docked at the foot of Canal Street. A young New Orleans

[34]"Louis Prima—The Chief," *WYES-TV*, Byer.

woman named Louise Polizzi went with her friends to dance on the ship and Prima made a point of staring at her, occasionally smiling slyly. Polizzi was unimpressed. She didn't think Prima was "very handsome," but admitted she was flattered by his attention. After several numbers, the band took a rest, and Polizzi left for the ladies room. Louis followed. When she came back out, Prima asked her to dance. It was the beginning of an inconsistent six-month courtship. "I'm going to be very famous," Louis blandly told Louise. "Someday you'll hear a lot about me and read a lot about me."[35]

Shy, Italian, dark-haired and of simple origins, Louise later admitted she had never quite met anyone like Prima. "He was very different," she said. "But he wasn't like people thought, he wasn't always happy and dancing around. Sometimes he'd be very sad. He'd cry very easily if something was bothering him. He didn't even have very many close friends, although he knew a lot of people."[36]

They were an odd couple: Where Louis was publicly exuberant, Louise was reticent. Louis had visions of conquest far beyond the narrow confines of Little Palermo, while Louise dreamed only of marriage. She got her wish on June 25, 1929, first in a ceremony by a Jefferson Parish justice of the peace and then in a repeat wedding ceremony supervised in its entirety by Angelina. The young couple moved into the St. Peter Street family home where Louise relegated all decisions to Angelina. At night, perhaps to get away from the overwhelming presence of her mother-in-law, Louise would sit for hours with Louis on the front door stoop, watching neighbors go by, and listening to Louis' comical stories about his club dates and the colorful characters who regularly patronized such establishments. On St. Peter Street Louise also experienced the paternal ways of Leon. Observing that Louis frequently sought out his older brother for advice, Louise began to do the same. "He always had an answer. He would always help either me or Louis out."[37]

Despite his seemingly passive personality, a natural temperament Leon claimed to have inherited from his father, the elder Prima son remained busy during the late 1920s and early 1930s. He operated the Hollywood open-air

[35]Louise Pollizi interview, May 1984.

[36]*Ibid.*

[37]*Ibid.*

dance pavilion, then started the Avalon, a medium-sized dance and music night club on Metairie Road, later renamed Prima's Beverly Beer Garden when it started serving fifty-cent buckets of beer after President Franklin Roosevelt repealed Prohibition in 1933.

On top of his business involvements, Leon formed the Prima-Sharkey Orchestra, which some considered one of the finest big bands in the city. Although popular for only about a year, 1930-1931, the Prima-Sharkey Orchestra played on riverboats, at supper clubs, and in Jefferson Parish gambling halls. Late in the evening, the orchestra frequently did live dance band broadcasts over station WSMB. On such occasions the Prima-Sharkey Orchestra broke one cardinal rule: They allowed black musicians to sit in with them—a distinct violation of the state segregation laws.[38]

The 1931-1932 season may have been one of the most formative periods in young Louis' life also. Although he was getting his fair share of exposure due to Leon's ongoing agreement to let him perform in the Avalon Club, he got his first genuine break when Lou Forbes, the director of the Saenger Theatre pit orchestra, hired him for the daily afternoon and early evening shows at the center.

The Saenger, then as now one of the largest and most beautiful theatres in the city, billed itself as a "Florentine Palace." Between showings of major motion pictures—talking pictures had been available to the general public for less than five years—the theatre orchestra whipped into action with colorful floor shows entailing elaborate dance numbers and lengthy orchestra movements. Members of the orchestra dressed in garb appropriate to the mood of the show and were trained to dance in rehearsed performances and sing—both individually and as part of a larger group.

Godfrey Hirsch, who played drums for Prima both in New Orleans and later in New York and California, called Forbes "One of the great conductors," noting that he purposely searched for young musicians like Prima who not only had the raw talent, but the enthusiasm to practice and play on a daily basis. "He would show you how to play," said Hirsch of Forbes. "He showed you everything there was to know, and he did the same thing for Louie."[39]

[38]Frank Driggs and Harris Lewine, *Black Beauty, White Heat* (New York, 1982), p. 35.

[39]"Louis Prima—The Chief," *WYES-TV, Byer.*

The shows at the Saenger encompassed variety at its best. On any given evening, Prima might find himself sharing the evening's honors with a spiritual quartet known as the Jubilee Singers, or with various local comedians, or with the dancing Strakova girls, or with a group known simply as the Four Horsemen. The emphasis was on musical comedy. If Easter Sunday was imminent, the Forbes cast would construct an elaborate set and dress as rabbits or chicks and sing both traditional and jazz-oriented numbers associated with the holiday. No matter how well-received a number might be, every week the entire show was scrapped and a new theme worked out.

Thus, during the first week of March 1932, Prima portrayed a singing and dancing policeman in a musical rendition of what goes on in a court of law. Forbes in this number was on trial, and the various cast members sang and danced out their roles as opposing attorneys, judge, and witnesses.

By the second week, Forbes presented a show called "The Green Hat." In this vignette, the director took a small green hat and randomly placed it on the head of any one of his orchestra members—usually with much coaxing and hooting from the audience. The supposedly surprised delegate would then have to sing or dance or do anything that Forbes deemed appropriate for the moment. In its weekly theatre review column, the *New Orleans Item* noted: "The hat goes to several, but Louis Prima gets the major amount of applause."[40]

Two weeks later, Prima was playing the role of "Goofus," a country hick character introduced to the ways of the city—all in song—and the *Item* responded: "The tune is sprightly and teasing and Louis Prima gives it color with his own style of syncopation."[41]

Not only was the work with Forbes strenuous, but Prima was getting a taste of his long-sought desire for fame—if only on a local basis. Within a matter of weeks, Prima's name was second on the bill only to Forbes—a significant accomplishment considering that the Saenger cast sometimes numbered well over sixty performers.

In addition, Prima seemed to have captured the hearts of both the regular theatre audience as well as the *Item's* theatre critic who regularly praised him. A typical review in May of 1932 went: "Lou Forbes and his music

---

[40]*New Orleans Item*, March 18, 1932.

[41]*Ibid.*, April 8, 1932.

got a rain of applause, especially after their last number featuring Louis Prima." For all of this training and professional exposure, Prima might have been tempted to pay Forbes. Instead, Louis made $65.00 a week for his work with the Saenger—a very good sum for a twenty-one-year-old musician in the midst of the Great Depression.[42]

With regular money coming in, a baby on the way, and the kind of copy that most local musicians could only hope for, Louis and Louise Prima should have been very happy in the early 1930s. Louis could afford to buy the kind of clothes his increasingly critical eye surveyed in the finest downtown stores, as well as making it out to the racetrack in Jefferson Parish to indulge in a growing interest in gambling and horses. But the nation's attentions had turned to New York, and Prima was painfully aware of it. Benny Goodman was organizing the band that would come to personify swing a year later. Larger orchestras such as Duke Ellington's and Fletcher Henderson's had already made their mark (Ellington, chiefly through the highly touted Cotton Club radio broadcasts), and a variety of lesser-known bands were struggling to find a place in the rapidly changing musical tides.

A Canadian-born bandleader who shared with Prima a similar background was promoting himself—and successfully, too—as the purveyor of "The sweetest music this side of heaven." At thirty-two, Guy Lombardo had his own big band and was about to make his first movie. He had performed in most of the largest cities in Canada and the U. S. and received favorable reviews in dozens of national publications. Like Louis, Lombardo had played the violin as a youth but gave it up out of boredom. Like Leon, Lombardo regularly dabbled in the club and restaurant investment business.

During the Mardi Gras season of 1934, Lombardo visited New Orleans and dropped in on yet another club venture of Leon's, this one called the Club Shim Sham. Louis was playing that night, displaying by now the professional refinement he learned from conductor Forbes. Exhibiting little modesty, Prima was also billing himself as "America's Hottest Trumpeteer."[43]

"It was springtime and warm enough so that the doors of the club were open," Lombardo later remembered of the night he met Prima. "Up and

[42]*Ibid.*, May 13, 1932.

[43]*New Orleans States*, July 11, 1934.

down the streets, sounds poured out, sweet, penetrating, Dixieland and improvised jazz. One night, walking alone, I heard the sound of a trumpet, different and more piercing than any I had experienced." Lombardo, who was known in the trade for his ability to spot new talent, headed toward the music, walking into the Club Shim Sham. The pub was "almost empty," Lombardo recalled, but on the bandstand was "an olive-skinned trumpet player, hardly more than a boy." Attracted by Prima's sound, Lombardo was even more impressed when he observed Prima performing, noting that Louis was "putting as much into the show as if the place overflowed with patrons."[44]

Lombardo ran back to his hotel and woke up his brothers Carm and Lebe. They had to come to the Club Shim Sham right away, Lombardo implored. "I wanted to find out if my brothers were as impressed with this different personality as I." After arriving at the club minutes later and listening, Lombardo reported: "They were." The brothers talked to Prima afterwards, complimenting his showmanship and asking about his aspirations. Louis was so taken by the Lombardos' attentions that he immediately invited them to one of Angelina's spaghetti feasts for the next evening.[45]

"I finally asked him if he would like to come to New York," Lombardo said. "I was sure I could find a job for him; I hadn't heard his type of music in the big city." Said Prima: "Lombardo wanted me to leave New Orleans and go to New York. But I knew if I left town my mother would be right up after me." Significantly, Louise's opinion concerning her husband's future was less important than what Angelina thought. The hardest part, as Prima saw it, was getting past his mother. Lombardo understated Angelina's resolve when he noted that she seemed "rather reluctant." In fact, Angelina was adamant. Louis should stay in New Orleans, she insisted. He had a wife and family to think of. Even when brother Leon intervened and reminded Angelina of Lombardo's stature and the potential his association held for Louis, Angelina remained unimpressed: "Why can't he be successful right here?" she asked. "He's doing fine right now. Why does he have to leave?"[46]

[44]Guy Lombardo and Jack Altshul, *Auld Acquaintance* (New York, 1975), p. 218.

[45]*Ibid.*

[46]*Ibid.*, p. 219; *New Orleans Tribune*, August 25, 1938; Leon Prima interview, May 1984.

"Mother said nothing doing," Prima recalled. But even Angelina's powerful influence on him, her arguments that he'd be lonely and a potential failure in the big city, that he had a wife and baby to care for and his entire family in New Orleans, all of these normally persuasive points went unheeded. Louis was only going through the motions in asking Angelina's permission in the first place. In reality, he had made his decision to leave the moment Lombardo suggested the promise of New York. Louis had a brand new trumpet, he later recalled, and "enough money for a week's bed and board."[47]

This was not to minimize Angelina's hold over Louis. Mother and son maintained an emotional bond that lasted for all of Louis' adult life. It was Angelina who prodded Louis to become a success, she was the one who gleefully saved his favorable newspaper clips and showed them to relatives. It was also Angelina whom Louis most enjoyed impressing. When he told her of how a club audience stood on their feet and cheered for more during one of his performances, Angelina gloated and fawned over her youngest son, confirming the security and confidence Louis already possessed in enormous quantity. But Angelina was eclipsed by the magnetic pull of New York. The Big Apple, for any budding musician in the 1930s, was simply *the* place to be seen and heard, and Louis knew he had to go there. Authors Frank Driggs and Harris Lewine may have put it best when they noted that "New York had become the vortex of the entertainment industry: recording, music publishing, and radio were centered here. It was the proving ground, necessary for individual players as well as bands of all sizes. Reputations meant little away from New York. One had to be seen and heard here, in the Apple, and then it was possible to join a name band, to challenge the giants in jam sessions . . . only then did you become a star."[48]

The route north from New Orleans, though, offered vastly different fortunes for many musicians. Some, such as Armstrong, achieved vast fame, while others met with humiliating rejections. Trombonist Henry "Red" Allen was not alone when he commented "I was leery of leaving New Orleans. I'd heard of too many New Orleans musicians getting stranded up North." New Orleans musicians loved to trade stories of disasters on the road. Many people still remembered New Orleans pianist "Jelly Roll"

---

[47]*New York Post*, March 30, 1938.

[48]Driggs and Lewine, *Black Beauty, White Heat*, p. 92.

Morton's debacle in California: the handsome and petulant Morton went west with a group of New Orleans musicians only to see the small combo angrily disband after Morton said he thought the Californians would think them "clowns" for the way they dressed and "kind of foolish" for eating red beans and rice—a New Orleans dietary staple—on the bandstand. Morton's self-consciousness symbolized how many New Orleans musicians behaved when they left their home city. Some did everything they could to distance themselves form their New Orleans roots, while others—such as some in Morton's band—returned home and vowed to never leave again.[49]

Prima, too, was pensive and aware that he could fail in a city far from the comforting confines of New Orleans. But he was also alive to the dreams of achievement. This was a vision which had come to dominate Prima's waking thoughts. New Orleans was too small. It had lost its national clout. Musicians like Armstrong had left and gone on to national acclaim and now Louis would too. It was his best chance, a break, the kind of opportunity he'd heard other musicians longingly hope for. In less than five months, Prima would be in New York.

What most stands out about Louis' final days in New Orleans were his weak ties to his wife Louise. It was Angelina, not Louise, to whom Louis turned for advice. And it was Angelina, not Louise, whom Louis felt compelled to convince on the merits of his move to New York in the fall of 1934. During his final weeks in New Orleans, Louis seemed every bit the starry-eyed musician entranced with visions of success and self-fulfillment. In his later written thoughts and through interviews, Prima gives little impression of being a married man with a small child concerned about his family's fortunes and whereabouts. Increasingly, Louise emerges as a shadow figure, married to Prima in name only, but discarded as both an intimate with an individual voice and a romantic partner with any influence over her husband.

Partly this was due to Louise's retiring manner. Partly it was due to Prima's "outside interests." Throughout his life, Prima was a vigorous and virile man. He was attractive to and attracted by women. In his teens and early twenties, Louis displayed a behavior trait that would stay with him all of his adult life—he regularly engaged in intimate and fleeting relationships with the many young women who caught his eye. His marriage to Louise

---

[49]Richard M. Sudhalter, *Henry "Red" Allen* (Alexandria, Va., 1981), p. 10; Chris Albertson, *Jelly Roll Morton* (Alexandria, Va., 1979), p. 20.

did little to inhibit such amorous inclinations and may have, in fact, only heightened the thrill of conquest. When Louis at last left for New York, he left behind him the commitments and responsibilities of a marital promise long since betrayed.

He was simultaneously embarking upon a dream of notoriety and chance that was shared by millions in the Great Depression. There were dozens of hungry jazz musicians equal to or better than Prima in New Orleans in 1934. But Prima was discovered largely because he *performed* so well. His music was high-spirited Dixieland, with the additional dimensions of an early swing influence. But it was Prima's ability as a showman, coupled with his talent on the horn, that won him his enthusiastic reviews while at the Saenger Theatre and most impressed Lombardo. The distinction would later become an important component in understanding the direction of Prima's career.

In 1934 show tunes were the rage—a perfect forum for Prima's talents. In addition, the record industry was booming along, despite the malaise of the Great Depression, providing millions of listeners and record-buyers with cheery, positive ditties that uplifted spirits as well as hopes. "A lot of money was made in the recording industry," author James Lincoln Collier has written. "Not only by the record makers, but by composers, song publishers, and, to some extent, musicians." As Louis packed his belongings for New York, the songs most requested on network radio programs included "Pop Goes the Weasel," "You're the Top," "La Cucaracha," and "On the Good Ship Lolly-Pop." Popular songs and commercial success pointed to comic lyrics, soft love crooning, and word plays—not the deeply intricate jazz riffs and mournful ballads that would later be associated with artists such as Benny Goodman, Billie Holiday, and Duke Ellington. As an interpreter of a comedy song or the performer of a snappy and even teasingly off-color tune, Prima had few equals. Upon leaving New Orleans, Prima was perfect for the spirited, happy, and somewhat mindless demands of the record-buying public of the day. He felt that his time had arrived. At twenty-three, Prima was beginning his long love affair with national success.[50]

---

[50]Collier, *Louis Armstrong*, pp. 95-97; *The Billboard*, October 13, November 17, and December 8, 1934.

Chapter II

The Famous Door

Throughout his nearly fifty years as a professional musician Louis
Prima took pride in his timing—not just an ability to keep the beat, but
also his tendency to be at the right place at the right time. Arriving by train
in New York in September 1934, however, Prima may have wondered if he
picked the wrong city for success in the wrong year. 1934 was, after all,
the fifth year of the country's Great Depression. Thousands of people in the
city were out of work. The New York streets were lined with downcast
men, shabbily dressed, selling apples—some of whom, five years earlier,
dressed in elegant splendor and sold stocks on Wall Street. Banks
foreclosed on homeowners, and small businesses, going broke, boarded their
windows. Songwriter E. Y. "Yip" Harbur, who became famous in the early
1930s for his Great Depression song "Brother, Can You Spare A Dime?"
summed up the bleak conditions: "The prevailing greeting at that time, on
every block you passed, by some poor guy coming up, was: 'Can you spare
a dime?" Or: 'Can you spare something for a cup of coffee?' . . . 'Brother,
Can You Spare A Dime?' finally hit on every block, on every street. I
thought that could be a beautiful title. If I could only work it out by telling
people, through the song, it isn't just a man asking for a dime. This is the
man who says: I built the railroads. I built the tower. I fought your wars.
I was the kid with the drum. Why the hell should I be standing in line
now? What happened to all this wealth I created?"[1]

Among those the Depression most severely affected were musicians.
Never a particularly lucrative trade, even in the best of times, the business
of being a musician in the early 1930s was an exercise in deprivation.
"About 60 percent of formerly employed musicians in the United States are
still out of work," the *American Mercury* declared in July 1934. "At the
height of the economic depression, unemployment in American industry as
a whole never went above 50 percent. The musician has thus got the worse
of it." The magazine surveyed musicians' job application cards in New
York and noted that in the space reserved for comments, many of the
musicians penned in things like "Needing badly, will accept any kind of

---

[1] Studs Terkel, *Hard Times* (New York, 1970), pp. 34-35.

position," or "Very great need, out of work four years," or even "My need is greater than my pride." The magazine said such comments revealed only part of the story: "There is nothing about the dispossess notices, nothing about the unpaid grocery bills, nothing about pawned overcoats or that last desperate resort—pawned instruments."[2]

Despite the gloomy conditions of 1934, many entertainment industry officials believed the worst was over. They pointed to the season of 1931-1932 when *Variety* noted "Show business . . . is in the most chaotic condition it has ever known." One historian later observed: "By 1932, in fact, every portion of the entertainment industry had plunged into crisis. The record business, sheet music publishing, movies, vaudeville, and theatres were all in desperate trouble as discretionary spending dwindled. Nightclubs were devastated . . ."[3]

A ray of promise shone through, however, in December 1933 when President Franklin D. Roosevelt's repeal of Prohibition took effect. In real terms, the repeal meant that hundreds of New York nightclubs, dance halls, theatres, and jazz pubs could once again rely upon the retail demands of customers whose first priority was to drink rather than be entertained. But because Repeal fostered a reawakening of New York's nightlife, it also directly benefitted entertainers who, starting in early 1934, began to see more club dates materialize. The sense of gratitude throughout New York's entertainment world was noted in June of that year when entrepreneur club owner Billy Rose presented his lavish show, *Here's to Broadway*, a musical tale depicting the ravages suffered by Broadway because of the Great Depression and the recovery expected through FDR's Repeal.[4]

Slowly New York was returning to the giddy glitz of its past life, a development observed by the *New York Times* which noted "From cocktail hour on to curfew the hotels that were dead and empty places (at least on the lobby level) are alive with gay throngs again." Fighting the economic doldrums of the times, Repeal also gave musicians their first glimpse of steady pay since the stock market crash in 1929: "The call is being broadcast throughout the land for orchestras," the *Times* continued.

---

[2]*American Mercury*, June 1934.

[3]*Variety*, January 7, 1931; Lewis A. Erenberg, "From New York to Middletown: Repeal and the Legitimization of Nightlife in the Great Depression," *American Quarterly*, (Winter, 1986), 763.

[4]*Ibid.*, 764.

> Hotels which formerly employed one to play for a chaste dinner
> hour are now hiring two to play throughout the entire evening;
> restaurants which never had music are today advertising their bands
> and bandleaders; nightclubs, cafes, beer gardens are sprouting up all
> over. . . . People are seeking to bury a dull past in a happy
> present.[5]

Prima knew too well the obstacles facing him. "I was only a kid when
I came up to New York," Prima said. "I either had to sink or swim on my
ability to play the horn." But Prima had Lombardo, a towering figure in the
dance band business, and Lombardo was convinced he could find work for
Louis. "I had one place in mind for him," Lombardo said. "A well known
spot on Fifty-Second Street." Lombardo couldn't have picked a better
location. In 1934, 52nd Street was about to become *the* place to be seen
and heard for a young jazz musician.[6]

Located in midtown Manhattan, 52nd Street—or Swing Street as the
musicians called it—was a place where music could be heard that was
"amusing and relaxed without succumbing to the leveling process constantly
at work on popular music," author Charles Edward Smith wrote, calling
52nd Street "The setting for virtually every type of jazz."[7]

Ever since its speakeasy days in the late 1920s, 52nd Street was the
city's fairway to the best jazz, comics, booze, strippers, and as a result, the
best fun to be had in all of New York. It was only a two-block area, but by
1934-1935, Swing Street was populated with such jazz establishments as
Leon and Eddie's, the Onyx Club, and Jack and Charlie's 21 Club. Author
Arnold Shaw, in a book examining 52nd Street, noted "Why the block
between Fifth and Sixth should have attained its undeniable notoriety cannot
be easily answered. In a sense, 52nd Street did not differ from all of the
other midtown blocks of Victorian brownstones. It was as narrow as any of
its undistinguished neighbors. But it did have a number of things going for
it." Those things, according to Shaw, were the large number of speakeasies
endemic to the Prohibition era when powerful and famous movie stars,

---

[5]*New York Times*, February 11, 1934.

[6]*New York Post*, March 20, 1938; Lombardo, *Auld Acquaintance*, p. 219.

[7]"The Street," Epic Records, linear notes by Charles Edward Smith, ca. 1963.

starlets, politicians, sports figures, and well-read columnists found the block particularly appealing. By the mid-1930s, 52nd Street was beginning to symbolize the struggle of the black singers and musicians who came downtown from Harlem in search of fame and at least a semblance of financial security. Most of the black musicians from Harlem and elsewhere would be disappointed in this quest. But some of the exceptional black performers of the era, people like Coleman Hawkins, Billie Holiday, and Count Basie, found that 52nd Street could serve as an effective launching pad for long, respected careers.[8]

"There was something about that street," Prima recalled years later. "I can't find the words. It always reminded me of old Bourbon Street in New Orleans. But it was more than just music. It was a feeling that it gave you . . . " Prima's first foray on 52nd Street, however, was a disaster. Lombardo wanted Prima to audition at Leon and Eddie's, one of the most popular clubs on Swing Street, located at 33 West 52nd. "I knew Eddie Davis, one of the partners," said Lombardo. "He was an ex-vaudevillian who emceed the show at his club and I felt I could talk him into hiring Prima." Davis was receptive to the idea, telling Lombardo, "Tell him to come. If he's as good as you say he is, I can use him." But when Prima and Lombardo arrived at Leon and Eddie's, Davis suddenly cooled. He took Lombardo aside and whispered "I don't know how to tell you this, Guy. But I can't use him. I just found out the union won't let me get rid of the band I was going to replace with him." But that was only part of the story, a bogus cover for what was really bothering Davis. Highly receptive to Lombardo's favorable reviews of Prima, Davis was ready to hire Louis. But when he met the musician he was startled—Prima is a Negro, Davis thought. That misconception abruptly ended any possibility of Prima performing at Leon and Eddie's.[9]

Although it was true that Prima, with his kinky hair, large facial features, and dark skin did look, at the very least, like a black Creole, it was also true that Davis' blatant bigotry underlined a darker side of Swing Street. As in New Orleans, blacks and whites were prohibited from performing together onstage and black musicians were generally shoddily treated on the street, a fact Billie Holiday remembered when she wrote

---

[8]Arnold Shaw, *The Street That Never Slept* (New York, 1971), pp. ix-x.

[9]*Ibid.*, p. 26; Lombardo, *Auld Acquaintance*, p. 219.

White musicians were 'swinging' from one end of 52nd Street to the other, but there wasn't a black face in sight on the street except Teddy Wilson and me. Teddy played intermission piano at the Famous Door and I sang. There was no cotton to be picked between Leon and Eddie's and the East River, but man, it was a plantation any way you looked at it. And we not only had to look at it, we had to live it. The minute we were finished with our intermission stint we had to scoot out back to the alley or go out and sit in the street.[10]

Lombardo deplored such practices: "The tragedy of our times," he called it.

The management of hotels and nightclub owners simply refused to break the color line, fearing financial consequences. Many of the best bands in the country were black—Duke Ellington, Louis Armstrong, Cab Calloway, Fletcher Henderson—but job opportunities were difficult to find outside of Harlem . . . Eddie Davis on first seeing olive-skinned and swarthy Louis Prima and knowing that he came from New Orleans, had simply assumed that he was a black man. The shame is not so much that he lost a gold mine but that he capitulated to the prejudice of the times.[11]

Said Prima, "For six months I couldn't get a job no matter what Guy or anyone else tried to do for me." One morning in November 1934 Prima called on trombonist George Brunis, an old family friend from New Orleans. "He didn't know anybody," remembered Brunis. "So he woke me up at nine o'clock in the morning and got me to go to the agent's office." But the initial check of Brunis' agents produced no work for Louis either.[12]

One door away from Leon and Eddie's, however, was the key to Prima's musical future. At 35 West 52nd Street a new club with the curious name of the Famous Door was just about to begin operations. By any reckoning,

[10]Billie Holiday, *Lady Sings the Blues* (New York, 1985), p. 97.

[11]Lombardo, *Auld Acquaintance*, p. 220.

[12]*New Orleans Tribune*, August 25, 1938; George Brunis, oral history, William Hogan Ransom Archive of Jazz at Tulane University, New Orleans.

the Famous Door would be a risky venture. Jack Colt, a Connecticut businessman and jazz fan, decided to raise funds in the winter of 1935 to form a club that local musicians in New York could call their own. For several weeks, Colt mused over the possibilities; where did the trumpet players, drummers, and singers go after the regular Manhattan clubs closed? How could they, too, find a spot where they could drink, listen to music and relax? Colt traveled in music circles and was personally close to bandleaders Jimmy Dorsey and Glenn Miller, as well as saucer-eyed comedian Jerry Colonna, and composer Gordon Jenkins. His friendships with these men inspired him to a plea for financial help. He didn't get much, most of his friends contributed about $100 each, while Colt and musician Lenny Hayton contributed exactly $2,000 from their own pockets, with the total investment from Colt's efforts coming to $2,800. Colt called it the Famous Door after his famous investors signed their names on the front door, inspiring other stars, starlets, and musicians to do the same. By March 1935 Colt held auditions for a band to play at his new club and he hired Prima after one audition. Prima had, by this time, established a fivesome with whom he hoped to invade New York. Frank Pinero landed the pianist's slot, Jack Ryan was on bass, gap-toothed Garrett McAdams on guitar, and, to Prima's credit, the legendary Pee Wee Russell on clarinet.

Lombardo and agent Irving Mills got Louis through the winter by making records for the Brunswick label, the first of which were recorded in September 1934. How this band, which was officially called Louis Prima and his New Orleans Gang, sounded was clear from their Brunswick sessions. The combo displayed a consistent and rhythmic tempo with Russell sensuously wrapping his clarinet around the central themes of the songs played, while Prima exhibited a strong, forceful trumpet style that usually executed the song's central theme. Almost from the beginning, Prima and Russell established a two-man musical challenge that marked the group as a vibrant example of the new Dixieland-swing style.

In early March, Prima and his New Orleans Gang made their debut at the Famous Door. Long-time New York entertainment columnist Robert Sylvester remembered that night well—he said that Prima's opening would be marked historically as the night that 52nd Street finally plunged headfirst into the Swing era. Prima, argued Sylvester, made such an impressive first-night appearance that he forever changed the way 52nd Street was viewed by jazz musicians. Before Prima, the street was a nice place to drink and listen to dance band music. After Prima, it was the only spot in town where hot, swinging jazz of a kind never heard before in New York could only be found. But things were slow in starting. "The early evening debut of the $2,800 Famous Door was anything but auspicious," Sylvester wrote. "On the stand, Louis Prima played his great cornet solos. The single bartender leaned back and bit at his knuckles. The two waiters huddled in the corner farthest from the music and sneered at themselves for not taking their union's offer of steady work in a chop house. Of customers, there were none."[13]

By 11 p.m., Colt was nervous and depressed enough to leave the club for a dark, chilly walk around the block. He never expected the Famous Door to be a roaring attraction, but a totally empty room—especially in a pub that seated at the most fifty people—this was too depressing for even the normally bouyant Colt. Prima, meanwhile, played on in seemingly blissful oblivion. An empty club with bored waiters plastered against the wall was nothing new to the young trumpeter. As his experience in New Orleans showed, the life of the professional musician was not always an easy one. Clubs would suddenly close, managers ran out with the pay, band members were indifferent and audiences were sometimes nonexistent.

On the night the Famous Door opened, Prima undoubtedly played some of the songs he had earlier recorded with the New Orleans Gang on Brunswick, probably favoring such crowd-pleasers as "Chinatown," "Way Down Yonder in New Orleans," and "Jubilee." The band played for more than two hours, without any noticeable difference in the number of patrons. "Just another flop," muttered Clot, as he left his club for a brisk evening walk. Colt walked several blocks, perhaps contemplating his lost investment and the unpleasant task of firing Prima, until he stopped on the corner of 6th Avenue and saw a crowd gathering around the front door of his club. "It looked like there was a gang fight in front of the joint," Colt recalled. "I was sure there was some sort of a drunken riot in the place."

Colt inhaled and ran to his club. It *was* a fight—a fight to get *into* the Famous Door. The word had passed that a new club had opened, and the trendy New Yorkers rushed over to get a piece of the action. "The sucker who owns this trap has disappeared," a waiter yelled at Colt, not recognizing the astounded the proprietor. "We sent down the block to borrow two cases of whiskey . . . " The bartender at the Famous Door, recognizing the growing crowd that would soon place demands beyond the tiny club's liquor stock, had run out of the club and down the street to Reilly's at 58 West

---

[13]Robert Sylvester, *No Cover Charge: A Backward Look at the Nightclubs* (New York, 1956), p. 73.

52nd Street to borrow two cases of assorted whiskey. The old saw for every night club and dive on earth held true that night: You're only as good as the amount of booze you sell. On the wonderful night Prima and the Famous Door burst upon Swing Street, the drinks and dollars were flowing—Colt's idea was a runaway success.[14]

"What had happened, of course," wrote Sylvester, "was that the prematurely discouraged Colt had forgotten the basic theme of his whole idea. He had opened a night club for musicians and forgotten that musicians don't go anywhere until after midnight—unless they're hired to go somewhere." Sylvester claimed that Prima's opening evening show signaled the birth of Swing Street. Author Shaw added: "In the view of many New York musicians, this was how a 'club of our own' was born." Prima, who called the Famous Door a "Little fun joint for musicians," was no less ecstatic: "The Door was an instantaneous success," he later said. "Winchell started boasting it, Sobol, Sullivan, and all the top columnists."[15]

The press was indeed immediately supportive: "Prima, with a five-piece combination, had the musicians congregating at the Famous Door until the delighted public crowded them out," reported *Down Beat*. The weekly entertainment magazine, *The Billboard*, gave Prima credit for giving rise to the "jam band" with his spectacular Famous Door debut. "The music of the jam band is the music of a hot Negro orchestra made more compact," the paper reported. ". . . that may explain why people like it—because it is savagely rhythmic, almost primitive in its quality." *The Billboard* also noted that the "Famous Door clicked from the beginning . . . being not only a rendezvous for musicians, but a favorite late spot for the laity as well . . . Something else the Famous Door did was to start the vogue for jam bands, swing music, bringing out Louis Prima and his torrid outfit and later causing other leaders to form similar outfits." It was the mighty publication *Variety*, though, that gave Prima and the Famous Door the loudest and most memorable round of applause: "The musicians' fave nocturnal haunt has been the Famous Door," the paper noted by the summer of 1935.

[14]*Ibid.*, p. 74.

[15]*Ibid.*; Shaw, *The Street That Never Slept*, pp. 106-108.

It's right next door to Leon and Eddie's and gets its name from an autographed portal whereon the professional mob inscribed their johnhenrys. Bankrolled by a musician's syndicate as a place to hang out after their working hours are through, that gave it enough impetus from the start, but apart from being just another bar it took Louis Prima and his New Orleans Gang to make it a metropolitan landmark. And such it is now.

Variety was especially astounded over the large number of teenagers who showed up nightly to sit and listen to Prima. "Considering that the kids have no place to dance, that's something to wonder about," the paper mused.[16]

Sam Weiss, the doorman at the Famous Door and later at the Onyx Club, chimed in: "Prima broke the street wide open. He was entertaining and funny . . . " Noting that Prima already had his own tag line—"Let's Have a Jubilee!" Louis yelled at the beginning of each show—Weiss said the motto caused "A lot of these sex-starved dames [to] practically have an orgasm. I think they thought he was saying 'Let's have an orgy,' in that horse, horny voice of his." The raw sexual appeal of young Prima was not to be understated. Noting that more and more young women were standing out in any type of weather to see Prima at the Famous Door, Eddie Davis— the man who wouldn't hire Prima—commented: "You could hear them breathing all the way down the street." Musicians who knew Prima at the time marvelled over the number of women who ran towards the bandstand and reached out for the trumpeteer's fast-moving feet. Other young female patrons screamed and fainted. In the always-crowded conditions of the Famous Door, such hysteria added both a touch of audience comedy and palpable excitement that fed on itself. Sam Weiss emphasized the point: "Don't minimize his appeal to the dames," he said. "Somehow the word got out that he was rather well-fortified, and there were lots of tables just bulging with females." Photos and film clips from this period underline Weiss's view. Tall, dark, and extremely agile, Prima had the physique of a young athlete. When he danced and coiled his way across the bandstand, he presented to his New York audiences a spectacle usually confined to the more suggestive black performances of Harlem. In fact, Prima's rather remarkable character traits were reminiscent of the more successful black

[16]Smith, "The Street;" *The Billboard*, December 28, 1935; November 30, 1935; *Variety*, July 31, 1935.

entertainers of the day. More than one reviewer likened Prima to Cab Calloway, the wild, frenetic, black bandleader.[17]

Beyond the simple physical capabilities which prompted observers to compare Prima with various black performers, was the simple essence of Prima's music and his scat style of singing. By the early 1930s, Louis Armstrong perfected the art of jazz and scat singing. With scat, Armstrong dispensed with words and substituted for them an odd, meaningless language of sounds. Essentially, Armstrong, and Prima, used their voices the way most jazz musicians used their instruments. With jazz singing, Prima, perhaps following the lead of Satchmo, moved in on the beat and changed a song's tempo almost at random. In addition, both Armstrong and Prima understood and easily expressed themselves in black jive rhetoric. This ability to sing as both a jazz and scat vocalist, as well as shout the language of jive, gave Prima an important edge in taking advantage of the new musical trends that, by 1935, were just beginning to take hold.

The rhythms and beat set by Prima in 1935 at the Famous Door proved to be the beginning of an entirely new era in jazz, one that spread through 52nd Street like a fast-paced riff. Jazz was reaching a new level of sophistication, one that would culminate, in admittedly bowdlerized form, into the full bloom of the swing age. In 1935, Prima played an interesting synthesis of both Dixieland and swing. His recordings from this period showed Louis firmly entrenched in the Dixieland tradition by both stating and embellishing the melodic line of a song with strong trumpet or cornet overtures. But at the same time he incorporated an early swing technique of playing off one instrument against another—primarily with Russell in both call and response and musical dialogue.

Just as jazz critics raved over Prima, so, too, did they attack him when they felt that too many of his Famous Door shows were less masterpieces of improvisation and more set, arranged programs. But the criticisms were sometimes shortsighted. When producer John Hammond, who later put on wax such diverse talents as Billie Holiday, Bob Dylan, and Bruce Springsteen, complained in *Down Beat* that "Prima persists in playing identical solos night after night and indulges in certain tricks that become a bit tiresome after awhile," he was missing the point and failing to understand Prima's sweaty, breathless appeal. Like a Southern evangelist who knew when to drop to his knees and rock the house with cries of

---

[17]Shaw, *The Street That Never Slept*, p. 109; *New York Post*, August 14, 1953.

salvation, Prima knew, by instinct, night after night, what songs could be used to build the audience into a state of exalted frenzy. His goal was mesmerizing entertainment. It would have been easier to put a gun to Prima's head than to get him to play in the manner typified by later jazz genius Miles Davis, who cooly turned his back to his audience and feigned complete disinterest. Prima believed in delivering to his audience a predictable set of songs on a nightly basis, but interpreting them in a totally unpredictable, but always entertaining manner. "Jazz has been handled all wrong," Louis later explained. "It was kept on an exclusive basis, as something that only a few were supposed to enjoy." Prima also said "I caught on in New York because I never changed the act."[18]

The adherence to an established act emphasized Prima's preference for entertainment over jazz. By sticking to a set program, Louis was free to explore more fully the possibilities available to make people laugh with his off-the-cuff remarks between songs, and make them tap their feet through his frenetic dance routines and on-stage acrobatics. Although the Famous Door was frequented by the purest of jazz fans, audience members responded warmly to Prima's penchant for entertaining the folks. Night after night, to Jack Colt's great satisfaction, the Famous Door drew SRO crowds. Obviously, from a popular perspective, Prima's method was successful. But the reaction of his fellow musicians varied. Claude Thornhill, who at times played piano for Prima at the Famous Door raved, "That man is a helluva horn player . . . knows what he's doing every minute . . . he gets into a jazz tune like getting into an overcoat." But old friend Brunis, who took Prima with him on his regular round of checking for work at the agent's office and played with Louis during the early days of the Famous Door, was disgusted by Prima's on-stage mannerisms, noting that he was too competitive. "Prima and I got into a little swivel," Brunis said, as the two musicians fought over who should get top billing. Confronting Jack Colt, Brunis waved his hand toward Prima and said, "Look, there's no use working with this guy. I'm detracting from the guy and he don't like it." When Prima ran over to complain about Brunis, Brunis snapped: "You're just two minutes too late, boy, I just quit you."[19]

[18]Shaw, *The Street That Never Slept*, p. 109; *Times-Picayune*, March 11, 1974; *Item*, undated clipping from the early 1950s.

[19]Record notes, "Louis Prima and His Orchestra," by John L. Escalante, Sunbeam Records, Inc., Van Nuys, California, 1979; Brunis, Tulane archive.

Such personal confrontations were trivialized, though, by the impact of succeeding in New York in the mid-1930s. Besides his spectacular success at the Famous Door, Prima could treasure the 52nd Street days for the exposure it gave him to major musicians, as well as well-known entertainers, comics, and even vaudevillians. Perhaps the greatest delight from the Swing Street days, certainly from a critical standpoint, was the happy membership of Pee Wee Russell in Prima's New Orleans Gang. Already a favorite with columnists and serious jazz lovers, Russell joined Prima in early 1935 and stayed with him for most of two years. For Prima it was a marriage made in musical heaven. Prima idolized Pee Wee's prowess with a clarinet, but also fretted over the clarinetist's well-known ability for consuming prodigious amounts of alcohol. "I was fortunate in having Pee Wee Russell with me," Prima once confided. "The most fabulous musical mind I have ever known. He never looked at a note. But the second time I played a lick, he'd play along with me in harmony. The guy seemed to read my mind. I've never run into anybody who had that much talent."[20]

Together Prima and Russell challenged one another to greater and more daring musical highs. Their May 1935 recording for Brunswick of "The Lady in Red," which became a big hit on the nation's jukeboxes that summer, is a prime example of the duo's musical acumen. The song was recorded in one try—and has since become a classic for hot jam band record collectors. Prima, in a simple and direct style, starts out the song in an engaging but only slightly swinging manner. After the bridge, Russell blares in over the song's beat. His sound is dirty and suggestive, as the song's pulse quickens. Prima sings in an energetic hybrid of words and scat. Suddenly Russell comes back to almost create an entirely new song, sailing his clarinet into the upper register. Prima fights back with a wailing, growling trumpet, and the two musical talents fight for the lead as the song nears its conclusion. Russell is at his best, displaying a fine, emotionally-wrought line that bounces out toward the listener. But in the end, Prima proves who's the bandmaster: he concludes in what one critic called "a sweeping glissando that covers nearly his entire working range on trumpet, from bottom to top."[21]

---

[20]John McDonough, *Pee Wee Rusell* (Alexandria, Va., 1981), p. 37.

[21]*Ibid*

A second profound influence upon Louis in both his professional and personal life during his Famous Door stay was comedienne Martha Raye. Night after night Raye happened by the club to take in Prima's show and eventually make spontaneous appearances in the program. Swing Street rumors suggested that the two performers' affection went beyond normal professional respect. Indeed, it would seem plausible that Prima and Raye may have had more than a passing interest in one another. Raye in many ways typified the physical type that Louis found attractive. Long-legged, with dark hair and a wholesomely pretty face, Raye was on the verge of national stardom as a comedienne, particularly after her appearance in the Bing Crosby movie *Rhythm on the Range*. But few people in later years realized the other side of Raye. During her visits to the Famous Door and other club appearances, she displayed a fine voice and a good sense for jazz singing. *Collier's* magazine caught the Louis-Martha show and captured the excitement generated by the two performers:

> Louis Prima stopped pushing that cracked voice of his around, waved his trumpet in an agitated circle and led a chorus which was yelling 'Martha!' 'Martha!' The sad-faced guitar player looked no more doleful than ever, the pudgy clarinet gentlemen beamed, the pianist looked over his shoulder with interest and the bozo operating the bull fiddle showed signs of pleasure. 'Martha!' everybody yelled and the coaxing didn't need to continue long, for Martha Raye got up from a table and started to sing.[22]

Prima was entranced. "So many great people started on the Street," he told author Arnold Shaw. "To me, Martha Raye was a great singer with a natural feeling for improvisation. But after she made that one picture, she couldn't help being a comedienne . . . If she had stuck to singing, she would have been a great one . . . " Said Sam Weiss: "Martha Raye and Louis became very close in this period. She copied his playing style in her singing." The Martha and Louis show became so popular with Famous Door audiences that by the summer of 1935 they were signed to appear on singer Rudy Vallee's national variety show "The Fleischman Hour," a format that gave both aspiring entertainers an audience far beyond the

[22]*Colliers*, May 1, 1937.

confines of Swing Street and introduced the nation to Prima for the first time on a regular basis.[23]

Another encounter with a New York personality left Prima less pleased. For years mobsters made it a practice to pressure club owners, demanding that they cough up a percentage of the profits for "protection" from other gangs and hoodlums. Sometimes Prima and Colt would be threatened. Other times a hood might simply sit in a well-placed seat near the bandstand and make everyone nervous. One such hoodlum was Louis "Pretty Boy" Amberg, who, when he visited the Famous Door, always ordered a table where he could sit with his back to the wall. Amberg was one of New York's bloodiest killers, having done away with more than 100 victims by stuffing them alive into laundry bags where they would suffocate. He made a fortune as a bootlegger, but his riches did little to curb his rather grotesque manners. For fun, Pretty Boy might walk into a restaurant and spit into someone's soup. If that someone dared complain, Amberg might spill the whole bowl in his lap. Few, or course, complained. Pretty Boy was dangerous, ugly, and, not surprisingly in a trade filled with thugs, intellectually limited.[24]

Although Amberg was later found dead in a burning car on a Brooklyn street, in the summer of 1935 he was very much alive and quite a figure of intimidation to Prima. "After someone introduced Prima to Amberg, Pretty Boy would feel insulted if Louis didn't come to his table and sit with him," Arnold Shaw later wrote. "Amberg made Prima nervous, but he'd have to go over because Amberg would begin to make things unpleasant for his waiter." Remembered publicist Eddie Jaffe: "Once Amberg showed Louis the picture of a girl on whom he was sweet—Donna Drake, who later achieved stardom on the screen, and who was then a close friend of Louis ... Things came to an unanticipated head one evening when Prima answered a knock at his hotel door and found Amberg outside. Amberg spotted a framed picture of Donna on Louis' dresser. It had an inscription like, 'To my dearest Louis.'" Prima had to be creative fast: "Donna gave it to me one night to give to you," Prima explained to Pretty Boy, remembering that the thug's name was also Louis. Pretty Boy fell for the explanation. On other occasions, though, Prima failed to escape Amberg's

---

[23]Shaw, *The Street That Never Slept*, pp. 108-109.

[24]*Ibid.*, pp. 114-115; Carl Sifakis, *The Encyclopedia of American Crime* (New York, 1982), pp. 19-20.

wrath. Although Prima later denied it, one New York columnist claimed he saw Louis get punched in the face one evening by Amberg for failing to play a requested tune. Prima would later even deny the presence of the mob or individual hoods at the Famous Door, telling author Ronald Morris that such stories were "Hearsay."[25]

But for all of the trouble they caused, mob members could also be useful. One night Pee Wee and Prima were cornered by two knife-wielding hoodlums who demanded $50 a week from Prima in protection money and $25 from Russell. "Well, I didn't want any of that," Pee Wee said later. "I'd played a couple of private parties for Lucky Luciano, so I called him ..." Both Prima and Russell were surprised when they saw who Luciano sent to protect them—none other than Pretty Boy Amberg. Arriving in a chauffeur-driven car, Amberg pulled up to the Famous Door. "Prima sat in the back with Amberg and I sat in the front with the body guard," said Russell. "Nobody said much, just 'Hello,' and 'Goodbye,' and for a week they drove Prima and me from our hotels, picked us up for work at night, and took us home after." Russell added the happy ending, "We never saw the protection money boys again."[26]

By the summer of 1935, Prima's world had abruptly changed. He had been in New York for less than a year, but his lot was transformed during that time from that of the Southern boy awestruck by the magnificence of the city, to a metropolitan success story steeped in the fast-trick life of glittery Manhattan in the 1930s. Prima's days in New York were comprised of spacious Manhattan hotel suites, friendships with the likes of Benny Goodman, Fletcher Henderson, and Coleman Hawkins, bets placed with mysterious bookies, afternoon visits to a harried theatrical agent's office, love notes from admiring women—from well-known starlets to well-proportioned hat-check girls—interviews with powerful Broadway columnists, weekends with the Lombardo family on Long Island, and even exposure to the ways and means of the city's underworld mob element. Prima excitedly read trade paper reviews of his club performances, angled for more recording time with Brunswick, and followed the success of his platters in the national jukebox surveys. He ate in expensive New York restaurants, performed with the likes of Goodman, Mugsy Spanier, and, of

[25]Shaw, *The Street That Never Slept*, pp. 114-115; Whitney Balliet, *Such Sweet Thunder—49 Pieces of Jazz* (New York, 1966), p. 37; Morris, *Wait Until Dark*, p. 16.

[26]Balliet, *Such Sweet Thunder*, p. 37.

course, Pee Wee Russell, and landed several short, but lucrative spots on nationally broadcast radio programs.

It was glamorous stuff, an entirely different universe from New Orleans' Little Palermo. Prima had wowed the caustic big-city crowd and, indirectly, assured the Famous Door's place in history. His appeal spread beyond Swing Street. He also won critical reviews and positive notice from such highbrow publications as *The New Yorker, Esquire,* and the elitist, glossy Broadway magazine called *Stage.* By August of 1935, Prima was even offered a chance to appear in a Hollywood musical. By any standard, such a track record—all of this happened in a short six-month period between March and September of 1935—would be considered phenomenally successful. But it was even more so given the fact that Prima was a young unknown from the hinterlands.

It was no surprise then that Louis, within weeks of his Famous Door debut, was asking for more money for both himself and his band. Considering the overwhelming critical and commercial success of the Famous Door, Prima's salary demands were justified. In the spring of 1935, Prima received only $60 a week, while the other four members of the New Orleans Gang were given $40. Prima demanded and got a substantial increase. But by midsummer, Louis had also made at least two more pleas for more money, and owner Colt became reticent. In late August, Prima went to Colt with what Colt supposed would be yet another salary increase request, but Prima instead surprised the Famous Door's owner when he announced he was quitting the club. Louis told Colt he had been offered the opportunity to set up his own version of the Famous Door in California and was going to take advantage of the plan. When word got out of Prima's impending departure from New York, columnists and musicians were astounded, wondering how Louis would dare to abandon his Big Apple success. This was, after all, still the Great Depression, and fame for many musicians and entertainers was a fleeting thing. "Somehow I'm of the opinion he's making a mistake," offered columnist Mel Washburn in the *New Orleans Tribune.* "All of us are interested, I know, in only what is best for Louis. We want to see him firmly planted in his own niche of fame and star there, reaping the harvest of his cleverness." But Washburn thought it was highly "unusual" for any performer to "rise to a choice spot in the Broadway firmament and then step out on a gamble." From the columnist's perspective, Prima was toying with fortune. He was on top in New York, and Jack Colt even told Louis if he stuck around he would undoubtedly be cast in a major Broadway show for the next season. "He shouldn't gamble with his own future unless he is compelled to," Washburn paternalistically warned.[27]

Louis, though, didn't listen to such dire thoughts. In early September, the entertainer waved goodbye to his friends and supporters of the previous year, smiled a victorious grin at the daunting New York skyline, and ducked into an express train headed directly for his hometown. Prima arrived in New Orleans and appeared in an emotional, triumphant "Welcome Home" spot at brother Leon's Shim Sham Club, while the New York columnists were writing of the Famous Door's decline in trade. Without Prima, the excitement was gone, and with it went the musicians, reporters, and groupies. Billie Holiday followed Prima with a September concert appearance at the Famous Door and was quickly dismissed when her sultry, sensuous style proved unpopular with an audience hooked on Prima's explosive brand of showbusiness. It was one of Lady Day's first and few club appearance defeats. Jack Colt was troubled enough by the state of receipts to board another express train for New Orleans and beg Prima to return. Prima, flushed with the adulation of his New Orleans family and friends, told Colt he was convinced that he could find greater professional achievement in Hollywood. Even Colt's offer of yet one more salary increase failed to sway Louis.[28]

But was it all just money and the potential for greater fame that drove Louis? Some associates didn't believe so. Sam Weiss, among others, thought the ongoing pressure from the mob put the fear of God into Louis. "He didn't want to get involved," said Weiss. "And he was smart enough to be scared about getting involved. So he left."

Prima didn't need to be told of the means employed by mob elements to get their way. Stories, some of them quite graphic, with an emphasis on river dumpings, shootings, and car bombings regularly circulated in the Manhattan clubs. What made things possibly worse for Louis, though, was his heritage. An Italian performer may have found the pressure from the mob more demanding than most musicians. He was, some thug might menacingly tell him, a "brother" and a "member of the family" by virtue of

---

[27]*New Orleans Tribune,* September 20, 1935.

[28]Melvin Maddocks, *Billie Holiday* (Alexandria, Va., 1979), p. 13. Returning to New Orleans just days after Huey Long's assassination, Prima was hailed as a city son made good. "He jumped from the train last night into the open arms of his mother and was almost as quickly torn away by wildly crowding friends," said the *New Orleans Item,* September 15, 1935, adding that a motorcycle escort, followed by "a long line of cars" took Prima to a welcome home blast in his brother's French Quarter nightclub.

his birth. Prima did not like to fight and enjoyed life too much to bear the constant threat of seeing it all come to an end. At the same time, he was a fiercely independent man and the idea of knuckling under and sheepishly paying protection money was more than he could take. California looked more inviting by the moment.[29]

When Prima left New York it was obvious even at the time that an integral part of his formative professional and personal life had come to an end. Even though Prima would return in the next several years for occasional stays at a renovated Famous Door under new management, the spirit and freshness of Louis' initial electric impact gradually diminished. So, too, sadly, did the general aura of Swing Street itself. Author Charles Edward Smith said the street gradually lost its magic, crumbling from "an air of almost-innocence to the cheap hustler's painted facade. It was a street that found itself, and, in the end, lost itself." Smith added that even in its dreary decline, 52nd Street was looked upon by musicians as a treasured old friend who had fallen on hard times. In later years, Prima would never admit to missing his Famous Door days, but he frequently despaired over the failed fortunes of 52nd Street. Zutty Singleton, Louis Armstrong's dynamic drummer, spoke for Prima when he sadly called the fabled Swing Street, with its clubs which were eventually boarded up and demolished, "The greatest that ever was." It was a fine moment in America's jazz history and perhaps one of the greatest times in Prima's life.[30]

[29]Shaw, *The Street That Never Slept*, p. 115.

[30]Smith, "The Street."

Chapter III

"It's Great to Be the Leader of the Band"

Rolling into California in the fall of 1935 was much easier for Prima than was his initial foray into New York a year earlier. In the preceding twelve months, Prima had become a nationally known figure in music circles as a result of his rafter-rattling success at the Famous Door. But another aspect of the business actually made Prima a national household commodity during the mid-1930s.

Even before his debut at the Famous Door, Prima had achieved notice from his jazz and swing recordings on the Brunswick label. Prima first walked into a recording studio in New York on September 27, 1934. With him were the members of his newly formed group, Louis Prima and his New Orleans Gang: George Brunis on trombone, Sidney Arodin on clarinet, Claude Thornhill on piano, George Van Eps on guitar, Art Shapiro on bass, and Stan King on drums. Within just a few weeks, this group would be replaced entirely by musicians more to Prima's liking. Specifically, Prima would hire New Orleanian Frank Pinero for piano, Garry McAdams on guitar, and, of course, Pee Wee Russell with his magic clarinet.

The recordings that Prima and his first New York sidemen made that day in September of 1934 are a good indication of where Prima's creative compass was pointing. Four songs made it to wax, each played without the benefit of any rehearsal, playback, or sound checks. Brunswick Records, with whom Prima would make records for the next two years, was typical of most record companies in the 1930s in that it spared almost every expense in getting its artists on platter. Artists were scheduled for limited recording schedules, perhaps two to three hours to cut a dozen tunes or more, and many times were rewarded with only a small "services rendered" check.

Musicians for Brunswick and other labels were also encouraged to make the songs as quickly as possible, preferably in one take. Perhaps realizing there was little time for innovation or experiment, or because he was intimidated by the auspicious event of his first actual recording session, Prima picked songs that were relatively conventional and played them in a hybrid fashion, mixing New Orleans Dixieland with the new elements of swing then just being heard in Gotham. Louis sang in two of the tunes: "That's Where the South Begins" and "'Long About Midnight." The vocals come off high-pitched and very much in the Louis Armstrong style—part words and part scat.

Two other songs rounded out the session, "Jamaica Shout" and the classic "Star Dust." If Prima expected fireworks from his first session, he didn't get them. While the four sides clearly exhibited his musical talent and energy, they fall short in presenting the kind of swing/jam band explosives that he would later be capable of recording. But the experience warmed him to the concept of recording and by November, Louis returned to the studios two more times to record a total of eleven tunes for Brunswick. From these sessions, things begin to happen. On November 1, Prima and his gang recorded "Let's Have a Jubilee," a song that Louis had earlier experimented with in New Orleans. There is some confusion here as to whose "signature" tune "Jubilee" really was. Apparently the November 1, version of the song went well—trombonist George Brunis began to play the song as his own in public after this session, and eventually Brunswick released this same song under the issue of George Brunis and his New Orleans Gang.[1]

But by the end of November, Prima recorded "Let's Have a Jubilee," one more time for Brunswick—perhaps to leave no doubt as to whose song it really was, but more likely to improve upon a ditty he seemed to like greatly. By the time Louis was packing the Famous Door, he was using "Jubilee" as his theme song. Posters of Prima in a tux, smiling and holding his trumpet, invariably listed the words "Let's Have a Jubilee!" right under the musician's name. It would be the first of many songs Prima would adopt as either an introduction to his club shows or as a means of securing a form of identification with the public.

Upon the release of the second Prima version of "Let's Have a Jubilee," *The New Yorker* commented that the Prima ditty was "Fast and loose and improvisational, with heroic solo passages . . . "[2]

During this same period, Prima also recorded one song that actually won him a significant amount of critical praise and popularity, "(Looks Like I'm) Breakin' the Ice." Recorded also on November 1, "Breakin' the Ice" was a typically fast-paced number highlighting Prima's singing and trumpet work. By December Brunswick publicists reported that "Breakin' the Ice" was the company's second-best seller in the crucial Chicago market.

[1] Brian Rust, *50 Years of Recorded Jazz—1917-1966, Volume 30* (New Rochelle, N.Y., 1976), p. 307. Also Rust's *Jazz Records, 1897-1942, Volume 2* (New Rochelle, N.Y., 1978), p. 1249.

[2] *The New Yorker*, April 13, 1935.

In February 1935, the song was still in the top five in Chicago and rated a number six slot in Los Angeles.

Prima's real hits, though, came when Russell climbed on board and Prima recorded "Chinatown," "Chasing Shadows," and "The Lady in Red," all in one memorable session on May 17, 1935. By late June, all three songs had made it to the top-selling national lists where they stayed for the duration of the summer. Abel Green in *Variety* called "The Lady in Red" a "rhumba fox, but you'd never know it as Prima plays and warbles it."[3] In July "Chasing Shadows" became the number one best-selling tune in the nation, while the following month "Gypsy Tea Room," another Prima song, climbed to number one in sheet music sales in the New York area as a direct result of the hit Prima platter. Los Angeles and Chicago also reported such strong showings for the Prima song that it hit the number one slot several weeks later, and by September Prima's "Lady in Red" was number one in Los Angeles, too.[4]

Three hit songs in three months is a level of professional accomplishment that many artists could envy. Even though it was limited to proportionately lower-selling albums than those later enjoyed by the likes of Frank Sinatra, Elvis Presley, or the Beatles, Prima nonetheless was experiencing in 1935 and 1936 the same happy exposure of watching various aspects of his career snowball into greater and greater public recognition. Those who lined up to watch his Famous Door appearances were the same people who purchased his Brunswick records. As Prima's reputation grew, specifically enhanced by favorable reviews in national publications, his Brunswick records began to sell well beyond the east coast markets. In turn, this national exposure gave Prima a perfect base for a successful opening in California in the fall of 1935.

Even from a critical standpoint, Prima's hit recordings were triumphant. The same music and jazz critics who would later accuse Prima of selling out to commercial interests, applauded his Brunswick work. Perhaps the greatest reason for these successful discs, next to Louie's abilities as a jazz musician, was the extraordinarily high-energy explosives issued by Prima and Russell as a duet.

[3]*Variety*, June 19, 1935.

[4]*Ibid.*, September 11, 1935.

Almost fifty years later, music critic John McDonough would write of the Prima-Russell chemistry on "The Lady in Red":

> Prima leads the group through a brief preface and the first chorus, sticking closely to the melody. His swing is direct and simple, his tone strong, penetrating and all on one level. After the bridge Russell comes marching in right on top of the beat, playing with a dry throaty tone. The first four or five bars are very much in step with the pulse, but then he takes a little splash of triplets and suddenly his solos take on a slightly tilted, asymmetrical shape, as if the notes and accents were dropping almost at random around the beat.

On "Chasing Shadows" a tune in which Prima warbles the lyrics in a distinct crooner fashion, McDonough notes: "Prima and Russell enter at the bridge and take it out smoking all the way, Russell playing along with Prima but initially shooting off a high-rising rocket of his own near the end."[5]

Russell's penchant for drinking, though, did add one disruptive note to the Pee Wee and Louie show. A story circulated that during their Famous Door days in New York, Prima felt relatively confident in his ability to curb Russell's intake by controlling his environment. As long as Prima could keep an eye on Russell, he could deter the clarinetist from overindulging. At the Famous Door, that was easy enough. But some people believe Russell outsmarted Prima anyway; during certain numbers, Pee Wee supposedly slipped off the bandstand and climbed out a window in the club's men's room. From there he'd run to Reilley's, a nearby saloon, grab a quick drink, and hasten to return to the Famous Door—all within the time frame of one song, and usually just in time to play a solo. Even Leon Prima, who joined up with Louis in California for awhile to manage the band, remembers calling on Pee Wee in his hotel room and learning that Pee Wee's room "Smelled like a gin mill, there'd be bottles everywhere; all over the floor." His drinking aside, Pee Wee's musical abilities were a decided plus for the Prima outfit, and not long after arriving in Los Angeles Prima

---

[5]McDonough, *Pee Wee Russell*, p. 37.

began to form the makings of a larger orchestra, one that would highlight both his and Pee Wee's playing.[6]

By late 1935, the movement was toward the larger swing bands and orchestras. Prima, who prided himself on spotting new musical trends, was interested in putting together a larger group, but was reluctant because of the potential trouble spots of such an organization: the larger payroll, the new arrangements, the demand for good personnel. He did, though, continue to hire new talent when various spots in his small band opened up and he saw the need to add new instrumental slots. Louis Masinter, a string bass player from New Orleans, came on board after Prima placed a long-distance call to the Crescent City native asking him to leave his birthplace for a tryout with the band. Masinter, who later recalled that Prima always "treated me and the other band members with respect," was interested in joining Louis because he knew that Prima was "getting up there," an obvious reference to Prima's emerging national status. One night Prima ran into his old guitar-playing friend Frank Federico in a California hotel lobby. "Go home and get your guitar," Prima yelled at Federico. "I just fired McAdams." Federico came back with guitar in hand, and stayed for the next eleven years.[7]

While the faces continued to change in the band and Prima contemplated life with a bigger orchestra, Los Angeles—and Hollywood—waited. Prima made good on his promise to start his own Famous Door, west-coast style. Several days after arriving in Hollywood in October 1935, Prima wandered into the Blue Heaven nightclub at Vine Street and Willoughby, which was owned by singer Gene Austin. "I got to talking with Austin," Prima said later. "When I told him that Red Calonna [Jerry Calonna's brother] and I were looking for a club location, he just turned the lease over to us. He said he was tired of the grind. Three days later, we had a new sign over the entry and Hollywood had its Famous Door. No connection with the 52nd Street joint."[8]

Prima remembered well what his new club looked like: "It was a small place," he said, "so small you couldn't get *out* when it was crowded. It was a fun joint. All the Hollywood stars came—and we got everybody to do something. Like we had a number called 'The Love Bug." After several

---

[6]*Ibid.*, p. 19; Leon Prima interview, May 1984.

[7]Louis Masinter interview, January 1986; Frank Federico interview, April 1985.

[8]Shaw, *The Street That Never Slept*, p. 126.

choruses, I would point to somebody in the audience, and he had to sing a chorus. He could make up his own words. Everybody got into the spirit of the thing . . . " "It was just for laughs," Federico recalled. "With the 'Love Bug' Louie liked to get people involved in the show. It was all for laughs. He'd point to you and you'd have to come up with some rhyme. It was all spur-of-the-moment stuff. None of it was rehearsed. If it was funny, we kept it that way." Prima, obviously borrowing from his latest theme, put it more simply: "We had a jubilee," he said.[9]

The Hollywood club led to opportunities that were perhaps not available even in New York. Nightly Prima subjected the well-known show business personalities in his audience, the directors, writers, actors, actresses, and producers, to his own particularly unique sense of humor. "All these young actors and actresses and kids like Mickey Rooney and Jackie Cooper would come and watch us play," bassist Masinter recalled. "They wouldn't serve them drinks because they were too young. They'd just sit there and listen. They'd invite us out to their homes." It was inevitable that Prima would get an offer to bring his talents to film. What is more interesting is that Louis eventually made more than twenty movies and always either played himself or the role of a musician. Maybe it was a good example of how permanently Prima's image had become etched in the public's mind. In any event, it was a gold mine of an opportunity. "The greatest source of publicity ever developed for bandleaders is the movies," advised *Metronome* in 1942. "First of all, the bandleader's name and photo appear in newspaper ads all over the country. Blowups go on display in thousands of theatres from coast to coast . . . When you mention film to a bandleader these days, he doesn't think it's something that collects on your teeth."[10]

One of Prima's first movie appearances had him dressed in cowboy boots, a dark shirt, and a large, flowing necktie for the mindless musical *Rhythm on the Range,* which went into production in early 1936. The movie was slated as a mixture of Western atmosphere and Broadway wisdom. Starring Bing Crosby and the newly-discovered Martha Raye, Prima's Famous Door friend, *Rhythm on the Range* presented Louis mugging happily in the background while Crosby and Raye sang around a

[9]*Ibid.*, p. 126; Frank Federico interview, April 1985.

[10]Louis Masinter interview, January 1986; *Metronome*, May 1942.

campfire "I'm an Old Cowhand." When his cue came up, Prima sang, "They fed me hot tamales the day I was born, I been red hot ever since that morn, when I start to cook, I just grab my horn." The Paramount release became a runaway box office success in an era when all forms of musicals, great and gaudy, dominated the silver screen. *Rhythm on the Range,* which also co-starred the hauntingly beautiful and poignant Frances Farmer, was one of Hollywood's top twenty hits of the year. Despite his limited participation in the film, Prima was soon making more movies for both Paramount and a variety of other Hollywood production companies. Between 1936 and 1938, he was one of the headline attractions in a short film called *Vitaphone Variete,* which presented him playing and singing in a night club setting; *Swing It,* which featured Louis and Pee Wee on "Basin Street Blues" and "Up the Lazy River" and also underlined the sometimes comic relationship between the two men in a remarkably clever scene showing them conversing with one another through their instruments; and *The Star Reporter,* which spotlights Prima in action at the Hollywood Famous Door. *Manhattan Merry Go Round* was released in late 1937 for Republic Pictures and starred an unlikely cast including cowboy singer Gene Autry and baseball star Joe DiMaggio. The plot was simple: a fast-talking con artist buys a recording studio and signs up the likes of Cab Calloway, Ted Lewis, and Prima, who appeared as himself. The film ends when the new owner's mother demands he makes an operatic recording by a famous Italian prima dona. "The barrage of Italian sprinkled throughout is comical, even if unintelligent," said *The Billboard.*[11]

That same year Prima also appeared in the musical *You Can't Have Everything,* a film about the fortunes and misfortunes of a young songwriter (Alice Faye) and the rich, sometimes drunk patron who falls in love with her (Don Ameche). In two scenes, Prima, again appearing as an orchestra leader, plays trumpet on "It's a Southern Holiday" and "Rhythm on the Radio."[12]

A survey of Prima's films would show that he never attained major star status in Hollywood. He rarely, in fact, had the opportunity to act in a picture because he was usually filmed as either a background musician hired

[11]William Arnold, *Frances Farmer—Shadowland* (New York, 1979), pp. 51-52; David Meeker, *Jazz in the Movies: A Guide to Jazz Musicians, 1917-1977* (New Rochelle, N..Y., 1977), citations 2118, 1914, 1585, and 1851; *The Billboard,* January 8, 1938.

[12]Jay Robert Nash and Stanley Ralph Ross, *The Motion Picture Guide—W to Z, 1927 to 1983* (Evanston, Ill., 1986), p. 3960.

to keep the party going or as himself playing in a concert at the Famous
Door or in a recording studio. But as a musician, Prima's frustrations in
Hollywood were not singular experiences. Evan musical giants such as
Louis Armstrong, Benny Goodman, and Billie Holiday were ill-served by
motion pictures. Hollywood instinctively seemed incapable of
understanding the social importance of jazz and swing, thus casting the likes
of Armstrong, Goodman, and even Prima in the roles of smiling, bland co-
stars who were there only to provide music—and usually traditional dance
band fare at that. Viewers rarely got the opportunity to see musicians doing
what they do best, that is, play music, unencumbered by a surrounding
romantic plot, dancing girls, and animal acts. "He would have never made it
if his career depended upon his Hollywood film appearances," observed jazz
film historian David Chartok. "Louis's films were only a means to
showcase his talent, however brief his appearances may have been. But
even in this limited context, Prima was able to project, to come across to
the audience primarily because he was such a superb performer."[13]

Prima had other interests in Hollywood, however, beyond his brief film
appearances. As in New York, women nightly approached Louis and let
their intentions be known. "He was sexually almost an animal," said one of
his sidemen. "I don't know if he could have been true to any one girl. He'd
be with this one for a couple of hours and then catch someone else's eye,
and take off with her. It was just incredible. Most of us in the band could
never figure it out."[14]

Prima's increasing interests in such matters were hastened by his
deteriorating marriage to Louise. As he became a headline attraction in New
York and Hollywood, Louise and New Orleans became less appealing to
him. Although the couple had a daughter named Joyce, trouble in the
marriage could be traced back at least as far as February 1933 when Louise
claimed to have discovered that Louis regularly visited a French Quarter
prostitute. Her lawyer petitioned the court, writing that Louise "has always
been a kind and dutiful wife," but that Louis, "regardless of his marriage
vows, has, since their marriage, been guilty of adultery, committed at
various times and particularly on the 24th day of February 1933, at the

[13]David Chartok interview, May 1987.

[14]Confidential communication.

premises No. 732 Toulouse Street, a notorious house of prostitution, with a woman named Alice . . . "[15]

It would still be three years, though, before Louis and Louise divorced. For her it was a painful experience. She was enchanted by Prima's success, his glamorous life and professional accomplishments. Even as their marriage crumbled, she clipped articles on Louis in the trade papers and magazines, treasured every letter he sent her, and listened, mesmerized, as he talked of the hotels, clubs, and music of the Big Apple.

During one Christmas visit to New Orleans, Louis woke up early at the St. Peter Street home and clipped a boxful of $10 and $20 bills to the family Christmas tree. To Leon, it was amusing. To father Tony, it was another sign that his youngest son couldn't handle money. To Angelina, it was proof that her son was a success, a reaffirmation of all the things she taught him. But to Louise, it was simply dazzling. "I'll never forget when he did that," said Louise. "He was always doing something like that. He could be so appealing sometimes. He had all sorts of charisma."[16]

Louis and Louise were divorced in early 1936 by decree in New Orleans, despite several attempts by both parties to save their marriage. By all accounts the divorce between Louis and Louise was amicable. Louise said he remained her friend, sent her regular checks, and kept in touch with her. She added that she was Prima's "best wife" because she loved him "when he didn't have anything. I think he always wondered about his other wives. Why were they really with him? With me, there was no doubt."[17]

Less than a year after the divorce from Louise, Prima was seen regularly escorting a leggy, dark-haired beauty in Hollywood named Alma Ross. Born in Minnesota but raised in Hollywood, Alma changed her last name from Raase to Ross and caught the attention of producers and agents who wanted her to sign a seven-year contract after she impressed them with a screen test. In an era—then as now—rife with intensely competitive starlets eager to jump through the Hollywood hoops for even a bit part in a film, Ross was singularly nonplussed by Tinsel Town's glamour and thoroughly indifferent to the opportunities available in film. "I had seen Hollywood up

[15]Civil District Court, Parish of Orleans, Division E, Docket 5, File number 202-140.

[16]Louise Polizzi interview, January 1986.

[17]*Ibid.*, May 1984.

close," Ross said later. "And I just wasn't that interested, to tell you the truth."[18]

In the spring of 1936, Ross and an escort stopped by the Hollywood Famous Door for an evening that would change her life. There was Louie, dressed in white, with his dark curly hair tumbling over his forehead, sending his club audience into a frenzy with that strange combination of humor, music, and sexual suggestion. Alma liked what she saw, but was even more attracted when she caught Louis after his show "sitting all by himself, looking so sad and lonely." When Alma and Louis were finally introduced to one another, the starlet was subjected to the full Prima treatment: the undivided attention, the sly smile, the sense that only she in the whole world was getting a glimpse of the private Louis, the inner man. "He was charming, and we were atracted to each other instantly," Alma said.[19]

Alma was elegant, beautiful, refined, and even-tempered. Her unassuming ways both captivated and infuriated Louis. When he learned that she held little affection for climbing to the height of Hollywood stardom, Louis was at first bemused and then indignant. "You don't want to work, that's your problem," he told Alma. "You could have a great career if only you tried a little harder."[20]

Prima urged Alma to sign the Paramount contract and appear in as many films as possible, to get her name before the public and become a major Hollywood star. Although Alma was still unimpressed with the Hollywood struggle, she and Prima continued to date. Increasingly, Alma was seen at the Famous Door or on Louie's arm as they attended the pool parties of the movie moguls or took part in the charity balls and concerts that are so much a part of Hollywood life.

In the summer of 1936, Prima took his band on the road, leaving behind the nightly duties of the Hollywood Famous Door, and presenting his music to ready fans in the midwest. From Madison, Wisconsin, Prima wired Alma in Hollywood and asked her to marry him. Alma said she almost fainted when she read Louis' wire, but she met him in Madison anyway, only to discover that the couple hadn't been in Wisconsin long

---

[18]Alma Ross interview, November 1986.

[19]*Ibid.*

[20]*Ibid.*

enough to satisfy the state's marriage requirements. Alma and Louis next went to Chicago, only to get similar news from that city's marriage license bureau.

That evening in Chicago, Prima encountered his mentor, Guy Lombardo, in a hotel lobby and told him of his troubles securing a marriage license. Lombardo, on his way to an appearance in South Bend, Indiana, called the courthouse in that town and then told the excited couple they could get married in South Bend. The ceremoney took place July 25, 1936. Lombardo was the best man, and the witnesses were composed of the several dozen musicians comprising both Lombardo's and Prima's bands.

The union was an explosive one, filled with fights, frequent separations, emotional letters from one city to the next, and tearful reconciliations. Alma rememberred that one of their biggest quarrels concerned Prima's daughter by his first wife. Louis, according to Alma, simply denied that he had any children at all. "He said he had never had any children," said Ross. "And there was no reason for it. When someone mentioned to me the possibility that Louis might be lying about this, I confronted him and told him that he had no reason to lie, that I thought it would be wonderful if he had kids. But he swore up and down that he had no children and asked who did I believe, a stranger or my husband? He had me apologizing to him for thinking such things."

The ploy even worked for awhile until Alma found a tax return addressed to Louie, asking about his dependant child. Alma sent the letter to Prima, who was appearing in New York at the time, and wrote on top of the correspondence: "You know more about this than I do." Prima's explanation was sheepish: "I thought you'd leave me if you knew I had a daughter."[21] His deception enraged Alma. But somehow the marriage survived, possibly because Louis and Alma were geographically separated for so much of their union.

To outsiders, Prima presented a picture of marital happiness. He told one reporter that he and Alma liked to listen to classical music in their Los Angeles apartment, never missed the Jack Benny radio program, and dreamed of buying a home in California and settling there. By 1937, Alma, due to Prima's coaxing, signed with Paramount, while Louis continued to nurture hopes of forming a Big Band on the east coast. Alma would, in fact, appear in a series of films, once even winning a fair share of critical notice for her

[21]*Ibid.*

role in *The Tuttles of Tahiti*, which starred Charles Laughton. Prima's film's on the other hand, continued to be artistically vapid but promotionally lucrative. Prima simply hoped to reap a rich harvest from the hundreds of movie posters bearing his name and face that appeared in theatres across the country from 1936 to 1939. But the best means of realizing his ambitions, Prima knew, came in organizing a big band that would travel the nation, hitting all of the biggest cities, best theatres and swanky clubs.[22]

Getting such orchestras organized was a big job, however. Initially Prima was discouraged from the idea by his agency, the powerful Music Corporation of America. Although Prima was relieved to have the mighty agency handle all of his promotional and scheduling arrangements, he soon resented MCA's scheduling practices, a topic of anger for bandleaders Goodman, Jack Teagarden, and Tommy Dorsey also. At the same time, Prima knew he would need MCA if ever he were to get the Big Band off its feet. Ironically, Guy Lombardo once again emerged as Prima's supporter, telling Prima to pursue his ideas of forming a Big Band. "Guy Lombardo was chiefly responsible for my big band," Prima said. "Lombardo was convinced I'd do great with a big band and he talked to MCA about it. But the agency wanted to stay with the small group, didn't offer any support at all . . . " Prima decided, nonetheless, to proceed with the Big Band format. He left Hollywood in the fall of 1936 to travel to Chicago—convinced that only in another city, far away from his normal support groups in New York and Los Angeles, could his project receive the kind of objective airing needed. Booked into the prestigious Blackhawk Club in the Windy City, Prima garnered a national radio connection from the club which he hoped would further the publicity needed to sustain a large orchestra. The Chicago debut received an unusual amoung of press attention with many columnists wondering if Prima would survive the sometimes fatal jump from small jam band status to Big Band fame.[23]

Prima opened at the Blackhawk during the first week of October 1936, appearing with a twelve-piece unit that included Russell, Federico, Masinter, and Pinero on piano, as well as female vocalist Velma Rae, and an entirely

---

[22]Unidentified newspaper clipping, Institute of Jazz Studies, Rutgers University, Princeton, New Jersey; *International Motion Picture Almanac, 1942-1943* (New York, 1942), p. 532.

[23]Dan E. Moldea, *Dark Victory: Ronald Reagan, MCA and the Mob* (New York, 1986), pp. 44-45; *Down Beat,* February 19, 1959.

new book of swing arrangements. The Blackhawk was packed, when the lights dimmed for Prima's walk-on, the crowd cheered with anticipation. After weeks of press speculation—would Prima's latest act be a big hit or a big boondoggle?—many in the audience may have showed up out of simple curiosity. Others may have come to be a part of the growing Prima legend, the tales of his career which Louis himself frequently promoted. Almost everyone who read about Prima's dramatic debut at the Famous Door in New York in early 1935 may have wondered if the same type of explosives would happen again in Chicago. Perhaps lightning would strike twice in Prima's career. If it did, the trendy Chicagoans wanted to be the first to say "I was there . . . "

Unfortunately for both Prima and his expectant audience, obvious problems beset the band from the beginning, and the press coverage chronicled his quick Chicago fiasco. Even though *The Billboard* took enthusiastic note of the first evening audience reaction and predicted "Prima is well on his way to becoming one of the most popular bands in town," the band quickly began to seem disorganized and aimless, a pattern *Down Beat* noticed several weeks later when it reported: "Prima's band is somewhat shaky in the rhythm section and also in the brass section . . . We're for you Louie, so get that gang of swingsters settled down." Three issues later, *Down Beat* observed that Prima's problems with his band had only gotten worse, and they bluntly reported: "Gargantuan is a good word to describe the sound of the flop made by Louis Prima at Chicago's Blackhawk . . . A hit with five men at the cat session in New York and a failure with twelve is a piece of history which only bears out the truth of Connie Mack's philosophy: 'Never change a winning line-up.'"[24]

For his part, Prima blamed the creative failure of his Chicago stay on his sidemen: "Every man was a master on his own instrument when he wanted to be," Prima later explained. "But they didn't want to play for me. They laid down . . . I don't know what happened. They sat there through my acts with long faces. They came late. It was awful . . . So we lost the Blackhawk job. We were out."[25]

Only a handfull of recordings from Prima's Chicago stay still exist. In mid-November, Prima and his twelve-man orchestra recorded several sides for Vocallion Records and his musical problems with the Blackhawk

[24]*The Billboard*, October 10, 1936; *Down Beat*, October 1936, January 1937.

[25]*Item*, undated clipping, ca. early 1950s.

appearance become quickly evident. Perhaps the greatest problem with the big band was that it lacked the Prima spirit. In his haste to emulate the Big Band styles of Goodman and Ellington, Prima had completely eliminated the spontaneity and sparkle that made his New York Famous Door stay distinguished. Gone was the energy of improvisation, replaced by a plodding, uninspired orchestral format that sounded overly rehearsed. Prima said it wasn't just the music from the Blackhawk stay that depressed him. He later claimed that his sidemen tried to rip him off. "The time came to break up," said Prima. "The boys wanted to go home. I had been lending most of them money from time to time and had a record of it. But I owed them $20 each for the record date [for Vocallion]. At the station I said I would just wash out their loans. I said 'Let's just forget the whole thing, boys. It just didn't work.' They understood that in cancelling their debts to me I also cancelled the smaller $20 fee I owed them. But a few weeks later the music union came to me on the West Coast and told me the boys had brought me up on charges back home. They accused me running out on the record payment. I cried like a baby."[26]

What really happened? Prima's claim that his New Orleans musicians just "didn't want to play for me" rings false. Any New Orleans musician worth his salt knew when and when not to lay back. Why would any one musician—let alone a group of musicians—make the big move from New Orleans to Chicago only to refuse to play? Especially when the New Orleans-Chicago connection, by tradition, after King Oliver and Louis Armstrong, was viewed as a sure route to bigger and better things? It seems more likely that Prima was simply unprepared to manage, program, and arrange his first big band. The jump from a hot jam band of five to the more professional big band with set arrangements and a thematic program was a big one. It's highly possible that Prima underestimated the job ahead and once he saw things fall apart in the Windy City looked for scapegoats. Long-time associates of Prima confide that in times of success, Prima could be very generous in his praise and that he was equally critical in times of duress.

Additionally, even Prima's biggest supporters in the band, men like Federico and Masinter, freely admit that Prima was known to be somewhat tight when it came to record royalties and regular pay. "He was just that way," said one long-time Prima sideman. "Money was important to him.

---

[26]*Ibid.*

In fact, I'd say he was obsessed with it. Even in the best of times, Louie was hardly loose with his dollars. After a disaster like the Blackhawk, he must have just closed his wallet. He wouldn't have cared who he'd owed money to at that point."[27]

Whichever version of the events at the Blackhawk were true, it's safe to assume that the first weeks of 1937 were unhappy ones for both Prima and his twelve-piece orchestra. If there were any hard feelings from the event, it's hárd to discern. The music business has always been rife with stories of musicians who failed to get paid for one gig or another—witness Prima and Federico's orange-picking excursion in Florida during the formative years. As if to explain away the entire ugly Blackhawk affair, Prima commented: "Maybe we all learned something."[28]

Between the winter of 1937 and late 1941, Prima would return to his big band idea on occasion, experimenting with new sounds, extra instruments and larger orchestral arrangements. Finally, as the United States entered World War II, Prima would abandon his jam band fivesome for good, fully throwing himself into the Big Band era of the booming 1940s. Bur first Louis returned to the scene of his greatest triumph: the Famous Door in New York, arriving in late 1937 with a newly structured New Orleans Gang that included Federico, Masinter, Pinero, and Meyer Weinberg on clarinet. New York critics rubbed their hands in anticipation: Here was the return of the prodical swingster—forget that messy affair in Chicago and all those tawdry Hollywood flicks. It was like old times. After his first triumphant week in the Famous Door, *The Billboard* enthusiastically reported: "Prima is a whole show in himself. He's a showman to the marrow of his bones, and his sensationalized style of trumpeting, reveling in high notes, bold attack, rapid changes of pace and mood, send the kittens who think they're cats into a frenzy."[29]

Prima's stay at the new Famous Door in New York lasted for more than twenty incredibly successful weeks. By May of 1938, Louis signed to appear at entertainment entrepreneur Billy Rose's Casa Mañana club, perhaps the most popular night club and vaudeville theatre in New York. Appearing with the Three Stooges on the bill, the Prima outfit grossed

---

[27]Confidential communication.

[28]*Item*, undated clipping, ca. early 1950s.

[29]*The Billboard*, December 11, 1937.

more than $250,000 in a seven-week appearance at the Casa Mañana,
prompting Rose to wire Prima: "Dear Louis—If you were a girl, I'd
propose."[30]

Prima's course suddenly became clear.   Almost a full year after the
Chicago disaster, Louis was now being booked by the Wiliam Morris
Agency into a variety of clubs spread from one coast to another. The Big
Band business was a national obsession, and Prima by late 1938 and early
1939 was no longer anchoring himself to one club, as he did with the
Famous Door in 1935 and his own club in Hollywood in 1936, but was,
instead, living the full-fledged life of a ragged and harried bandleader on the
road.

"Those one-nighters were really something," bassist Masinter later
recalled.

> We used to travel by car. We didn't travel by bus or train or
> anything like that. We'd go the cheapest way we could get there.
> We'd pile in a car, and, you see, that was dangerous too. He was
> with the William Morris Agency and the bookers didn't care where
> you played a job . . . You'd get through one place and they'd have
> you booked 400 miles away for the next night. You'd get out of
> your tuxedos after one show, get into something more comfortable,
> jump in the car, and drive all night. We'd switch off driving, but, I
> tell you, it was hard living.

Throughout the late 1930s and early '40s, Prima and his band—eventually
increased to a fourteen-piece organization with female vocalist Lily Ann
Carol—saw the countryside through the windshield of their sedans. Like
many big bands, the Prima orchestra travelled in a geographic arc that started
around Boston, swooped down through New York on its way to Baltimore
and Washington, D. C., and then swerved back to Philadelphia and various
cities in New Jersey. As his orchestra gained public attention and
acceptance, he would occasionally venture out to places like Miami Beach,
New Orleans, or St. Louis, but the northeast corridor consistently proved to
be his most lucrative circuit.[31]

[30]Gia Maione's private files.

[31]Louis Masinter interview, January 1986.

A good example of the Prima path and schedule could be found in their September 1942 travels. At the beginning of the month, the Prima band appeared at the stately Summit Theatre in Baltimore. From there they played a stop at the RKO Theatre in Boston; the Palomar Theatre in Norfolk, Virginia; the Earle Theatre in Philadelphia and then, finally, one last week at the Royal Theatre in Baltimore, ending up more than 1,000 miles on the road and a hectic, typical month back in the same city in which they started.

Sometimes the pace resulted in frayed nerves. During the same week in which the Japanese bombed Pearl Harbor in December of 1941, Prima was booked to appear at Boston's Rymor Ballroom, but two of his trombonists were arrested in Hope Valley, Massachusetts, for speeding. With their arrests, all of the band's uniforms, instruments, and music were held up in the truck they were driving. One of the trombonists called Prima and told him of their predicament. Angry, Prima yelled into the phone: "Tell that cop I hope his mothers dies and I'll call you back." Noted the *Providence Journal:* "State police do not like to be told that someone hopes their mother will die. They are not eager to speed things up for anyone who says anything like that." Four hours after the arrest, the men were released and continued on their way to Boston. "And Louis 'Be Happy' Prima was not happy," said the *Journal.* "Nothing but trouble," Louis snorted.[32]

In a calmer presence of mind, Prima could joke about the life of a bandleader. In a poem written for *Esquire's* annual Jazz Book, Prima said the bandleader's life was a "lot of grief for me on every hand." He then talked about the song pluggers who stopped him on every visit with ditties that are supposed to be the best, and waiters who write songs, "You know the pest." He mentioned the fights with song arrangers, the photos for picture magazines, the teenagers who mobbed him at every stop, and the reporters who want "just a peek behind the scenes!" Admitting that at first he thought "the life was simply grand," Prima said it was now "more than flesh and blood can stand." But he ended the verse with a wry acceptance of his fate, noting that he always told his men to "pack 'em up and let's get going," and signed off sighing "It's great to be the leader of the band."[33]

[32]*Down Beat,* December 1, 1941.

[33]*Esquire's 1947 Jazz Book,* p. 34.

While it took some of the more reserved columnists awhile to accept it, Prima by the early 1940s had organized his big band around entertainment, rather than purely musical, themes. "I don't want any of that schmaltz that's been identified with the corny bands of swing music," Prima told one reporter when he organized his larger group. But increasingly, "corn" was what the buying public got. For almost a ten-year stretch, Prima was rated by his fellow big band musicians across the nation as a pure corn performer. Defining the "corn" list regularly compiled by *Down Beat*, the magazine's editors noted: "The list is composed by other musicians who select them not because they are bad (although some 'corny' musicians are notoriously bad) but only means musicians do not think their styles are in good taste. They lean more toward the tastes of a large public." If Prima was bothered by such kidding, he rarely acknowledged it. "I offer them comedy routines between numbers," he explained. "Dance bands that are only that are dead. I use my musicians for much of the comedy. Every guy I got is a hambone." On another occasion, Prima remarked: "They all put us down as a novelty band. They don't appreciate the fact that you can't draw crowds if you can't draw dancers, and dancers come here for the beat and not the novelty."[34]

Sometimes Prima even lashed back at his detractors: "Look, people have been unfair to me," he said. "They see us on the stage clowning around and they call us a show band . . . They forget that we can play very good dance music when we feel like it . . . We adapt ourselves to moods. The sooner a lot of bands realize that they can't live forever if they play strictly dance music, the better." Prima was proud of his ability to entertain. But he was equally adamant in his belief that his music was good, that it had a beat, and that audiences enjoyed his band as much for their intended levity as their musical merit.[35]

The domestic scene during World War II was one full of pitfalls and opportunities for many big band groups. Some of the larger organizations like Glenn Miller's and Tommy Dorsey's were financially successful due to the enormous popularity of their music. When the draft came and raided such groups of talented men (Prima was classified 4-F due to a knee injury), there was an abundant list of other young, ambitious msuicians waiting to replace their predecessors. A lesser known and financially entrenched band

---

[34]*Down Beat*, November 1, 1939, November 1937; *Item*, August 3, 1948, undated clipping, ca. early 1950s.

[35]Story by syndicated journalist Betty Brown, 1945, uncited clipping, Institute of Jazz Studies, Rutgers University, Princeton, New Jersey.

like Prima's could only suffer through their World War II losses. Prima was equally strapped by the gas rationing decrees from Washington which severely cut back on his band's energy reserves for travel.

But, in an interesting change of fate, Prima greatly benefited from one domestic development that most musicians steered clear of: the racial politics of the day. In the early 1940s, First Lady Eleanor Roosevelt became widely identified as an ardent foe of segregationist practices and racist policies throughout the land. Mrs. Roosevelt wrote in 1941 that many problems, including the prevalence of tuberculosis and rising crime were attributable "not just to lack of education and to physical differences, but are due in large part to the basic fact of segregation which we have set up in this country and which warps and twists the lives not only of our Negro population, but sometimes of foreign born or even religious groups."[36]

Accordingly, the president's wife encouraged public examples of integration wherever possible, sometimes with disastrous results. Bandleader Charlie Barnet remembered one interracial concert for a predominantly black audience in Los Angeles which Mrs. Roosevelt helped to sponsor that turned into a "full-scale riot," in which he and Louis Armstrong narrowly escaped with their lives.[37]

For Prima, the idea of integrated entertainment was nothing new. As a New Orleanian, he watched many black and white musicians play together, although it was always in informal settings. Because Prima joined in many of these same jam sessions with black musicians and learned some of his greatest musical lessons from them, he was open and receptive to the idea of whites and blacks playing together. Although the New Orleans jams were impromptu affairs, Prima's sessions with black musicians in New York were always well organized and highly public events. He played in at least one battle of the bands with Count Basie, who followed Prima into the Famous Door and whom Prima always admired for his musical talent. During his Second Coming at the Famous Door in 1937-1938, Prima's intermission act was the legendary black pianist Art Tatum, who brought in a sizable number of black followers. In addition, Prima and his New Orleans Gang frequently invited such Famous Door guests as Teddy Wilson

[36]Joseph E. Lash, *Eleanor and Franklin* (New York, 1971), p. 532.

[37]Charlie Barnet and Stanley Dance, *Those Swinging Years: The Autobiography of Charlie Barnet* (Baton Rouge, 1984), p. 119.

and Lionel Hampton, who were then the black half of Benny Goodman's interracial quartet, to sit in on a few numbers, and the two musicians always obliged.

By 1939, Prima and his band were under contract to appear in a number of black theatres in New York, Baltimore, Boston, and Washington, D. C. But his appearances at the famed Apollo Theatre in Harlem were most noteworthy largely because of the historic importance of the hall and Prima's extraordinary success there.

"The Apollo Theatre probably exerted a greater influence upon popular culture than any other entertainment venue in the world," author Ted Fox wrote. "It was primarily a black theater presenting the finest black entertainers performing the most innovative material of their day. For blacks it was the most important cultural institution—not just the greatest black theatre, but a special place to come of age emotionally, professionally, socially, and politically." Sammy Davis, Jr., who made his first appearance at the Apollo with Prima's orchestra, said he thought Louis was successful at the theatre because many people in the predominantly black audience were unsure what color Prima really was. "Half the people who came to the theatre thought Prima was black anyway. Mixed. So he was a big favorite." But long-time Apollo host Ralph Cooper had his own reasons for Prima's success. "He was one of the few white bands to play here," said Cooper.

> But his style merged with the Apollo. Being from New Orleans, and the Louie Armstrong-Joe Oliver background, I suppose that was one of the reasons his music appealed to us. Besides that, he was a hell of a good entertainer. That was good enough reason right there to play the Apollo. The question we always had was if you were a singer, either you could sing or you couldn't. If you were a musician, you were a good musician, a fair musician, or exceptional. Prima was in the exceptional category. He was quite an artist.[38]

Even the reviews were good: "Way up in this darktown section, trumpet man Louis Prima is turning on the heat in a performance that

---

[38]Ted Fox, *Showtime at the Apollo* (New York, 1983), pp. 4, 160; Ralph Cooper interview, April 1987.

knocks those of all hues right out of their seats," said *Variety* in November of 1941.[39]

But such events were not without their reminders of the racial mores of the day. Although he could perform in front of black audiences, Prima was still prohibited from appearing onstage with blacks. "They used to put a curtain down between us and the black showgirls," remembered Masinter.

> That's the way it was segregated. They put down that curtain and then we played while the girls danced. Then when it came time for our act, the girls would run off and the curtain would rise. We could look through the curtain at the girls, but the audience could never see through the curtain to see us.[40]

When Prima appeared at the predominantly black Howard Theatre in Washington in January of 1942, an enthusiastic Eleanor Roosevelt waited in the audience. "Mrs. Roosevelt heard about this white band that was playing all of the colored theatres," Prima recalled. "So she came to see us and invited me to the President's birthday party a couple of days later." What happened when Prima got to see FDR and the First Lady surprised even the normally jaded Louis. Ushering him into the White House's East Room, Mrs. Roosevelt introduced Prima to a number of Washington political officials and a gathering of entertainment figures including Mary Pickford, Lily Pons, Lucille Ball, Red Skelton, and Joan Fontaine who turned out to wish the president well. Louis, however, was afraid to meet FDR. "Waiting in line to meet him, I really got nervous," Prima said.

> What would I say: 'Howdy do,' 'pleased to meet ya,' 'the pleasure is mutual?' Finally I got to meet him and was amazed to hear my own voice saying 'Hello, Daddy!' The president burst out laughing. I sure felt better when I found out he understood hepcat talk.

But that was not the only surprise at the White House party. Before lunch was served, news photographers asked the party guests to gather around the

---

[39]*Variety*, November 5, 1941.

[40]Louis Masinter interview, January 1986.

president and Mrs. Roosevelt for a group shot. Prima kneeled down in the farthest corner of the picture with his mentor Guy Lombardo. And then something happened. "When they started taking pictures, all of the big names jockeyed for position, to be near Mr. and Mrs. Roosevelt," Prima said. "But I was way off in a corner. Mrs Roosevelt stopped the photographers and waved me over to her side. The next day my picture was in every paper in the country." Louis added: "The publicity was tremendous and the bookings started coming in."[41]

More than two decades later, Prima fondly gave credit to the Roosevelts and particularly the First Lady, for boosting his career. An habitual telegram sender, Prima was one of the first to wire a message of congratulations to Franklin D. Roosevelt, Jr., upon his election to the U. S. House of Representatives in 1946, prompting a kind word of thanks in return, and told reporters for years afterward that his 1942 White House visit was his "proudest memory."[42]

While ambitious bandleaders in the 1940s used any means of publicity they could get to bolster their career fortunes, Prima, by at least late 1942, was also riding high on the musical success of his band. The same idea that bore disastrous results for him in Chicago in 1936 was now bearing fruit. Recordings of Prima's band from 1942 to 1948 indicate a strong, unified sound rivaling the works of some of the greatest bands. In May 1944, Prima was featured on the radio program "One Night Stand" at the Hotel Commodore in New York. The fare for the evening included such standards as "San Fernando Valley," "I'm in Love With Someone," "Chinatown," and a straightforward version of the sultry "Stella By Starlight." Preserved on record, the outtakes of this radio performance present a band confident of its own musical abilities, swinging out in the kind of full arrangements, with an emphasis on saxophone and trumpet lines, that made the Glenn Miller and Tommy Dorsey bands so popular.[43]

In addition, the frenzied emotions Prima once generated at the Famous Door were now being reproduced in big city theatres across the land. In places like the Hippodrome Theatre in Baltimore and the RKO Theater in Boston, publicists noticed an interesting sight: ticket buyers lining up as

[41]*New York World Telegram*, May 11, 1965; *Chicago Tribune*, March 12, 1950.

[42]Gia Maione's private files; *Chicago Tribune*, March 12, 1950.

[43]"One Night Stand With Louis Prima," Joyce Records, 1067, New York, New York,.

early as 7 a.m. for a Prima matinee or evening concert. One writer described Prima as a "guy who's getting ten thousand a week from theatres that wouldn't book him fourteen months ago." In addition, he was breaking the house attendance records set by such giants as Goodman and Dorsey.[44]

It was a circuitous route from his Famous Door success in New York and California to the egg dropped at the Blackhawk in Chicago. But by the early 1940s, certainly after 1942, there was a distinct change in the air. Columnists could feel it, record producers saw it in raw numbers, and Prima heard it from the roar of the SRO crowds greeting him night after night. Prima was a success again. He left New York after less than a year as a triumphant entertainer, became a Hollywood regular in film and club appearances, took a bath with his first Big Band, but finally emerged victorious with a band that was winning national acclaim and a solid, loyal following. Yet, as ever, Prima remained an essentially private person. Those who thought they knew him well could detect little difference emotionally between the struggling musician and the popularly acclaimed band leader. One who did, fellow band leader Woody Herman, said the changes in Louie's fortunes could be reflected in his personality traits, but you had to look closely. Seeing Prima regularly in the halls of New York's Decca recording studios, Herman noted that if Louis "greeted you with a big hello, things were not that great. But if he was really swinging and getting ready to do a movie or something . . . he'd give you a little nod." Herman laughed at the memory. But the story rings true. By the mid-1940s, Prima was likely giving his "little nod" to dozens of professional peers. Things had never been better.[45]

---

[44]Uncited, undated clipping, Institute of Jazz Studies, Rutgers University, Princeton, New Jersey.

[45]"Louis Prima—The Chief," *WYES-TV*, Byer.

Chapter IV

Playing It Pretty and Private

Strangely enough, as Louis Prima became well known nationally, less was known about him personally. When reporters from high-circulation magazines and big-city newspapers sought the bandleader out, what inevitably emerged was a man who was often extraordinarily quiet and gave little indication of his private self. Interviews with sidemen and professional associates confirm this enigma. Few people felt they ever really "knew" Prima. He wasn't, many said, the type who would talk about his innermost desires and dreams.

What emerged instead was a mixed brew of behavior traits and character patterns portraying a restless, sometimes angry and brooding man, who lived for professional achievement and only rarely gave in to moments of retrospection and reflection. Temperamentally, Prima could be explosive. More than one associate tells of how Louis singled them out for scorn or ridicule on a particularly bad day. He was professionally demanding and financially preoccupied. There was always a new deal in the works: a recording contract, a concert schedule, a film commitment. If you were willing and pliable, you could be the perfect Prima band member. If you had personal problems or concerns about your pay, you might find yourself out of the band within minutes.

Prima's professional concerns were an unending obsession. Romantic interests of the bandleader say Louis was never really married to any of his wives—he was married only to his career. The women were a secondary preoccupation. And, admittedly, the small details of running a big band in the 1940s could be endless. But Prima gradually exhibited a drive that could best be described as relentless. There may have been a thousand details and angles to the business, but Prima saw to it that all of them worked out to his satisfaction.

In the middle of 1945, when Prima had a series of hit records blazing across the nation's airwaves, Warner Brothers offered the bandleader and his group a part in a new movie depicting singer Helen Morgan's life. Prima indicated an initial interest in the project, but from the outset complained about the money offered. The Hollywood producers and agents, long accustomed to extravagant financial demands, decided to stay the course. They met with Prima a number of times, gradually hoping to arrive at a financial agreement. But instead of getting closer to a consensus, Prima and Warner Brothers fell further apart. He wanted to know what role he and the band would plan in the new film; he mentioned the expense of travelling with the entire band from the east coast to California; he talked about the concert commitments he would have to curtail. The folks at Warner Brothers listened politely and then offered Prima $60,000 for a picture contract—a sum he wouldn't have had a chance of being offered just two years earlier. Prima rejected the bid. He wanted more, he said. The sum jumped to $75,000. Prima just smiled and shook his head. When the bandleader wired his demand for $100,000 and artistic control of his role, Warner Brothers quickly dropped the negotiations.[1]

Nor did his demands limit themselves to high-time contract clauses. On one occasion, Prima entered a nightclub in New Orleans, took one look at several large posters and photos of him, and snapped: "Get rid of it. We said one picture. That's it."[2] An aide dutifully wrote down the demand. After getting booked into the prestigious Astor Roof in New York, Prima threatened to cancel the whole date when he learned that a rival bandleader who was appearing at the club during the same week was going to get four of the five broadcast spots over the CBS radio network. Prima told reporters he would not play the date unless he got equal radio time. Nervous agents at MCA pleaded with the Astor Roof management to give in to Prima's demands. Perhaps because Prima's reputation by this time gave every indication that he would carry out his threat, the Astor Roof people capitulated, giving Prima a combination of two national hook-ups, and doubling his on-air radio time.[3]

During the same summer in which he asked for an upped salary from Warner Brothers, Prima exhibited his aggressive business nature again with the famous Strand Theatre in New York by refusing to honor a contract which pegged him for a lower $7500 a week during his four-week run there. Prima said a clause in his Strand Theatre contract pegged his salary there on how well he did or didn't do at the tough Earle Theatre in Philadelphia earlier in the month. "That date was enough of a success to draw Prima a $1,000 bonus from the Earle," *Variety* reported as the Strand-Prima dispute got

[1]*Variety*, July 18, 1945.

[2]*Times-Picayune*, January 15, 1973.

[3]*Variety*, June 21, 1944.

under way. Four months later, the Strand management gave in and agreed to pay Prima $50,000 for a four-week run.[4]

No sooner had Prima settled his dispute with the Strand than he found himself involved with a new row concerning his contract with Majestic Records, a company he had recorded for since 1943, cutting such hits as "Robin Hood," "My Dreams Are Getting Better All the Time," and "I'll Walk Alone." Prima claimed he didn't sign a new two-year contract with the firm and was looking around for another company that might be interested in recording him. The thinly disguised threat sent the Majestic lawyers scrambling. When the merits of Prima's contract were made known—he was going to be given 5 percent of all royalties for his big-selling albums plus artistic control over the variety and number of tunes— Louis quietly dropped the issue.

If Majestic learned anything from the brief dispute with Prima, it wasn't evident when the contract came up for renewal again in 1947. Prima accused the company of handling his promotion poorly and limiting the national distribution of his records. Said *Down Beat:*

> At the time of his entry on the Majestic label, Prima was guaranteed top publicity breaks among the label's rosters. Another provision of his gilt edge contract gave him the right to terminate the pact if Majestic failed to sell a given quarterly quota of platters. Taking advantage of this clause, Prima served notice on Majestic on June 6 as of July 6, he'd blow on someone else's wax.[5]

Within weeks, Prima signed an exclusive new contract guaranteeing him greatly increased distribution potential with RCA Victor Records.

Obviously, most of Prima's professional demands pertained to the nitty-gritty of getting the best possible deal from giant recording companies and concert halls—entities for which Louis felt little personal sympathy when he behaved particularly aggressively. Sometimes his peccadilloes could even be comic, as when he announced he would not play New York's 400 Club because there were too many large posts in the ballroom that could obscure a good audience view of him. (He eventually played the club

---

[4]*Ibid.*, February 18, 1945.

[5]*Down Beat*, July 2, 1947.

anyway.) But, on the other occasions, his manner seemed to be nothing more than mean-spirited as when he had lawyers at MCA order long-time Prima songstress Lily Ann Carol that "under no circumstances" could she use the Prima band name for advertising purposes. Carol, who had been with the Prima band for more than five years, had decided to go solo just one month earlier. Her offense? On a sign during a recent solo Boston appearance was the legend under Lily Ann Carol's name "Formerly featured with Louis Prima's orchestra."[6] It was enough to send Prima into another legal skirmish.

In the midst of this ongoing preoccupation with business matters, though, was a private Prima who many times revealed a tender, affectionate, and diffident presence to friends, fans, and family. One afternoon during his successful stay at New York's 500 Club, Prima stopped by his enterprise offices at 1619 Broadway. As he began to make a series of phone calls to business associates and entertainment connections he was interrupted by a visit from a sixteen-year-old school boy breathlessly carrying a box of 78-records. After Prima asked the boy why he wasn't in school and discovered that the student was one of his biggest fans, Prima asked "Well, what can I do for you?" The boy, Bob Pepitone, asked Louis to autograph "fifty or sixty records in white ink." When Prima asked why white ink, Pepitone told him it wouldn't rub off and he could see it on the black labels. Louis then ordered his secretary to fetch a straight pen and a bottle of white ink and, after the supplies arrived, signed each and every record. "The whole time I was there, he was nice to me," Pepitone recalled. "He thought it was all pretty funny. He got me a Coke, gave me some doughnuts, and even asked me how I was doing in school. Whenever I saw him after a show, he was always nice to his fans. He never refused to sign an autograph or pose for a photo."[7]

Prima received a similar visit during this same time from Barbara Belle, a young songwriter. After sending a series of scores to Louie's address, she arrived one afternoon backstage at the Strand Theatre during one of the bandleader's appearances there. Convinced that she should call up to Prima's dressing room to find out what happened to her sheet music and that Louis would let any female in, she asked a messenger to announce her and

---

[6]*Variety,* July 17, 1946.

[7]Bob Pepitone interview, July 1986.

Prima replied "Send her up." Belle, who described herself as a "little fat butterball with glasses," said Prima grandly opened the door in his bathrobe, looked stunned, and then quickly signed a photo of himself and handed it to her. "You don't understand," said Belle. "I'm here to see if you got all of the music I sent you. I'm a song writer." Prima invited her in , pointed her in the direction of a small white piano and said to Belle "Take a look and see if you can find it, it's somewhere over there." Belle did, in fact find the song, and seventeen others she had sent in recent weeks. When she showed Prima the efforts of her labor, he smiled and said, "If you want a job, you can write musical openings for me."

It was the beginning of a long relationship in which Barbara Belle would become Prima's majordomo, handling most of his songwriting work, scheduling, and even financial management. But more importantly, Prima gave Belle, who was an orphan, the affection and authority of a father. "He was very good to me, very protective and caring. Like a father, he made sure I didn't get into any trouble."[8]

Prima also exhibited less of a robotic business nature when he made it to the race track, a growing interest throughout the 1940s. Prima caught the horse fever during his salad days in New Orleans. When he first began to play late into the evenings in the French Quarter, he'd while away the wee hours of the morning with fellow musicians and then make a pre-dawn appearance at the horse track where he'd watch, ride, and bet on the fillies with his pals. During the horse's regular runs, Prima would sometimes spend in one afternoon more than he made in a month. But his lucky moments—he once claimed to have won more than $45,000 on one race— fed his enthusiasm for the sport. By the mid-1940s, Prima's fondness for ponies was so well known that a joke made the New York rounds in which two Broadway song pluggers tried to devise the best way to meet Prima and show him their music. When all the possible solutions seemed exhausted, one of them suggested: "I know what, throw a saddle on my back and ride me in. Prima will never be able to resist that."[9]

As his disposable income increased, Prima steadily spent more money buying a stable of horses and betting what he called "smart" money on them. In 1945, Louis purchased five horses for $32,000 to add to his

---

[8]Barbara Belle interview, July 1986.

[9]*Item*, August 3, 1948.

previous stable of two housed at Aqueduct, New York. Three years later, when Prima decided to cut back on his gambling expenditures, he adamantly refused to give up his two-year-old filly named "Pennymaker," because she had yet to return her earning potential.

"The relaxation is worth it," Prima once told a reporter from the *New Orleans Item*. The paper noted that "Louis says he wins races with his ponies—sometimes—and they only cost about $5,000 a year . . . He is also a very moderate bettor, he says. Never more than $10 on a race. A few moments later he said he might bet a thousand if he's winning."[10] Once a reporter from the *Philadelphia Inquirer* watched Prima make the rounds of his stables at Aqueduct, petting his horses "Solid Chick," "Modulate," and "Mr. Preem," squirting belts of imported olive oil down their throats, which he said helped to lubricate their moving parts, and avidly reading a book called *Training Horses for Fun*.[11] "Hosses, Man! I'd like to get me five, six horses!" Prima enthusiastically told columnist Earl Wilson in 1945. "They get me up early in the morning, get me into the open air," he explained, adding "they give me plenty of excuse for horseback riding and provide a most satisfactory combination of exercise and relaxation."[12]

But even within the guise of this consuming recreational interest, Prima's promotional side remained ever active. The official colors for the Prima stable were a traditional tomato red and snow white. But the reverse side of the flag showed Prima's always-present trumpet. Even the horse's names were used to remind folks of Prima's other business. The man who "Played Pretty for the People," as he called himself throughout the 1940s, also had a racing horse named "Play Pretty,' another one called "King Pretty," and still a third named "That's Pretty."[13] By the late 1940s, Prima could boast of owning more than a dozen horses and investing upwards of $100,000 in his stables. "I've always been crazy about horses," Prima explained of his extraordinary investment. "I can read a racing form and not figure I'm just another Tin Pan Alley two-buck bettor."[14]

---

[10]*Item*, undated clipping, ca. early 1950s.

[11]*Philadelphia Inquirer*, August 14, 1952.

[12]*New York Post*, July 2, 1945.

[13]*Buffalo Courier Express*, May 3, 1950.

[14]*Ibid.*

Prima's other major expense was his clothing.   As with the horses, Prima acquired his taste for fine clothing from his days in the Crescent City. In a day that put a premium on men wearing suits, ties and hats as part of their daily wardrobe—a far cry from the clothing fare exhibited by similar young musicians in the 1960s and '70s—Prima liked to wear the best and the flashiest. Additionally, Prima in New York learned the strategic importance of having his clothes tailored to accentuate certain parts of his anatomy. One Prima sideman recalled how the bandleader would hike his tight-fitting pants up over his hips and then suggestively dance before groups of females in his club appearances. "Tom Jones and Elvis Presley weren't the first ones who turned on the girls by dancing funny," said Louis Masinter. "Louie did it all the time."[15]

Despite Prima's fast-track living, he kept in daily touch with relatives back home in New Orleans, particularly Mama Angelina, who regularly advised him on the merits of certain songs, business deals, and musicians he might hire for his orchestra. Her influence directly affected Prima's professional fortunes in a variety of ways, but perhaps never as dramatically as when Louis decided to try out a song called "Angelina."

"I was playing an engagement at the famous Paramount Theatre on Broadway," Prima wrote. "I was in my dressing room between shows going over a song entitled 'Angelina' that had just been submitted to me by Mr. Frank Kelton, one of Broadway's leading publishers. Suddenly the phone rang and it was my mother Angelina Prima, calling long distance from New Orleans . . . I got the chills."

"Mama, what a coincidence—I'm just going over a song called 'Angelina,'" Prima said. "Let me sing it to you and you tell me if you like it." Louis sang the fun-loving song about the Italian waitress in a pizza joint, and his mother responded enthusiastically: "Take it. Honey, its got to be a big hit." Explained Louis: "The rest is history. Millions of records were sold. A new trend was started and then we followed up with many more wonderful novelties. . . ."[16]

It was a risky venture to perform the Italian novelty songs at the time Prima first did. In the middle of World War II there was a certain amount of

---

[15]Louis Masinter interview, January 1986.

[16]Record notes by Louis Prima, "Angelina" (Prima-1 Records, 1974).

unease on the domestic front with regards to the Germans, Japanese, and Italians who lived in the United States. The Japanese-Americans fared the worst of these groups during the conflict when thousands of West-coast citizens of Japanese origins were forced to leave their homes and live in evacuation camps. Italians also met with discrimination and fear when they attempted to find employment in war work. One labor union, the International Longshoremen's Association in New York, made it official policy to place all Italian workers in special working gangs. In Great Britain, anti-Italian prejudice reached a fever pitch when an innocuous song called "Papa Nicolini," which portrayed an elderly Italian merchant in a kindly light, was banned as "stirring friendly feelings toward an enemy nation."[17]

Obviously performing Italian songs was an act of bravery, and Prima didn't stop with "Angelina." In a three-year span, Prima also released such ethnic fun songs as "Please No Squeeza Da Banana," "Bacci Galupe (Made Love on the Stoop)," and "Felicia No Capricia," among other tunes. All of the songs took a playful, kidding look at the Italian-American experience in the big city, and some of the numbers seemed to be directly related to Prima's personal experiences. In "Bacci Galupe," Prima fans heard of Bacci and his girlfriend Maria who had to make love on the front door stoop because "Mama was in the kitchen, sister was in the hall, brother was in the parlor, there ain't no room at all."

"Felicia" told of a young girl who went on a date to Coney Island and "ate a fortune in sazeech and macaroni." But when her boyfriend tried to kiss her, "Felicia No Capricia." The lyrics stirred up a controversy in New York. Suddenly the city's license commissioner wanted to know if "Capricia" meant anything sexual. *Life* magazine asked Mayor Fiorello La Guardia to mediate and he reassured the nervous censors that "capricia" means "understand."[18]

Prima also scored political points with these tunes, singing in "Please No Squeeza Da Banana," of the Italian fruit vendor who daily endured the indignity of silently watching as a police officer pinched and squeezed the vendor's vegetables, before finally settling on an apple or banana he never paid for. "You touch-a this, you touch-a that, you take me for a fool,"

[17]Lawrence Frank Pisani, *The Italians in America* (New York, 1957), p. 78.

[18]*Life*, August 20, 1945.

Prima sang, giving voice to what must have been a widespread frustration. But he prevented the song from becoming an angry diatribe by offering a comic solution: "If you please; officer, pleasa; squeez-a the watermelon; squeez-a the coconut; But Please No Squeeza Da Banana."

Many of the songs were nonsensical, particularly when Prima playfully substituted certain phrases in his songs with words like "macaroni," "zucchini," and "lasagne," but the tunes were also a strong reminder to his audience that Prima was a fellow *paesano* as bemused and confused over the differences in the Italian and English cultures as they were. "It struck a nerve," brother Leon said. "Wherever he went people would come up to him on stage and give him big pizzas and Italian candies. They loved him for singing those Italian songs. There'd be pretty girls and their mothers wearing black, with the dark shawls and all. It was crazy."[19]

Perhaps the tremendous reaction was predictable. Ever since the greatest migration of Italians to the U. S. during the first part of the century, a certain amount of intolerance and ridicule had plagued the collective psyche of the newly sworn-in American citizens. Many of the poor and illiterate Italians arrived in the U. S. lacking the proper identification, thus being stamped "With Out Papers." The acronym WOP shortly became a slur reflecting upon the immigrant's ethnicity, social lot, and economic status.

In the movies and in the popular literature of the day, Italian-Americans were frequently portrayed as loud and arrogant buffoons who liked to eat a lot and drink vino, or as crass underworld mob chieftains such as Al Capone, who ruthlessly wiped out their criminal rivals one moment and then enjoyed their ravioli and garlic bread in a neighborhood Italian restaurant the next. Mussolini's wretched dictatorship in the Old Country only further focused the negative fears and doubts about these new citizens.

Now, for those thousands of young and old people who followed every trend and turn in popular music, Prima's Italian lyrics were providing a healthy outlet, one that allowed for a certain amount of sentimentality coupled with self-parody. Not everyone, though, enjoyed Louie's ethnic act. New York disc jockey Barry Gray sardonically complained that the Italian trend meant nothing to those of a more Anglo background. "The Italianisms obviously mean something hilarious to dancers from New York's Little Italy to San Francisco's North Beach," said Gray. "But

[19]Leon Prima interview, May 1984.

Prima's affected accents leave a non-comprende group cold . . ." Gray also said that "Felicia, No Capricia," brought out the "worst in Prima's personality—his voice."[20]

The Italian novelty songs came during a time of extraordinary popularity for Prima and his big band. As World War II came to its bloody ending in the spring and summer months of 1945, Prima broke box office records and topped the pop chart lists week after week. The sheer numbers were incredible: In a six-week run at the Strand in New York, Prima brought in more than $440,000, a figure that the theatre's management said was the biggest sum in the thirty-year history of the concert hall.[21] At the Downtown Theatre in Detroit on Good Friday—a traditionally slow day in the business—Prima broke all existing records by garnering more than $38,000 for an afternoon performance. Outside the Adams Theatre in Newark, a line of teenagers—many taking leave from their high school duties of the day—lined up at 7 a.m. for the afternoon performance and helped make up the theatre's all-time best week with Prima in mid-April at $31,000 in receipts.

Strangely, Prima was chasing his own shadow at the Adams Theatre: the last best week there was also due to a Prima appearance, in October of 1944. "You smashed every existing attendance record at the theatre," Adams Theatre managing director Ben Griefer wrote Prima after his show left town. "Secondly, from the standpoint of showmanship and entertainment, yours was one of the finest shows ever presented at the Adams. This was borne out by the fact that business the closing day was 40 percent better than the opening day."[22]

In addition, Prima had the particular pleasure of making a triumphant return to Chicago, the scene of his disastrous Blackhawk Cafe opening nine years earlier. This time Louis and his band appeared in the luxurious Panther Room in the Windy City and the results couldn't have been better: More than 12,000 people turned out for Prima's two-week stay at the club, filling the place to capacity. On opening night autograph hounds lined up across the dance floor and rushed Louis when he walked onstage.

[20]*Variety*, November 28, 1945.

[21]*Ibid.*, July 25, 1945.

[22]*Ibid.*, November 1, 1944.

Additionally, Chicago's frequently ascerbic critics welcomed Prima back and applauded his exuberant showmanship.

Fans of Prima—there were more than 20,000 members of a New York-based club called the "Prima Donas"—kept in touch by a monthly newsletter and had their interests whetted by a series of cover stories in some of the nation's most widely-read publications, including *The Billboard* and *Down Beat*. Calling Prima the "talk of the music business," *Life* magazine—during the same week that the Japanese surrendered to the U. S., thus ending World War II—ran a two-page photo spread showing dozens of bobbysoxers gleefully gathering around Louis after a concert. "He and his band had just scored a sensational hit at New York's Strand Theatre," *Life* said. "The demand for their Majestic records far exceeded the supply. Prima's antics and dialect songs had endeared him to teenagers who were taking 'Play pretty for the people,' as their new slogan. After years of scuffling, Louis Prima had hit the jackpot."[23]

The newfound popularity, though, didn't for a moment silence the critical debate swirling around Louie's artistry. George Simon in *Metronome* called Prima's success "both a healthy and happy phenomenon. For it proves once again that even if you're not the world's greatest musical genius, you still don't have to invest a lot of rickety tricks to make folks like you and to make money for yourself. All Louis does is go out front and have a hell of a good time, acting like a natural showman, kidding around, poking fun at folks out front, at guys in his band, and, most of all, at himself." Simon also credited Prima with being a much better trumpeteer of the Satchmo school than most people gave him credit for and added "Louis has a fine ear, good musical sense and taste, a feeling for right tempos, a feeling for jazz."[24]

Prima's artistic relevance prompted an internal debate in the editorial columns of *Metronome*. Two months after Simon's glowing tribute to Louis appeared, Barbara Hodgkins, the magazine's assistant editor, took pen in hand under a headline blazing LOUIE PHOOEY and wrote: "Judging from this pathetic show [at the Strand] Louis Prima has sacrificed his musical abilities to become a buffoon. Prima carries most of what weight the band has on his shoulders, but why does he feel it necessary to

[23]*Life*, August 20, 1945.

[24]*Metronome*, June 1945.

constantly monopolize the spotlight?" Noting that Prima usually made even his vocalists laugh while they were trying to sing or deliver a serious song, Hodgkins added: "I agree with George Simon that there's no percentage in taking yourself too seriously. But there's a limit even for money-mad bandleaders. And I don't believe that Prima can be having a helluva good time making a living which consists solely of repeating the same questionable Italian jokes, wild-arm-and-leg waving, and screeching of idiotic lyrics, jitterbugging with girls from the audience, and in general wearing himself out until even his frantic public can't take any more . . ."[25]

The debate even raged in the letters column of *Life* magazine two weeks after the Prima portrait appeared. "We read with extreme disgust your article describing Louis Prima and his band in their crude bid for publicity," wrote three cadets from Phillips Exeter Academy. "How any self-respecting female could lower herself to such an extent as to even attend such an exhibition, let alone shove herself against a balcony merely to touch him is utterly incomprehensible to us." But a Prima fan in Lancaster, Ohio, offered this opinion: "With the possible exception of versatile Lionel Hampton, no other bands have caused such widespread acclaim from central Ohio's jazz-crazy juveniles as have Louis Prima and Benny Goodman. Prima's rendition of "Please No Squeeza Da Banana" sent thousands of us into ecstasy . . ."[26]

Prima's name also stayed before the record-buying public throughout 1945 with songs not connected to the Italian trend. A prolific songwriter, Prima spent hours in various hotel rooms trying out different themes he was convinced would prove popular with the public. One ditty that caught Louis' attention was a sprightly, finger-snapping tune called "Robin Hood," that had as its basic musical theme an introduction he previously used for another song. When Prima applied the chord progressions to the lyrics for "Robin Hood," he hit paydirt. The song, recorded on Majestic records, became a top seller and one of a handful of numbers which would be his personal property throughout his career.

Another song he wrote nearly a decade earlier, "Sing, Sing, Sing," was used by Benny Goodman as one of his signature tunes, particularly after

[25]*Ibid.*, August 1945.

[26]*Life*, September 10, 1945.

Goodman's wild, run-away jam session in 1938 at Carnegie Hall. Louis' song-writing ability was one of those talents that kept serious musical observers interested and perhaps even more chagrined when Louis increasingly turned to the Italian and novelty songs which sold so well, but were less musically valuable. The "Sing, Sing, Sing," number, for example, is generally viewed as one of the greatest jazz riffs, with a dramatic and extended drum solo, of all time, even though as the years went by Goodman, rather than Prima, became more publicly linked and associated with the tune.

1945 was a good year for Prima in songs, too. In March of the year "My Dreams Are Getting Better All the Time," a record featuring both Prima and Lily Ann Carol entered *Billboard*'s "most played" list at number thirteen. From there it gradually rose to number one and stayed on the top ten list for most of the spring. Simultaneously, another Prima number, "Bell-Bottom Trousers," also made the *Billboard* list and remained a top-selling platter for almost twenty weeks during the spring and summer of 1945.

Determining exactly how many recordings of some songs were sold was a tricky business in the 1940s. Many times a hit record such as "Star Dust" or "Laura" would have a variety of singers and musicians releasing various versions of the ditty at the same time. Thus, when Prima came out with "Bell-Bottom Trousers," there were also at least six other versions of the song by such artists as Guy Lombardo, Kay Kyser, and comedian Jerry Colonna. The emphasis in the record business was on the song, not the singer—the complete reverse of Top 50 lists in the 1950s and '60s, when the singer or musician was emphasized first and the song second. Perhaps because of the confusion over which singer "made" which song, Prima enjoyed the popularity of his Italian novelty numbers. With a song like "Please No Squeeza Da Banana," no one could identify it with anyone else but Prima.

While all of these entertainment and business highs were materializing, Prima's personal life once again took a drastic change with his separation and eventual divorce from Alma Ross. By March 1947, lawyers for Prima and Ross met in a courtroom in Los Angeles and talked about a letter Louis had sent to Alma calling her "gorgeous and terrific" and then suggesting they part. It was a surprise move, but perhaps an inevitable conclusion to a marriage riddled with fights, suspicion, and long separations. Alma, like Louise before her, remained stoic when she heard stories suggesting that Prima was less than true. She believed only a portion of what the columnists suggested, but had a good deal of her suspicions borne out by fact. During the first year of their marriage, Alma discovered a letter written from Angelina to Louis in which mother and son engaged in a conspiracy of silence concerning Prima's latest romantic exploit with the legendary film actress Jean Harlow. Columnist Whitney Bolton, recalling the sultry atmosphere of the Hollywood Famous Door, remembered seeing Harlow "in a trance" as she sat night after night and listened to Louis play.[27] Harlow, who would die tragically in just a matter of weeks at the age of twenty from uremic poisoning, found in Louis the qualities that so many other women seemed unable to resist: his uncanny ability to charm and his little-boy innocence that only partially masked a strong sexual appetite.

In 1937, Jean Harlow was one of the most popular and well known film actresses in Hollywood. Her presence in a movie guaranteed a box office hit and prompted dozens of platinum imitations in films of lesser status. She was, by any reckoning, a major film star, and perhaps her status was more than Prima could contend with. Excitedly he wrote to Mama Angelina of his romantic escapades—one sideman recalled seeing Harlow's chauffeured limousine pick Prima up outside the Hollywood Famous Door at night—and Mama responded in conspiratorial fashion, warning her son that Alma might find out: "Don't let your right hand know what your left hand is doing," Mama wrote.[28]

After Alma read the letter from Angelina she confronted Prima, and the couple went through a ritual that would be replayed throughout their marriage. "It was always the same thing," Alma later said. "Whenever Louie was sleeping with someone or having an affair, I'd leave him, and, of course he'd deny all along that something was up. But then after I was gone, Louie discovered that he loved me and he'd do anything to get me back. After a couple of weeks, the letters and the calls would start and it would get more intense all the time until he'd finally quit work altogether and come out to get me."[29] After he asked Alma for a divorce, he told her to "get a lawyer and file suit against me."[30] Alma did as requested, claiming in

---

[27]Alma Ross interview, December 1986; Keely Smith interview, May 1986; Louis Masinter interview, January 1986; column by Whitney Bolton, *The Morning Telegraph*, ca. 1947.

[28]Alma Ross interview, December 1986.

[29]*Ibid.*

[30]*Ibid.*

her divorce petition that Prima treated her in a "cruel and inhuman manner," inflicting upon her "grievous mental and physical suffering."[31] Ross was awarded $15,000 alimony or 7.5 percent of Prima's yearly earnings.

The actress disappeared from the gossip columns for years after that, returning to a reclusive life in Hollywood that saw her only rarely attending parties and social events. On one such occasion, she encountered film actor William Powell who told Alma that Prima's affair with Harlow "destroyed" his relationship with the actress. But Powell counseled Alma not to be bitter. "And I never was," said Alma. "I thought that Louie just couldn't help himself, that this was the way he was and always would be."[32]

In 1958, however, Alma won national headlines when she charged that Prima was $60,000 to $80,000 behind in his alimony payments to her. A new settlement in Los Angeles gave Ross a $45,000 cash payment and $250 weekly.[33] As the years passed, Prima kept in touch with Alma and even suggested on several occasions that they reunite. "I chalked it up to Louie just wanting me because he couldn't have me," she said later. "That was how Louie always was."[34]

Prima remained single for slightly more than a year. In June 1948, he married his former secretary, twenty-one-year-old Tracelene Barrett of Tacoma, Washington. Barrett first met Prima in 1944 when she approached him for his autograph. A friendship ensued and eventually Prima gave her a job as his New York-based business secretary. Dark-haired and slim, Tracelene had a number of goals which Louis claimed to find troublesome. One was her desire to become a model. Reversing the stance that he took with Alma, in which he encouraged his second wife to pursue her professional aspirations, Prima tried to talk Tracelene out of a modeling career. As their romance gathered momentum, Prima, according to columnist Earl Wilson, "wanted to keep her the sweet and simple girl she

---

[31]Superior Court of the State of California, County of Los Angeles, Complaint for Divorce, no. D317-395, p. 2.

[32]Alma Ross interview, December 1986.

[33]*States-Item*, December 19, 1958.

[34]Alma Ross interview, December 1986.

was. He figured the only way to keep her sweet and simple was to marry her. So it was done."[35]

Prima was equally bothered by Tracelene's penchant for airplane flying. To his dying day, Prima remained terrified of planes and jets and in the 1940s did most of his major travelling by train or auto. Partly to encourage Tracelene to consider other means of travel and partly to find something to substitute for the ponies—by the time of his marriage to Tracelene, Prima had sold several horses and promised his new wife to limit his time and money at the track—Louis suddenly became greatly interested in boats. As his wedding gift, he gave his bride a thirty-three foot cruiser called Tracelene II and promised her a wonderful honeymoon off the Hudson River in his new toy. "I like to go up the river and groove," Prima told columnist Wilson. The bandleader purchased a jaunty yachting cap, $75 worth of nautical maps, and a compass "he wishes someone would show him how to read," Wilson said.[36]

The wedding was a family affair: Mama Angelina and Papa Anthony came up to New York for the big event in the Essex House. Anthony complained about taking the time off from his Jumbo Soda Pop route, and Angelina sang an aria for the festive occasion.[37] When it came time to depart, the newlyweds drove to the dock off the Hudson River and smiled and waved as family and friends threw rice and old shoes. Louis put on his cap, started the engine and piloted the cruiser toward the middle of the river. Far away from the watchful eyes of family and well-wishers, near sunset, the Tracelene II hit a sandbar and Tracelene I flipped through the boat's instruction book and read: "When in distress, fly your flag upside down." Prima turned the flag upside down and together they waved frantically at passing boats. The people in the boats smiled and waved back. Tracelene returned to the charts as Louie fumed. She told her new husband that it looked as though they were only a foot or so from a ten foot shaft of water. With a lurch, the honeymoon party was off again, headed for Lake Geneva—unfortunately by way of the Erie Canal.

Now imagine this scene: Here's city slicker Louie with his little cap and limited or no experience in a boat trying to maneuver the difficult locks.

---

[35]*Item*, August 3, 1948.

[36]*Ibid.*

[37]*Ibid*

"Sailing through the locks almost finished them off," wrote gossip columnist Dorothy Kilgallen in a column on honeymoons that were almost fatal.

> It meant going through different levels regulated by water pouring in. There were stairs along the walls. Louis would hang on for dear life, while Tracelene would run hundreds of steps up the ladders with a rope so that when the boat got even with the top it would be secure . . . After they had undergone a half dozen of these dangerous and highly acrobatic experiences, they found themselves in a lock with nothing happening. No water poured in , and the boat did not rise.[38]

A man appeared at the top of the lock and yelled "Moor your boat!" Prima just looked blankly at him. The man yelled again "Moor your boat! Moor your boat!" Finally Prima answered "I don't dig you, Jack." The captain explained that Prima should tie his boat to the top of the ladder. Suddenly it dawned on Louis that the way to go through the locks was not horrifically grasping for the sidewalls as the boat rose and sunk, but calmly mooring the vehicle when the water dipped and holding on as it came up again.

After they cleared the locks and checked and re-checked their maps for Lake Geneva, Prima turned and smiled at Tracelene: "Isn't this a wonderful honeymoon, baby?"[39]

Married life with Louis was probably somewhat calmer. He rented an apartment in New York, and purchased a large tract of land near New Orleans called "Pretty Acres" where he and his new wife spent increasingly large amounts of time. Tracelene took on her new duties as Prima's wife with a relish, fixing up both his New York and New Orleans residences, and planning the kind of family that Louie had never started on his own.

After his latest scaled mountain of professional success in 1945 and 1946, Prima began to curtail his career goals, relaxing at home and spending more private time for golfing, sailing, and being with his wife than he had in years. If Prima was considering reducing the amount of time spent pursuing his career aims, he couldn't have picked a better time than the late

[38]*Chicago Herald-American*, September 17, 1949.

[39]*Ibid.*

1940s. Despite Prima's enormous triumphs in big city theatres, on radio, and with recordings on more than six different labels between 1936 and 1946, there were signs all around him that the big band business was changing—and not for the better. As early as 1946, there were indications that pointed toward tough times head. TOO MANY OF 'EM, NOT ENOUGH DATES, headlined *Variety* in a July 1946 story talking about the large number of orchestra bands and decreasing number of clubs and halls that wanted to hire them. "One of the major agencies feels so strongly about the future of new bands at the present time that it will not take on a single new property," the publication reported.[40]

A variety of factors contributed to the decline of the big bands. Solo acts like vocalists Frank Sinatra, Perry Como, and, later, Frankie Laine, made it possible for thousands to hear and see favorite artists without the benefit of any one particular accompanying band. When Sinatra was the vocalist for Tommy Dorsey's band, where he went, they went. Now he was a solo act, and his name caused packed theatres wherever he went, but it didn't help out any one band in particular.

The end of World War II brought about an abrupt change in entertainment values. During the war years, thousands of young girls spent their evenings jamming various nightclubs and theatres to hear the big bands. Now their Johnnies had come marching home, and more people were starting families, buying nests out in the suburbs, and generally staying away from the big-city entertainment houses by the droves. "When the war ended in the fall of 1945, the big bands were dominant," James Lincoln Collier later wrote. "Eighteen months later they were gone."[41] Louis Armstrong, Count Basie, and Earl Hines were but a handful of big band leaders who were forced by economic necessity to either eliminate their groups completely or drastically reduce them. Prima, at first, didn't change the makeup of his band, but the maddening pace of the war years began to show on him. His vacations were longer, he seemed to be more the happily married man, and, on several occasion, he even deviated from his cherished comedy music program to deliver songs completely different from the "Robin Hood—Angelina—Felicia No Capricia" norm.

[40]*Variety*, July 24, 1946.

[41]Collier, *Louis Armstrong—An American Genius*.

In the fall of 1947, Prima bucked the big band decline with the hit single "Civilization" on RCA Victor which remained on *Variety's* chart for more than three months. Sometimes, Prima the musician played the kind of straight jazz which the critics had raved over in the late 1930s. In the fall of 1947 Prima recorded straight, jazz-oriented versions of "All of Me" and "Sweet Nothings," which reminded the critics of the Prima of old.

Prima's new RCA Victor contract was lucrative enough to signal an incredibly creative and productive period, beginning in July of 1947 when Louis arrived at RCA's studio number two in New York to record "Civilization," "You Can't Tell the Depth of the Well," and "Say It With A Slap," with vocalist Cathy Allen and his entire orchestra. He followed that date with a September 22 session in which he recorded "Valencia" and "My Flame Went Out Last Night." During a two-day session on November 11 and 12, Prima recorded nine songs, including the hit "Thousand Islands," and one month later put thirteen more songs to wax, among them the classic "Mean To Me" and "Tutti Frutti Pizzicato." In all, during a short four-month period in late 1947, Prima put more than thirty songs on wax, with two of them—"Civilization" and "Thousand Islands"—making the hit charts just weeks later.

Despite his recording activity, Prima had perceptibly curtailed many of his professional involvements by 1947 and 1948. Prima now seemed more content than people ever remembered seeing him before. By 1948, he was grossing as much as $500,000 annually and owned his own record firm, a nightclub in New Orleans, two sheet-music publishing houses and at least five horses that he kept and raced at the New Orleans Fair Grounds.

Every one of the musicians he had started out with in New York in 1935 had left; most went on to other opportunities, and some, like Federico, returned to New Orleans to raise families. Tracelene gave birth to a baby girl, and many people began to openly wonder if Louis was now going to settle down and put his career on the back-burner for awhile. Times were no longer the same, his pals told him; the days of the traveling musician were over. Records were selling at a fraction of the rate they had commanded during the war years and now television had become the dominant entertainment vehicle, one that Tracelene encouraged Louis to investigate.

But despite the changing shifts and the rotting of the nation's big band industry, Prima revealed no inclination to stop. "I wouldn't think of quitting," Prima told one reporter. "The excitement of the business keeps me going, keeps me young." He scaled back the orchestra, but continued his weekly travels along the northeast corridor. Tracelene stayed home for the most part, either in the New York apartment, or at Prima's Pretty Acres compound across from New Orleans on Lake Pontchartrain, or even with Mama Angelina and Anthony, who now lived in a big mansion on Canal Boulevard in New Orleans, courtesy of Louis.

Everything seemed downright calm and quite—a very unusual state for the normally restless and kinetic Prima. Then one day in August of 1948, Prima and his band took an afternoon break from their rehearsals at the Surf Club in Virginia Beach and went for a lazy, bucolic ride. Prima gazed out the passenger window, and suddenly asked the driver to stop. Coming out of the water, in a dark-fitting swim suit, was a dark-haired woman with an incredibly taut figure and a deep tan. Louis was spellbound. The woman's name was Keely Smith.

CHAPTER V

Keely

By the late 1940s, when Prima first encountered Keely Smith, it was clear that he had an uncanny ability to accentuate and promote himself not just as a musician or singer or comedian, but as a *personality*. The emphasis is important. While many entertainers won public acceptance because of their talent in a particular field, few performers floated to the top and stayed there decade after decade unless they somehow established a personal relationship with the audience. The trick was to make the people think they knew you, that by conveying a certain personality on a consistent basis a sense of affection and caring on the part of the audience would gradually emerge, keeping the entertainer in solid favor during both good and bad commercial times.

Prima sold himself as a gay Lothario who frequently got into trouble for his meandering eye, but was impossible to hate simply because he was so lovable. This image was conveyed through Prima's up-tempo music, his off-the-cuff remarks, and, most significantly, through his dancing. During his appearances at such giant dance halls as the RKO Boston and the Strand in New York, Prima usually had a large stage floor for himself and his band. His strict set-up requirements, thoroughly detailed by his advance agents at MCA, called for the band to be seated in a particular fashion and for Prima to have plenty of room to move around in. Move around he did, usually jumping, jogging, wiggling, and even crawling from one end of the stage to the other.

But when Prima danced, if that was what it was called, he suggested the art of the mime. Depending upon the tonal suggestion of the song being played, Prima could dance as an enchanted schoolboy in love, a suggestive older man looking for romantic trouble, or even a jealous lover hovering over whatever girl singer happened to be with him at the time. It was almost always funny, entertaining, and highly visual.

This was an integral part of the personality Prima presented to his adoring masses. Because most of these dancing suggestions were also silent, that is, no one specifically called out "And now Louis Prima is going to dance like a happy husband in love," various members of the audience could interpret Prima's movements to their own liking. Undoubtedly many people just liked Prima because he made them happy.

Fan Bob Pepitone once said that "no matter how sad or upset you were when a Prima show began, you always left just feeling good about everything when it was over. That's why his personal appearances were so successful."[1] Like the physical antics of Charlie Chaplin or Buster Keaton in the silent comedy films of the 1920s, Prima's acrobatic agility was presented as a blank check to the audience, with no strings attached. There was no narrator telling the folks what was supposed to be funny, or a laugh track signaling to us the humorous scenes. It was only Louis acting like a crazed *paesano* or an innocent troubadour or a slick hep cat or any of dozens of other images his performances conjured up.

Perhaps people warmed to Louis during these engagements because his antics reminded them of a loved one, or a happy time in their life. Perhaps people just liked Prima because he was so adept at self-parody. Maybe he was perfect for the brassy, flashy, and noisy 1940s, the same decade that also gave rise to such crazies as Danny Kaye, Red Skelton, Abbott and Costello, and even Yosemite Sam. Whatever the reason, Prima knew he had unearthed an engaging public personality which proved highly popular in his concert hall appearances. He presented this persona again and again in theatre shows from coast to coast.

He also exhibited his acumen for developing talent and personalities in others. Members of Prima's big band frequently were singled out by the bandmaster to portray women, or old men, or love-happy soldiers. Sometimes a certain way a musician walked or gestured would be enough for Prima to create an entire stage personality for him.

Whether Prima saw such onstage possibilities for the seventeen-year-old Keely Smith as she strode out of the Atlantic at Virginia Beach, or whether he was simply dazzled by her physical beauty remains unknown. What is certain is that Keely's entrance into Prima's life ignited perhaps the most exciting, passionate, and vibrant chapter of Louie's professional and personal existence, and her onstage persona and offstage image became probably his greatest creations.

Born to Irish and Cherokee parents, Dorothy Jacqueline Keely took her stepfather's name, Smith, and started singing at the age of eleven in her hometown of Norfolk, Virginia, as a regular cast member of a local show called "The Joe Brown Radio Gang." A dark-haired belle with wide eyes, delicate features, and light brown skin, Keely at an early age developed the

---

[1]Bob Pepitone interview, July 1986.

unusual habit of staring blandly ahead, showing no emotion of any kind while she belted or whispered a tune. Because of her minimal physical interpretations, many talent scouts may have written Keely off as an unlikely candidate for the kind of choreographed, Broadway musical vocals that were the vogue in the late 1940s.

But what she lacked in stage dramatics, Keely more than made up for in her uniquely warm and wide-ranging singing style. Her voice suggested a freshness and innocence far removed from the smokey, nightclub female vocalists Prima had grown accustomed to hearing in places like New York and Chicago.

Part of it may have had to do with her background. Keely came from humble beginnings, and by the age of seventeen her family's financial lot had not improved greatly. "My stepfather, Jesse Smith, was a carpenter," Keely once said. "He was a wonderful man. We were poor, but happy. We are a close family . . . My three brothers and I never minded, nor did we miss, having extras. When I needed a gown for a show Mother earned it for me by taking in laundry. We all had pride but, fortunately, not the kind that would make us ashamed of being poor."[2]

Friends in Norfolk said they liked Keely because of her quiet demeanor, coupled with her candid ways. "You see, I have this problem," Keely later said. "I'm me—just me. I've been completely honest all of my life, and I just don't know any other way . . . I guess I'll just go on thinking what I want to think, saying what I want to say, and doing what I want to do."[3]

As a teenager, Keely spent many comfortable hours, particularly in the summer, listening to her favorite radio and recording artists and visiting the local dance clubs with her friends where she'd jitterbug until she knew her parents expected her home. The Surf Club in Virginia Beach was just such an establishment. During the summer months, the Surf Club brought in a different band every week, placing them in an outdoor patio area, with a large dance floor surrounding the stage. When Prima and his big band arrived there in August of 1948, several months after Louis' tunes "Civilization" and "Thousand Island" were national hits, Keely made a point of stopping by the club.

---

[2]*TV Reporter*, August 1958.

[3]*Ibid.*

"Our family had gone up to New York the year before and seen Louie in person," Keely said. "He was working at the Steel Pier in Atlantic City and I fell in love with the band. I just thought it was the greatest band I had ever seen or heard. When we returned home to Norfolk, I found all of the records I could get by Louis. And I played them constantly. I learned all of the arrangements."[4]

By the time Prima came to perform at the Surf Club—less than two months after his marriage to Tracelene—he was looking for a permanent female vocalist, someone who would make the public forget the more successful Lily Ann Carol and especially the less successful singers Florida Keyes and Bronx-born songstress Tangerine. On the first Friday evening of his stay at the Surf Club, Prima impulsively announced he was looking for a new female singer. Within hours he had listened to several dozen contestants, but selected none of them. By Sunday afternoon, Keely's brother got word to Prima that his sister had a good voice. Prima told him to bring her on stage, and suddenly there was a mad search for Keely. Found calmly sunning herself on the beach, she was given the good news and told to come to the Surf Club immediately for a tryout.

"I had a bathing suit on and you weren't allowed inside with a bathing suit," Smith said.

> I had to borrow a blouse and a skirt to get in, and I was barefoot, but no one seemed to care about that. I went up to the stage and sang 'Embraceable You' and 'Sleepy Time Gal." What I remember most is that I had picked the wrong key to sing in—I didn't *know* what key I sang in—and I ended up singing too low. In the middle of the song, Louie had the boys suddenly change the key. Well, I must have heard a chord that signalled the change, because I changed just a little ahead of them, and I think that impressed Louie.[5]

After Keely sang, Louis stopped between his songs and told her "If you work real hard and get over your shakes, I'll give you a try."[6]

[4]Keely Smith interview, May 1986.

[5]*Ibid.*

[6]*Item,* January 14, 1953.

Prima also made Keely promise not to smoke or drink and to "work very hard and listen to me . . ."[7] Prima's attraction to Keely, beyond a certain physical magnetism, was an instant appreciation of her vocal capabilities. Louis thought Keely had a "voice with a heart."[8] Hiring her on the spot, Prima took Keely on the road with the big band the following Thursday. Because of his sharp sense for talent, Louis was obviously impressed with Keely for her raw, magnetic, natural vocal ability. But Keely's sheer physical presence was not to be underestimated. She was stunningly attractive, glowing in an ethereal manner. Several days later Prima told his assistant Barbara Belle that he hired Keely because he saw her first in a bikini: "When I saw her walk away from me, I knew she had to be a good singer," Louis remarked.[9]

In a four-month period, directly after Keely joined the band, Prima's outfit appeared at the Paramount Theatre in New York, a club called Orsatti's in Sommerset, New Jersey, the Royal Theatre in Baltimore, the Apollo Theatre in Harlem, the Convention Hall in Asbury Park, New Jersey, and Summer's Point, also in Asbury Park, among other spots both in Canada and the U.S.

As the Prima caravan of five cars rolled from city to city, Keely got to know more of Louis than she probably ever thought possible as she sat listening to "Civilization" on her radio back in Norfolk just weeks earlier.

What she saw was the same personality in action that mystified so many other Prima associates. In the sedan with Louis and his third wife Tracelene, Keely saw the couple argue and protested to Prima: "I don't think I should be in your car all of the time. I'll go sit in another car with the boys."[10] Although Prima reluctantly agreed and warned his new singer not to develop any romantic interests in her co-workers, Keely was back in Louie's car by winter after Tracelene returned to New Orleans in preparation for the birth of her first daughter.

[7]*TV Reporter*, August 1958.

[8]*Newsweek*, June 9, 1958.

[9]Barbara Belle interview, July 1986.

[10]Keely Smith interview, May 1986.

"Louis hated to be alone," Keely remembered. "So I went back into his car." This time Louis pointedly invited drummer Jimmy Vincent to join them in the front auto.[11]

If Louis had romantic notions about Keely in their early days, she did not share them. While Keely thought Prima was a "nice man," she was troubled because he was "not easy to get to know," and nonplussed by Louis' physical presence. "I didn't think he was very handsome," she said. "And he was so hairy, I couldn't stand it. When we did afternoon tea dances, he always wore short sleeves, and he'd put his arm around me, and I would just cringe."[12]

Keely also initially had a difficult time getting used to the wry ways of the Prima band members. Barbara Belle thought the new singer was a "real Southern belle and you had to be careful what you said around her." When Prima first told Belle about his new find, the songwriter made a special trip just to hear Keely and was surprised when she encountered "this adorable little girl in her graduation dress. She didn't even have a gown." But Belle, who was awed by Keely's singing abilities, shocked the Virginia songstress when she remarked "Louie's finally got a chick who can sing her ass off." Keely found the language highly offensive.[13]

Beyond the difference in etiquette, Keely found herself in good company with the Prima outfit, especially with Louis. Noticing that Keely seemed to stare at him in amazement when he played and sang, Louis encouraged her to do this even more so. Her reactions were natural and authentic, Prima told Keely, advising her to "be herself" on stage. "The boss started shaping me," Keely later told reporter Dee Phillips. "And I didn't even know it, most of the time. He worked on my arrangements, my phrasing, the little bits of me—naturally that he wanted kept in."[14]

Prima also began to pick out certain numbers perfectly fitted for Keely's low and open vocal abilities, always emphasizing her seemingly innocent and reserved bearing.

[11]*Ibid.*

[12]*Ibid.*

[13]Barbara Belle interview, July 1986.

[14]*TV Reporter*, August 1958.

Her wardrobe, or lack of one, didn't escape Prima's attention either. Although he bought her several gowns, Prima most liked to show Keely off in a white crepe dress, splattered with silver beads that was, significantly, tight in front, with a neckline sloping to the waist.[15]

The obvious sexual overtone was established early. During one of her first appearances with Prima at the Paramount in New York, Keely wore a light, revealing gown on stage that, Prima later said, "caused so much comment" among the kids in the audience he was forced to tell Keely to wear something else for the next show.[16]

But, despite Keely's erotic potency, Prima insisted that she stay far away from any form of mugging or vamping, that she remain totally unaffected, only adding to the sensuous air of possibility. Gradually, Keely's image merged in a variety of personality traits—innocent singer, sexual young woman, the proper debutante, the slyly flirtatious girl next door.

The image was rounded out when Prima developed yet another stage personality for himself, this one the naughty older man constantly vying for his youthful companion's attentions. Because of Keely's extremely laid back singing style, Prima counted on the audience to conclude that she was completely put off by his mannerisms.

Eventually, Keely would add sharp off-hand remarks pertaining to both Louis' antics and his possibilities as a love god. "I think I'm too much for him," she'd remark, taking a discrete but well-placed glance below Prima's belt. The chemistry did not make itself known instantly. In fact, such personal dynamics between Louis and Keely took months to work out. But as it did, the two performers developed a new-found respect for one another both personally and professionally.

Unfortunately, developing Keely's stage personae was the least of Louis' worries in the late 1940s and early 1950s. The decline of the big band trend that Prima had so long bucked finally caused him to break up his organization and perform with Keely in various localities backed up by whatever house orchestra was available.

Many of the large orchestra halls in metropolitan areas were also suffering reversals, fed by the public's desire to stay home and watch

---

[15]*Item*, January 14, 1953.

[16]*New York Post*, July 27, 1958.

television.   Between 1950 and 1954, the number of households with television in the nation leaped from 3.8 million to more than 20.4 million, one of the greatest marketing success stories in the history of the United States.[17]

Prima's attitude toward television, however, was not unlike his attitude toward radio—he simply had no use for it.   "Most fans I've talked to lately throughout the country have explained that the reason they are not at home watching TV is because they are tired of repetition," Prima said in the summer of 1952, trying to put a brave face on things.   "I am slow in even thinking about going into this medium," he added, charging that most of the vocalists appearing on the small screen had no idea how to captivate their living room audiences.   "So many of them don't know how to use anything but their vocal chords.   Until they learn, there won't be a single singing star to come out of television."[18]

In addition to the declining fortunes of the theatres, concert halls, and clubs, Louis also had to contend with both a commercial and artistic drop in his recordings.   Once again the record industry was in the throes of a major upheaval.   Strange names and new voices were becoming familiar to millions of record buyers in the early 1950s and Prima was disappearing as a viable recording star.

Johnnie Ray scored a number one hit in 1952 with a morose ditty called "Cry," which was followed by Percy Faith's "Where Is Your Heart?" Juke box listeners were plugging down their coins for Vera Lynn's "Auf Wiedersehen, Sweetheart," and Tex Ritter's "High Noon."   That latter recording came from the Gary Cooper movie of the same name and was so popular that even President Dwight Eisenhower whistled it for months. Historian William Manchester summed up the times perfectly when he noted, "In none of the lively arts was there anything startling or jumpy, anything that rocked the boat."[19]

The trend was noticed at Columbia Records, also.   In charge of the company's popular music division, conductor Mitch Miller emphasized

---

[17]Peggy Charren and Martin W. Sandler, *Changing Channels: Living (Sensibly) With Television* (Reading, Mass., 1982), p. 82.

[18]*Item*, August 8, 1952.

[19]William Manchester, *The Glory and the Dream: A Narrative History of America, 1932-1972* (New York, 1975), pp. 643-644.

songs that were simple and sweet. His own recordings, an endless series of "Sing Along With Mitch" albums, sold more than 100,000 copies a month. But it was in his managerial position at Columbia that Miller came to dictate national tastes. In 1951, two typical Miller productions were Patti Page's "Tennessee Waltz" and Guy Mitchell's "My Heart Cries For You." Both songs were chart busters.

When Frank Sinatra, then at his singing nadir, came under Miller's supervision, the conductor suggested several gimmicks he thought might salvage Sinatra's career. First he had Sinatra record with a busty blonde named Dagmar. Then he put Frank to the accompaniment of musical washboards, and finally he asked Sinatra to bark out a song called "Mama Will Bark." Said Sinatra: "I growled and I barked on the record, but the only good it did me was with the dogs."[20]

Even the physical appearances of records were changing. Rapidly becoming obsolete were the heavy 78s that Prima had recorded on since his first session in 1934. Once again, Columbia led the way through its parent company, CBS, by introducing long-playing LPs at the speed of 33 1/3. The use of 45s, first marketed by RCA-Victor, only added another marketing change to the business—the growth of the single record as a viable commercial product.[21]

While Columbia records was at the nerve center of an always-changing industry, none of it did Prima much good. Although he scored a number of hit records for RCA-Victor in the late 1940s, Prima was unable to rely on his long-standing song-selling success when he joined Columbia Records in the fall of 1951. Part of the problem, undoubtedly, was the material he chose to record. A series of singles in which he shared billing with Keely ended up as bombs on the market. Songs like "Ooh-Dahdily-Dah," recorded in October 1951; "Chop Suey, Chow Mein," recorded in March 1952; and "Chili Sauce," recorded in July of that same year, were painful attempts to recreate the exaltant silliness of his earlier Italian and novelty hit records of the 1940s.

But Prima at Columbia was also frustrated in his attempts to record the kinds of songs he knew his public would like. Hearing a demonstration recording of the tune "Come On-a My House," Prima walked into Columbia

---

[20]Arnold Shaw, *Sinatra: Twentieth Century Romantic* (New York, 1969), p. 174.

[21]Robert Metz, *CBS: Reflections in a Bloodshot Eye* (Chicago, 1975), pp. 153-154.

to record it but was told by Miller that the song had already been selected for singer Rosemary Clooney. "But it's for me, it's an Italian song," Prima argued. Miller refused to back down, telling Prima to abide by his decision, "because I told you so."

"The hell with you," Louis answered, walking out of the studio and privately vowing never to record for Columbia again, thus ending a short sixteen-month relationship which saw him record fewer than twenty tunes, most of them forgetable in both a commercial and artistic sense.[22]

What must have been especially annoying for Prima was the success Clooney enjoyed with "My House"—it was a giant seller for her, even though she claimed that she hated the song, and it additionally established her as a national singing star.[23] Not surprising, the market forces took their toll on Prima's personal fortunes. Even though he had eliminated many of his expenses by disbanding his big band, he still had considerable financial overhead with his New York enterprise offices which oversaw his music publishing business, his horse stable in Louisiana, and several choice pieces of land he held title to.

"We started working the dumps, really," said Keely. "Things got bad rather quickly. We worked at all sorts of God-awful places. And we'd go in and work with whatever band was available. Two pieces, three pieces, six pieces, whatever. Just the two of us."[24]

Keely also remembered the horses becoming the biggest drain on Prima's pocketbook. "They were not good racing horses," she said. "They just cost Louis a lot o f money. We were doing one-nighters everywhere just to support Louie's horses. I'm telling you—we'd go 700 to 800 miles to do a one-nighter, pick up something like seven hundred dollars, and then hit the road again—all for the horses."[25]

Prima would also drive nearly as far just to see one of his horses run. In 1952, the *Philadelphia Inquirer* noted that Prima had sometimes travelled as far as 450 miles for one race. On one occasion, Prima drove from a club appearance in Camden, New Jersey, to the race grounds at Aqueduct, New

---

[22]Bob Pepitone interview, July 1986.

[23]Rosemary Clooney and Raymond Strait, *This For Remembrance* (Chicago, 1979), pp. 133-134.

[24]Keely Smith interview, May 1986.

[25]*Ibid.*

York, in the middle of the night in order to see one of his fillies run the next morning. When he arrived at the stables, he parked his car in front of the barn and fell asleep. "He woke up the horses with his snoring," said Prima's horse trainer, Leon Silva, whom Louis hired to watch over his horses, setting him up in a small apartment at the end of the stables. "Some of the horses didn't like getting up that early."[26]

In the middle of Prima's concerns over his career, he separated from Tracelene and obtained a divorce from his third wife on June 18, 1953. Tracelene, in Volusia County, Florida, obtained $75 a week in child custody from Louis.[27] Louis also declared his love for Keely. "Mr. Prima, who falls in love with the subtlety of a ton of coal going down a chute, fell for the fourth—and probably final—time of his life," columnist Jim Bishop later wrote of the Louis-Keely romance.[28]

Calling Keely "half woman/half child," Louis proposed to her and the couple drove back to Keely's hometown in July 1953 for the wedding ceremony—less than one month after his split from Tracelene. Prima was forty-two and Keely, twenty-one. Prima's physical attraction to Keely was clear from the outset. But initially it may have been nothing more than that. Prima was long used to attracting all sorts of women—starlets, social climbers, groupies—in numbers that most men could only dream of. Certainly Louis was open to the romantic and sexual advances from well known stars and little-known fans. But the chasm between a fling and a protracted relationship in Prima's life was a great one. What usually bridged the gap was the attitude of the woman in question.

"Louie had to be the boss," one associate said. "He had to dominate women completely, much in the same way his mother dominated him."[29] Columnist Jim Bishop said Prima was possessive. "When he's in love, he wants to control everything," Bishop wrote. "Keely likes a man like that. So life has become a ball for these two. The deadpan Indian princess

---

[26]*Philadelphia Inquirer*, August 14, 1952.

[27]*Louis Prima* v. *Tracelene Prima*, Case File 22,516, Circuit Court, 7th Judicial Circuit, Volusia County, Florida.

[28]*New York Journal-American*, undated clipping, ca. 1959.

[29]Confidential communication.

insists, loudly, that Louis is the Chief in the wigwam, and what he says goes . . ."[30]

Keely, on many occasions, expressed her willingness to comply with Louie's requirements. "Louis is the boss," she said, several years after they were married. "Everybody calls him the 'Chief'—he's strictly boss at home and in business. It doesn't really matter to me . . . When a woman really loves someone then she's happy—his way."[31]

Keely also told *Newsweek* magazine that her entire life's fortunes were due to "God, luck, and Louis Prima," adding "I don't think I'll ever do anything unless Louis OK's it or supervises it or directs it."[32] Prima's songwriter Barbara Belle called him a "male chauvinist pig," but she also said that Louis could be enormously worthwhile for any up-and-coming starlet if she was willing and pliable. "If you had the initial talent, he brought it out," said Belle. "When Louis realized the magic of Keely's deadpan ways, of having her just watch him, he developed it further."[33]

The integral factor, though, was always the willingness to be subjugated. Without such submissiveness on the part of the woman, Prima was unable to sustain a romantic relationship.

"I was very much in love with Louis by the time we were talking about getting married," Keely remembered. "I fell in love with him and I grew to love him even more. I didn't care where we went or what we did, as long as I was with him."[34]

To ensure marital bliss, Prima's women additionally had to exhibit unconditional surrender to the wisdom, ways, and will of Mama Angelina, who continued to exert an extraordinary amount of influence on Louis even as he reached middle age. Keely told Louis during the beginning weeks of their marriage "I'm going to handle your mother, because I can't fight her. I'm not going to fight her. I'm going to let her think that she is getting her own way in everything."

[30]*New York Journal-American*, undated clipping, ca. 1959.

[31]*TV Reporter*, August 1958.

[32]*Newsweek*, June 9, 1958.

[33]Barbara Belle interview, July 1986.

[34]Keely Smith interview, May 1986.

"Babe, do whatever you have to," Prima answered.[35]

All the proper roles in order, the marriage of Louis and Keely seemed destined for success, even given Prima's dismal track record. Unlike his past three wives, Keely gave Louis the perfect opportunity to mix marriage with his professional goals. Now the raison d'etre of his life would be Keely. More specifically, Louis set out to make his wife a star, perhaps even eclipsing him if need be. Entire programs were to be tailored around her vocal abilities. Prima would provide the comic relief. It was an exciting prospect for Louis, a chance to do for someone else what had already happened to him. It gave him a sense of power. With Keely he found a marketable product that could reflect his considerable entertainment acumen. Not only did Prima select the proper song material and wardrobe for his wife, he also gave her what turned out to be her most recognizable trademark—a short-banged school girl haircut. "At one of our one-night stands, I saw a girl whose hair looked the way I wanted mine," Keely said. "So? Louis looked at her hair, looked at my long hair, and agreed. *He* cut it just the way I still wear it."[36] Keely's little girl hair-cut, coupled with Louie's fleshy face and his ever-present trumpet turned out to be a cartoonist's delight. Caricatures of the couple in the 1950s invariably showed Prima as a daffy, ape-like sport, bearing an uncanny resemblance, people told him, to the Indian chief on the U.S. nickel. Keely, on the other hand, always seemed wide-eyed with surprise, chaste and salacious at the same time, innocently calm in her suggestive gowns topped by her school girl haircut.

Prima's problem, beyond trying to sell Keely to a national audience unaware of her talent, came with his business. By 1954, his old concert hall route was bankrupt and most of his music outdated. Stories circulated that he would join the lengthy list of displaced big band leaders and announce his retirement. Even Prima encouraged the speculation, telling friends he was thinking of settling down permanently on his 97-acre property dubbed "Pretty Acres" in Louisiana. Prima said he spent some of his most relaxing hours there, playing golf, tending to his horses, and overseeing the maintenance on a number of structures including a large wood-frame country club, with a circular driveway in front of it, a small

[35]*Ibid.*

[36]*TV Reporter*, August 1958.

hotel behind it, and a club office located near the front of the sprawling, hilly property. "The idea of retiring to that farm and playing a lot of golf looked awfully good," Prima said, noting that Pretty Acres and his other remaining business enterprises "wouldn't take too much work."[37]

But even Prima's closest associates and family members doubted he was serious about the retirement thoughts. "I heard talk about retirement then, but none of us took it seriously," remembered Madelyn Prima, the wife of brother Leon. "What he talked about instead was Keely and how he was going to make her a star."[38]

Prima also decided by late 1953 that Keely should be surrounded by a new musical sound, something far removed from the big band format with which he had become identified. "I got to thinking that we might do better if I bought some special material, you know, written just for us," Prima said later. "I'd given up the big bands and was trying to get established with a small group."[39] His idea was to highlight Keely with the new sounds of the day, perhaps incorporating the rock n' roll rhythms that were just beginning to dominate the airwaves.

Once again, Prima was demonstrating his ability to incorporate the latest musical trends into an act that might prove financially lucrative. Additionally, he was exhibiting the ceaseless demand for change within his own industry. An avid reader of the musical trade papers, Prima thought rock n' roll was soon going to account for a large chunk of the record-buying public's dollar. By 1952 Specialty Records in Hollywood had already released Lloyd Price's "Lawdy Miss Clawdy," which hit number one on the rhythm and blues charts across the country and sold a million records in six months.[40] Soon the Specialty producers would sign a little known Southern black singer by the name of Little Richard and the new musical expression would find one of its first legends.

During these same years in Memphis, a truck driver for Crown Electric walked into the tiny recording studios of Sun Records and cut one very bad version of a country ballad called "I Love You Because," and then one

[37]*Times-Picayune*, May 22, 1960.

[38]Madelyn Prima interview, July 1986.

[39]*Oakland Tribune*, September 30, 1959.

[40]Charles White, *The Life and Times of Little Richard* (New York, 1984), pp. 43-44.

electric, historic rendition of "That's All Right Mama," and rock n' roll in a matter of months had its first king—Elvis Presley.[41]

Prima's generation found it difficult to accept the beat, sound, and stage antics of rock n' rollers. Frank Sinatra spoke for millions of his contemporaries when he called the music "the most brutal, ugly, degenerate, vicious form of expression it has been my displeasure to hear . . . It fosters almost totally negative and destructive reactions in young people . . . It is sung, played and written for the most cretinous goons . . ." Jackie Gleason shared Sinatra's opinion, telling one columnist that Elvis Presley was a flash-in-the-pan: "He can't last," predicted Gleason. "I tell you flatly—He can't last." But Prima had his own views, as usual far different from the conventional wisdom. "There's nothing, but nothing, wrong with rock n' roll," he said. "It's got that beat, and as long as the kids keep listening to it, they'll keep out of trouble—Don't sell those kids short—they've got an instinct for the kind of music that's fun to listen to and dance to." Prima also challenged the "Ozzie and Harriet" set: "I don't know what their parents are complaining about. They used to dance the black bottom—and that was downright vulgar."[42]

What Prima's interest in rock n' roll displayed was his desire to find a musical style not only complimentary to Keely, but also different enough to firmly etch her in the public's mind as unique. Prima had an idea about music in the 1950s: The best sound, he decided, would be one that mixed aspects of Dixieland, jazz, swing, and rock n' roll. This was a revolutionary thought in the business. In 1954 the lines between such styles were firmly drawn with musicians rarely venturing to cross such borders, much less combine elements of each genre. But Prima had freely mixed musical influences in his songs throughout his career, and suffered the hostile reviews of critics less imaginative than he for it. To detractors, Prima's plan to synthesize the major musical styles of the day would be further proof that he had long since abandoned whatever remained of the musical integrity he exhibited during his New York days. Here again was evidence that Prima was eager to sell out to the latest noise blasting over the country's juke boxes. Prima was, his critics charged, something of a musical whore.

---

[41] Albert Goldman, *Elvis* (New York, 1981), pp. 131-132.

[42] Kitty Kelly, *His Way: The Unauthorized Biography of Frank Sinatra* (New York, 1987), pp. 277-278; *This Fabulous Century*, Volume VI, *1950-60* (New York, 1970), p. 145; *Chicago Tribune*, September 30, 1959.

But characteristically, whatever lack of enthusiasm Prima may have encountered with his plan did little to inhibit him. For Louis the only questions were where he would unveil his new act and what musicians he would play with. The first question was answered in the fall of 1954 when Prima placed a call to Bill Miller at the Sahara Hotel in Las Vegas and begged for a booking. Prima told Miller he was working up a new act, one that would spotlight Keely and would be somewhat unusual musically. Miller, who was trying to convince casino executives to use the hotel's lounge for musical acts rather than as simply an adjunct to the casino pit area, listened to Prima's offer and gave a limited counter-offer: a two-week stay at the Sahara. But, Miller cautioned, Prima and Smith were targeted for the lounge, not the hotel's swanky night club. This was a tremendous comeuppance for Prima. Ten years before, perhaps even five years before, Prima would have headlined the night club, no question about it. But Prima in 1954 had not had a hit recording in more than seven years. He no longer had a big band. He was not a television star, he made no regular radio programs. It did not matter that for nearly two decades he was a musician of national prominence. It was forgotten that he recorded more than a dozen hit songs between 1935 and 1948, that he packed the giant Strand Theatre in New York and the Earle Theatre in Philadelphia, that he was the toast of the town because of his Famous Door show in the mid-1930s. No one seemed to care that he was a hero and cultural phenomenon to thousands of Italian-Americans in big cities throughout the northeast. Despite all of this, Prima's desultory record of the past few years had severely affected his professional status.[43]

Prima was a proud man, but he was equally ambitious and accepted Miller's offer immediately. He excitedly told Keely of the date and made plans to drive out to the nation's gambling capital to begin what he hoped would be his third run up the ladder of American entertainment success. There was only one problem—this new show had to be dynamic, it had to take Las Vegas by storm. Nothing less would do. And, more importantly, Louis and Keely would have only two weeks in which to do it.

---

[43]Don Knepp, *Las Vegas: The Entertainment Capital* (Menlo Park, Calif., 1987), p. 99.

CHAPTER VI

Lamisters in the Casbar Lounge

Louis Prima and Las Vegas were made for one another. When Prima and Keely Smith blew into town in the fall of 1954, the casino city was wild, full of late-night, exotic entertainment, and ripe for hype. "*Who* comes here?" the colorful author A. J. Liebling asked of Hank Greenspun, the publisher of the flamboyant *Las Vegas Sun*, during an early 1950s visit. Greenspun replied "People on the lam." Liebling thought for only a moment: "Lamisters," he called them.[1]

A town of only 8,422 in World War II when the casinos operated on a restricted schedule, Las Vegas by 1954 was the fastest-growing small city in the country with a population of more than 45,000. Mobsters and molls infiltrated the city. Money and the promise of more—much more—were everywhere. "It must be something in the air, man," entertainer Sammy Davis, Jr., said of the gambling mecca. "I'm positive that this was what Nero had in mind." Davis may have been right. Everywhere one turned was a sense of glitter and kitsch; all-night club shows, dance revues, high-stake poker parties. Texans with ten-gallon hats mixing easily with New York businessmen in shiny suits smoking large cigars. It was an oasis for a carnival in the middle of the desert, a place in the sun, and a city where poker chips could be used as money at the local grocery store.[2]

Surrounding Vegas like a permanent cloud of vapor was the omnipresent emphasis on money and the exhilaration of winning great amounts of it. "Show me a man without money, and I'll show you a bum," joked Joe E. Lewis, the consummate Las Vegas comedian. At the Horseshoe Club, multi-millionaire oilman and gambler Joe W. Brown, typically decked out in a voluminous cowboy hat, put on display in the club's lobby an exhibit of $1 million in $10,000 bills. The awe-struck line of visitors and would-be lucky gamblers formed an almost continuous wave at the club. This ongoing lure of quick riches provided Las Vegas with a

---

[1]*Harper's*, June 1982.

[2]Neal R. Pierce and Jerry Hagstrom, *The Book of America: Inside Fifty States Today* (New York, 1984), p. 706; Eugene P. Moehring, "Las Vegas and the Second World War," *Nevada Historical Society Quarterly*, (1986), 14-15; *Harper's*, (June, 1982); "That's All," Sammy Davis, Jr., monologue in concert at the Sands Hotel, (Reprise Records, Hollywood, California, 1966); *New Yorker*, March 27, 1954.

growing annual income throughout the booming 1950s. It also produced an assortment of personalities, characters, and celebrities that might dumbfound even the most imaginative novelist. A future president of the United States, Ronald Reagan, attempted an ill-fated dance revue at the Last Frontier Hotel. Another soon-to-be chief executive, John F. Kennedy, drank and played all night with the likes of Frank Sinatra, Dean Martin, and Sammy Davis, Jr.—the famed "Rat Pack"—at the Sands Hotel. Later Kennedy's staff wisely collected all photos and negatives of the event. Playwright Noel Coward was seen in his tuxedoed splendor in the desert sun just outside the Strip before the opening of *his* nightclub act, while former heavyweight legend Joe Louis genially served as host at the Moulin Rouge, where the "Tropi Can-Can" provided a nightly "dazzling revue" with 50 well proportioned female hoofers.[3]

"Las Vegas still has, week after week, the greatest galaxies of entertainment to be found anywhere," noted the *New York Times,* in an article marveling over the fact that the town seemed to thrive through national boom and bust times alike. "A typical week," reported the paper, "will bring such an assortment of stars and headliners of hotel shows as Liberace, Judy Garland, Joe E. Lewis, Danny Thomas, Donald O'Connor, June Powell, Cab Calloway, Cesar Romero, and Denise Darcell." The Strip's well-lit marquees might showcase Vera Ellen at the Dunes in a "Magic Carpet Revue—with a cast of 60," or the "Fabulous Dorsey Brothers—Tommy and Jimmy," at the New Frontier, with the durable Mary Kaye Trio in the Cloud 9 Lounge.[4]

If these entertainment explosions weren't enough, there were the actual explosions waiting to be witnessed by wide-eyed tourists some 100 miles northeast of the city. Noted the *New York Times:*

> This is the best year in history of the non-ancient, but nonetheless honorable pastime, of atom-bomb watching. For the first time, the Atomic Energy Commission's Nevada test program will extend through the summer tourist season, into September . . . several of the explosions will be larger than the ones detonated on Japan in

---

[3]*Times-Picayune,* March 11, 1962; Shaw, *Twentieth Century Romantic,* p. 270; *New Times,* January 23, 1976; *Life,* June 20, 1956.

[4]*New York Times,* June 9, 1957; *Life,* June 20, 1956.

World War Two, and at least one will be three to four times as large.

Not surprisingly, the AEC's atomic testing, rather than alarming local residents, became just one more excuse for gaudy promotion Las Vegas style. The Flamingo Hotel's hair stylist, GeeGee, designed an "atomic hairdo" shaped like a mushroom cloud. Bartenders reported increasing orders for an "atomic cocktail," with equal parts of vodka, brandy, and champaign, while people danced to the "Atomic Bomb Bounce," a boogie-woogie written by pianist Ted Mossman, and watched the explosions from their rooms at the Atomic View Motel.[5]

This obviously was a town tailor-made for Prima. Given to promotion, carnival hoopla, and endless partying, Las Vegas was the home Prima at the age of 43 never had before. Where once Prima's endless publicity stunts might cause resentment and embarrassment within the industry's musical purist department, in Las Vegas Louis' happy hucksterism was a sign that he was "one of us." If a resume had to be presented to enter the borders of the city, Prima's would have merited a gold star stamp of approval. After all, it was Prima, who, in the early 1940s, laughingly took a bet that he wouldn't dare march his band into the Atlantic Ocean. Prima did, got everyone's pants wet, and made sure the wire services covered the story. In the summer of 1946 Prima became convinced buried treasures were lying beneath the sands of Pigeon Key, Florida. He announced to the Associated Press that he was giving up his career as a bandleader to search for the loot. "Prima disclosed he's negotiating for the purchase of Pigeon Key, between Miami and Key West," the report duly announced. "He said he has a cache of army surplus mine detectors in a Miami warehouse and is ready to go to work in earnest." It was all part of Prima's unending quest for publicity. In the mid-1940s, Prima engaged the services of Luce's Clipping Bureau, a firm that would provide Louis with the stories that mentioned him by name and what newspapers ran the stories. Thus, Prima could gauge which stories most impressed newspaper editors and readers. The band excursion into the Atlantic Ocean proved a popular item in more than fifty newspapers nationally, while Prima's pipedreams about treasure hunting in the Florida Keys also won wide notice. His World War II meeting with the Roosevelts was good for coast-to-coast

---

[5]*Ibid.*, June 9, 1957; A. Costandina Titus, "A-Bombs in the Backyard: Southern Nevada Adapts to the Nuclear Age, 1951-1963," *Nevada Historical Society Quarterly*, (1983), 250-251.

coverage, as was a 1952 wire press photo showing Prima tooting his horn at his magnificent two-year-old filly "Solid Chick," as the horse seemed to swoon, rolling her eyes in ecstasy.[6]

Promotion was a large part of Prima's life, and in a variety of ways, he proved to be an imaginative and innovative press agent for his interests, once, in 1948, making the cover of *Down Beat* for sharing his horn with a puppy named "Pizza." But even Prima's endless fountain of promotion and fondness for gimmicks had its limits. The slot provided for Louis and Keely at the Sahara by Bill Miller was a death zone for live entertainment, or so it seemed. Miller slated the couple to go on in the hotel's lounge after midnight. The crowds were boisterous, frequently extremely drunk; smoke filled the air, slot machines whirled and rang, and raucous table conversations dominated the room. This was no place for the timid. "It was a comedown for us, having to work in the lounge," said Keely. "The last time Louis came to Las Vegas, when things were going better for him, he was the headline attraction at the El Rancho in the showroom there. But when Miller offered us the lounge in the Sahara, things were so bad, we felt we had to take it."[7]

The Sahara, which opened in October 1952, quickly became a Las Vegas favorite. The first gambling palace heading south from Las Vegas' downtown, the hotel featured such stars as Ray Bolger, Artie Shaw, Esther Williams, Marlene Dietrich, and Mae West in its luxurious nightclub. Called "The Jewel of the Desert," by its developer, Milton Prell, the Sahara was known for its statues of camels standing as sentinels in front of the hotel, with an African motif inside. By 1954 Miller hoped to enclose the hotel's Casbar Lounge and make that, too, a magnet for big-name entertainment. He started with Louis and Keely.[8]

The Casbar Lounge looked formidable. It provided its entertainers with one of the smallest stages in town, roughly no wider than thirty feet across. To reach it Louis and Keely walked up a few stairs behind the bar's cash register and then landed on a platform with barely enough room for a piano, several instrumentalists, and Louis and Keely. The ceiling was quite low in the lounge, thus reducing the sense of illusion audience members probably

---

[6]*Item*, undated clipping, ca. early 1950s; *Times-Picayune*, July 12, 1946.

[7]*Down Beat*, January 28, 1948; Keely Smith interview, May 1984.

[8]Knepp, *Las Vegas*, pp. 82-83, 99.

felt when they watched Prima perform in such lush arenas as the Strand Theatre in New York or the Saenger in New Orleans. There was also little space separating Louis and Keely from their audience. While the air may have been more intimate, it was also as classy as a neighborhood amateur night show in someone's basement. "Really, I'm talking about a place that seemed to us like the bottom of the barrel—we could hardly move," said Keely. "The only thing was, this was part of a major Las Vegas hotel."[9]

For Prima, the size and state of the lounge were secondary concerns—a far cry from his sometimes persnickety demands during his heyday as a big band leader. What the Casbar Lounge offered to Prima was an opportunity to present his singing wife in a format that could rock the audience, and, hopefully, give him one more shot at the national market. But before Louis and Keely even performed their first show, the couple almost walked out of the hotel in anger. Following a successful Sahara visit by entertainer Cab Calloway, an old musical pal from Prima's New York days, Louis saw the energetic performer, who gained national fame during his frantic performances at the Cotton Club and the Apollo in the 1930s, in the Sahara's lobby and invited him to the lounge for a drink. As they approached the bar's door, Prima was told that Calloway couldn't sit with him, that it was a distinct violation of the city's segregation laws. While black superstars like Calloway, Sammy Davis, Jr., and Nat "King" Cole might be able to headline a luxurious showroom performance, they weren't allowed to drink or eat in the same establishment's restaurants or pubs, or even stay in the swank suites usually reserved for the stars. "Why can't this man have a drink with me?" Prima demanded of the waiter. The waiter looked nervous and got the lounge's manager who told Prima that he would break the rules and let Calloway sit with him, but under no conditions could the two entertainers drink together in public view. "In the South I expect this, but here?" Prima asked. Then Calloway told Louis he had a trailer in the back of the hotel where he was supposed to stay and invited him over for after-show drinks. Trying to reduce his friend's growing humiliation, Prima smiled and said he'd take him up on the invitation. But things didn't end there. "I don't want to work for this place," Louis told Keely. "Let's get out of here." Said Keely: "I really thought Louie was going to quit. In fact, I know he would have. But no one could find Bill Miller, who was, in fact, on his way to Mexico that night. Louie didn't think he should quit

9Keely Smith interview, May 1984.

under the circumstances. And under the circumstances, I'm glad we stayed. It was right after that that everything started to happen."[10]

Prima *did* open at the Casbar Lounge in late November of 1954, but not with the musical combo highlighting jazz and rock themes. That would come later. For now, Louis hoped to wow the merry Las Vegans with his stage antics, trumpet prowess, and Keely's voice, in the hopes that Miller might sign the duo to an extended stay. Giving it their all, Louis and Keely caused an upheaval, prompting gamblers to leave the crap tables and reporters to take note. Ralph Pearl of the *Las Vegas Sun*, a widely read columnist who would someday bolster Louis and Keely almost as much as he criticized them, raved that the husband and wife team were "absolutely the hottest combo to hit this town yet . . ." More and more people began to show up for the midnight shows, making gambling a secondary attraction. "The drop in the casino between midnight and 6 a.m. was more than at any other time," recalled Miller, who, upon his return from Mexico was startled by the size of the crowds Louis and Keely were drawing. It didn't happen overnight, but the trade steadily increased with each successive show in late November and early December 1954, enough so to convince Miller to sign the couple up for an extended stay after the holiday season and Las Vegas' annual Helldorado Week. To build up suspense for the next Louis and Keely show at the Sahara, Miller took out large ads in trade publications and Las Vegas newspapers, some with Picasso-like art designs, billing the couple as "all-time record holders for Las Vegas lounges."[11]

But the program was still far from what Prima musically hoped for, although he was encouraged by the popular reaction and warmed by official Las Vegas' open arms. For all of its fun-loving, carefree atmosphere, Las Vegas could be a ruthless town for those entertainers who went unaccepted by the entertainment establishment. A certain ritual in the gambling mecca almost dictated popular approval—if an entertainer was an accepted "in" with his or her peers, then his/her nightclub act would more than likely prove successful also. The other entertainers, people like Red Skelton, Danny Thomas, or Frank Sinatra, would show up for a lounge show highlighting Louis and Keely and make their presence known in the audience. Sometimes they'd even get involved in the act, other times they'd happily wave and joke to the performers onstage. This extra added attraction of

[10]*Ibid.*

[11]*Las Vegas Sun*, November 24, 1954; April 28, 1955; *Las Vegas Review-Journal*, August 24, 1978.

seeing powerhouse entertainers showing up for another performer's program added a dimension of excitement to the night's festivities and also gave people like Louis and Keely an added measure of respect from their regular audience. From the start, Louis and Keely were embraced as welcome newcomers to the city. Three weeks after their opening at the Casbar, Prima was invited to play in the prestigious "Tournament of Champions" golf classic at the Desert Inn Country Club. By Christmas week he and Keely were listed prominently as two of the entertainers slated to perform at a local high school's "All Star" party, including Jimmy Durante, Sophie Tucker, and Lena Horne.[12]

Relieved by the popular reception to his Sahara show, Prima realized he needed a new sound, that no matter how entertaining he and Keely might be, their novelty would quickly dull without a musical freshness. Several days before Christmas, Prima called New Orleans saxophonist Sam Butera, one of the musical mainstays in Leon Prima's 500 Club in the French Quarter. "Sam, you got to come out to Vegas, and bring three guys for a rhythm section," Prima begged Butera. "Don't worry about the money—it's gonna happen." Louis was so excited about the prospect of Butera joining him— brother Leon said Butera was "the best player there is"—that he asked Butera to fly to Las Vegas on Christmas Day. Butera resisted, explaining that he was going to be with his family in New Orleans for the holidays, but Prima insisted. "We're going to have a brand new show, man. I need you as quick as I can get you," Prima urged. Butera wasn't so sure: "In 1954 I had my own group, Sam Butera and the Night Trainers," he recalled later. "I was just about to go back on the road when I had an automobile accident which caused me to play while sitting down . . . I was already doing quite well with records and the exposure I was getting . . . but I decided to take a shot."[13]

Nurtured as a Dixieland musician, Butera spent his teenage years in New Orleans listening to a wide variety of sounds. Butera emulated the rhythms of bebop, jazz, and swing—almost anything that caught his attention he played and usually did so energetically and deftly. "When I started playing tenor in New Orleans in the mid-'40s, when I was with Ray McKinley, Tommy Dorsey, and those bands, I was playing jazz tenor. I

---

[12]*Las Vegas Sun*, December 14, 1954.

[13]*Times-Picayune*, January 15, 1984; *The Italian-American Digest*, Spring 1983.

loved players like Vido Musso and Charlie Ventura," Butera said. "When I had my own group, that was when rock n' roll came out. The record companies wanted that, and didn't care about the jazz saxophone. Of course, having a family, I was looking to make some money rather than being a martyr to the jazz cause. Then came Louie."[14]

Like Prima, Butera lived a colorful New Orleans boyhood and knew success early. A graduate of Holy Cross High School who attended the school on a music scholarship, Butera started playing saxophone at the age of seven and by the time he was fourteen was working in several Bourbon Street strip joints as part of the clubs' bands. "I was in awe seeing the ladies taking off their clothes," said Butera, who added that his parents were opposed to such work for their talented son. "But I had to get my experience somewhere . . . Working as a strip joint musician gave me a chance to improvise." The work paid off. In 1946, Butera was selected by an impressive panel of judges composed of Nat King Cole, Spike Jones and bandleader Les Brown as *Life* magazine's "Best High School Saxophonist in America." By the early 1950s, Butera was a regular attraction in Leon's club. One night, years before their eventual Las Vegas meeting, Louis walked into his brother's club, listened to Butera wail, and predicted "One day we'll get together."[15]

That day arrived on December 26, 1954, the same day, Butera later recalled, "When the ball started rolling." Butera's arrival at the Sahara during the final week of that year was akin to a life raft saving the passengers of a downed cruiser. Prima told Butera he would have complete creative control and that he wanted a sound highlighting Keely's singing and incorporating the rock n' roll beat. Keely later divided her success at the Sahara as Before Sam Arrived and After Sam Arrived: "Until Sam came, the group didn't really cook," said Keely. "They were nice guys and they were pretty good musicians, but Sam was the front Louis needed to work off of." Butera quickly developed the grinding saxophone style heard in the background of many rock n' roll hits then making the airwaves. He formed the Witnesses—a name Louis thought up—to back Prima with well-placed beeps and bops, while Butera shuffled back and forth in cadence. In addition, Butera used his saxophone as an adjunct to Prima's voice. If Louis crooned

[14]*Times-Picayune*, January 15, 1984.

[15]*The Italian-American Digest*, Spring 1983; *Las Vegas Review-Journal*, September 23, 1984.

and moaned, Sam did likewise. When Prima sang in sad ballad fashion, Butera followed suit. If Louis screamed and hollered, wailed and jived, Butera was there to follow him and meet him, beat for beat. It was the perfect marriage of man and instrument, what one writer later called "a natural merging of exceptional New Orleans talent."[16]

Some of Butera's arrangements included jazz singing, harmonizing, rock n' roll structures, and swing overtures—sometimes all within one song or medley. His arrangements required lengthy rehearsals because of their abrupt tempo shifts and the singing and instrumental specifications outlined in Butera's charts. Butera was a perfectionist who took his music seriously. From the start, Prima respected such professionalism, but he also attempted to exert a personal dominance over Sam, who was seventeen years his junior, telling the young saxophonist to address him as "The Chief."

An integral part of Butera's success was derived from his backup group, the Witnesses. From 1955 on, the Witnesses were composed of a series of young musicians whom Louis studied for their strongest attributes and then told them how to sell their talent. Drummer Paul Ferrara said Prima taught him to play for the audience's enjoyment and not to be a musician's musician trying to impress his peers with complicated musical techniques. "He really taught me the business and how to handle an audience, how to excite people," Ferrara said. The young drummer was also amazed by Prima's penchant for innovation: "Why don't you get thimbles and try them on the cymbals?" Ferraro remembered Prima asking him. "He was full of ideas." Prima also took the Witnesses' trombonist Lou Scioneaux aside and told the tall, hefty musician to change his name, explaining that few people outside of Louisiana would know how to pronounce it. "Lou Sino" was the result. "He was a leader, man," said Sino. "If you had basic talent, he could project it onstage, and that's what the whole act was. Everybody in the band did something."[17]

As the Witnesses under Butera became a regular and potent component in Prima's Sahara show, more and more critics singled them out for praise. "Butera and the Witnesses are a vital adjunct to the layout," said *Variety*, "providing a driving musical background and joining in the clowning." Perhaps it wasn't so surprising that Butera and the Witnesses should be

[16]"Louis Prima—The Chief," *WYES-TV*, Byer; *The Italiaan-American Digest*, Spring 1983.

[17]*Las Vegas Sun*, August 25, 1978; "Louis Prima—The Chief," *WYES-TV*, Byer; *Times-Picayune*, August 1, 1986; *WWIW* radio tribute to Lou Sino, New Orleans, July 31, 1986.

singled out for critical acclaim. All of the members of the combo were accomplished musicians—if not well-rounded entertainers by Prima's standards. Author Roger Krinkle said Butera's arrangements were "often fast and intricate" and that such programs as the Sahara Hotel's show "required good musicianship." Thirty years after Butera and the Witnesses first put their talents, with Prima and Smith, on record, music critic Art Fein wrote:

> The music they were playing, and that Prima sensed was vital and even visionary, then had no name. It's taken historians 30 years to pinpoint it for what it always was—rock n' roll . . . At first there is an easy shuffle beat, and often a vocal call-and-response between Prima and his chorus, deceptively similar to the '40s stylings of, say, the Andrew Sisters. But as the verses wrap up and lead into the instrumental break, the structure begins to wobble. Prima very excitedly begins to lose the formality of the song and begins scat-calling in Italian doubletalk. The sax player responds hurriedly to answer the vocals, the voice recedes, and an explosive sax solo rocks in! Add to that the other inputs of trumpets and trombones and you have a musical sound salad that was, frankly unprecedented at the time, and frankly misunderstood.[18]

Fein's contention, later supported by a number of critics, has as it basic argument that Prima and Butera were playing frenzied rock n' roll to the very parents in the 1950s who condemned musicians like Elvis Presley and Little Richard for corrupting their children. Whatever description it went by, the Prima-Smith-Butera-Witnesses show, after its initial public outing in April 1955, was a Las Vegas sensation, winning critical reviews and prompting long lines of fans into the casino. Author Don Knepp later said the Prima-Smith-Butera-Witnesses show was "the strongest lounge package on the talent-laden Strip," a judgement quickly borne out by visiting journalists and critics who, from 1955 on, singled out Keely for their praise, focused on the exciting entertainment themes, and rarely forgot Butera's musical beat. "No this isn't jazz," said *Down Beat*. "In fact, it's down right rock n' roll— except when Keely sings—Then it's a musical delight." The *Chicago Tribune* called Keely the "most provocative deadpan since Buster Keaton, she just stands there while husband Louis Prima cavorts and doodles his way

---

[18]*Variety*, September 11, 1957; Rogert D. Krinkle, *The Complete Encyclopedia of Popular Music and Jazz, 1900-1950* (New Rochelle, N.Y., 1974), III, 78; Art Fein, record notes, "Zooma Zooma—The Best of Louis Prima," (Rhino Records, Hollywood, California, 1986).

through a song. Everyone in the house usually breaks up as Louis performs—everyone except Keely, of course . . . Then Keely steps out and in that smokey voice of hers sings everything back into place again." When *Newsweek* magazine decided to write about the entertainment explosions at the Casbar Lounge, they focused on Keely, calling her a "deadpan with a voice," and noting that "Keely is currently classed in show business as a new 'overnight sensation'."[19]

What may have particularly ignited the national press attention to the Casbar Lounge show throughout the rest of the 1950s, was Prima's decision in 1955 to sign with Capitol Records—his first major recording company contract in more than five years—and attempt to package the magic of the lounge shows through a series of Capitol albums. The decision to focus on Louis and Keely's live shows, rather than bringing the duo to Hollywood or New York for studio sessions, turned out to be highly beneficial for both Capitol and Louis and Keely. All of the albums, beginning with "The Wildest," released in September 1956, turned out to be brisk sellers, but historically, were of an even greater value because they came the closest to capturing the vibrancy of Louis and Keely's live shows. The Capitol albums, in fact, are practically the only recorded evidence of what Prima must have been like on stage. The album titles gave a hint of what to expect: after the release of "The Wildest," came "Call of the Wildest," "The Wildest Show at Tahoe," "Las Vegas Prima Style," and into the early 1960s, "The Wildest Comes Home."

Capitol's release of "The Wildest," in 1956, the first in the live club series, also contained one remarkable song that set the Butera arrangements, augmented smartly by Keely and Louie's vocalizing, in a maze of rock n' roll rhythms, hip harmonizing, and swing up-tempo beats. A musical medley of "Just A Gigolo" and the song "I Ain't Got Nobody," the Butera arrangement is a *tour de force* clearly exhibiting the saxophonist's artistic penchant and creative imagination. Its musical influences seem to be an eclectic mix of every major musical strain of the twentieth century. In addition, the song became a top seller that year, even though it ran for nearly five minutes, far beyond the two minutes, thirty seconds barrier for hit singles.

---

[19]Knepp, *Las Vegas*, p. 99; *Down Beat*, October 31, 1957; *Chicago Tribune*, July 12, 1959; *Newsweek*, June 9, 1958.

With the positive press reception of 1955 and 1956, coupled with the popular success of "The Wildest," and Prima and Smith's next Capitol album "The Call of the Wildest," in 1957, Prima orchestrated Keely as a single recording star. To the duo's relief, Keely's individual albums, also on Capitol, sold as well as the Louis-Keely ventures. That same year, Keely and Hollywood arranger Nelson Riddle, one of the city's giants in his field and a regular orchestra leader for Frank Sinatra and Ella Fitzgerald, produced the album "I Wish You Love," which by the end of the year was a million-selling album and won a Grammy nomination in 1958. In addition, Keely's public profile by 1957 was strong enough to win for her the role of Francie Wymore, Robert Mitchum's love interest in the film *Thunder Road*. A rollicking movie centered around moonshining, Smith, one critic later wrote "with her unusual mannerisms and unique appearance, was an inspired choice . . ." Keely also sang the theme song of the movie, "Whippoorwill," which was written by Mitchum.[20]

Critical response to Keely's single recordings was equally positive. "Her style has always a freshness, an insouciance, that makes her one of the most delightful singers around today," said *High Fidelity* magazine, "and when she had the chance to work alone, she seems freer in spirit, as well as more assured, than when partnered by her husband, Louis Prima." *Down Beat* noted the same phenomenon, reviewing a Prima-Smith-Butera-Witnesses club date in October of 1957, the publication noted:

> Throughout the general riot, however, the imperturbable Keely poses deadpan by the piano. When her number comes up, she delivers a clean bill-of-goods well calculated to hit the audience in its musical solar plexus. (One wonders, in fact, why Capitol Records chooses not to record more often this potentially major pop vocalist with accompaniment other than by the roughhouse Prima boys.)[21]

But for all of their professional success, however, Louis and Keely's single source of power came from their Casbar Lounge shows, those late-night, uninhibited forays into musical madness that started out as a two-

[20]Jay Robert Nash and Stanley Ralph Ross, *The Motion Picture Guide, T-V, 1927-1983* (Evanston, Ill., 1986), p. 3438.

[21]*High Fidelity*, August 1960; *Down Beat*, October 31, 1957.

week trial stay in the fall of 1954 and ended up as a permanent Las Vegas institution from 1955 to 1959. As the Casbar act grew in popularity month after month throughout 1956, 1957, 1958, and 1959, Louis and Keely looked at the gambling capital as their home. They purchased a sprawling ranch home within the city's boundaries, and, after the birth of two daughters, sent them both to Las Vegas schools.

In the summer of 1956, *Life* magazine attempted to provide its readers with a glimpse of what a daily routine must be like for the couple, showing Louis and Keely filling in for a sick nightclub performer as the main floor attraction from 10 p.m. to midnight, then, said the publication "they worked form 1 a.m. to 6 a.m. in the lounge where their unusual act competed with the chant of the gambling casino's croupiers. It was 8 in the morning before they had breakfast at home with their 18-month old daughter." Reporter Dee Phillips also tried to capture daily life for the Primas, and was surprised when she noticed that Louis and Keely headed "directly for the coffee shop," during intermissions at the Casbar Lounge. It may have been two or three in the morning, but Louis went "immediately to the table where Barbara Belle . . . sips coffee, waiting to get busy." Phillips then observed Prima talking with Doyle Gilmore of Capitol Records about the recording schedule for "Las Vegas Prima Style," making arrangements with Belle to run through the charts with Nelson Riddle for Keely's single album, and accepting a TV appearance for later in the year. Wrote Phillips: "The 'Chief' glances at his watch, then looks across at Keely. It's time for another performance. The look of intense concentration leaves his face. He becomes the Louis Prima the world knows . . . and so it goes until six a.m.: One half-hour of entertainment, one half-hour of business. For their three-thirty show, entertainers from all the other hotels have dropped in to see the 'Wildest'." By six a.m., Louis and Keely left for home to have breakfast with their two daughters. The couple would go to bed generally by seven a.m., with Louis rising just before noon, and Keely shortly afterwards. Prima divided his afternoon between endless business calls and golfing. By five p.m. Keely and Louis dined with their daughters, napped between 7 p.m. and 11:30 p.m., and at midnight were dressing, getting ready for their Sahara show at 1 a.m. Wrote Phillips: "Time-wise, of course, their home life is like an upside-down cake."[22]

[22]*Life*, October 22, 1956; *TV Reporter*, August 1958.

The frenetic pace seemed to fit Louis and Keely fine. "I enjoy performing and playing," Prima said, "and the family feeling of my band keeps us together and encourages honest criticism. We have a couple of dozen children between us—Sam Butera, Jimmy Vincent, and the others— we live in Vegas, support the good schools, and, well, I guess I try to create the kind of loving family I grew up with." Band members recalled how Prima and Keely invited almost the entire staff of the Sahara Hotel to their home for the holidays, and how the inevitable Mama Angelina would be on hand, supervising kitchen activities and making her own spaghetti pasta. "Everyone would be there," remembered Lou Sino, Jr., "and Louie and Keely knocked themselves out being nice to us. I was only a kid then, but my father took me there for Christmas. It was always a fun time. There'd be all sorts of commotion, people everywhere and lots of gifts. Louis and Keely were in the middle of everything. Everyone really liked them a lot."[23]

It was, indeed, a happy time for the Primas. Louis had taken a gamble and won splendidly. His idea to merge jazz, swing, and rock n' roll was a success, his launching of Keely as a single recording star brought the couple millions of sold records, and his decision to sign on at the Casbar for an extended stay that lasted more than four years, gave the act, but Prima in particular, a sense of stability and national recognition previously lacking in his career. As always, Prima had his own reasons for the success of the Casbar show.

> The audience never knows what's coming up," he told one reporter. "And to tell the truth, neither do we. We're always throwing 'em surprises and they love it. It's something different. Why, in one show we give an audience seven or eight samplers of different material . . . We may work out a rough routine—for myself, for Keely, for Sam and the boys. But there are always a lot of changes when we get going onstage. It depends on the temper of the audience . . . When I get the feel of the people out there, I may change everything. To put it simply, the audience controls us.

[23]*San Francisco, Examiner*, September 9, 1968; Lou Sino, Jr., interivew, July 1986.

Prima added that he thought his act would continue to improve because both
he and Butera insisted on daily rehearsals: "We're the one act in show
business that's constantly rehearsing," he noted.[24]

Whatever element sparked the public's reaction may have been
immaterial; all the owners of the Sahara cared about were the SRO crowds
Louis and Keely were drawing on a nightly basis. Said *Time* magazine: "

> The Sahara, which pays him $10,000 a week, goes all out to clean
> up while he is there. Waiters rush into the Casbar Lounge with
> extra tables, each the size of a phonograph record. By midnight,
> the space between the lounge and gambling room piles up ten deep
> with waiting fans.

Columnist Ralph Pearl also enjoyed the Louis and Keely hysteria,
recalling the lounge dynamics through the frantic eyes of Pancho Aliati, the
lounge's maitre d'. "People waiting to see Louis Prima and Keely Smith,
who didn't and couldn't get reservations, formed in lines outside the
showroom an hour before in hopeless agony," Pearl wrote in the *Las Vegas
Sun*. "There was always furious confusion around showtime and Pancho
Aliati, one of the most reserved and cool gents in the business, was starting
to feel the pressure, as was his captain and waitresses," continued Pearl.
"As always, after the room was filled to the walls, Pancho walked out to
survey the people in the non-reservation line. He'd give them a helpless
smile before explaining he could seat nobody else." On one evening in
particular, Aliati was touched by the determination of three young New
Zealand women standing in line three nights in a row without getting to see
Prima and Smith. "Such bravery over and beyond the call of duty touched
the genteel Aliati," Pearl recalled. "He immediately got them a table, even
though they had to be squeezed between an unbending wall and seven other
crowded tables. Today, somewhere in New Zealand, the name of Pancho
Aliati is being whispered with reverence by three happy New Zealand ladies
who finally got to see their favorites, Louis Prima and Keely Smith."[25]

Such stories were typical of the impact Louis and Keely had on the
times. Looking back, Keely said the Casbar Lounge stay—the two-week

---

[24]*Down Beat*, February 19, 1959.

[25]*Time*, September 7, 1959; *Las Vegas Sun*, August 28, 1961.

engagement that stretched into more than four years—was "one of the happiest times of my life. I was just very happy with Louis and being with my kids and singing and living." Butera was equally entranced by what seemed to be a magical time: "If I could do it again, it would be a pleasure," he said, recalling the Casbar and the late 1950s. "That one time around was beautiful." By all accounts, everyone else experienced the same ecstasy. By the late 1950s, Prima nd Keely were bringing in $20,000 a week, before Prima broke his engagement with the Sahara and signed with the competing Desert Inn for a record-breaking fee of $3 million, committing the Louis-Keely act to twelve weeks a year for five years.[26]

With Butera and the Witnesses in tow, the Keely-Louis show seemed like the place to be, the center of hip Vegas action, sly sexual suggestions, and finger-snapping rock n' roll music. The *Miami Herald* said the Louis-Keely show created an entertainment revolution, calling it a "venerable style of showmanship that, if it didn't launch a thousand ships, launched 10,000 Vegas acts that are now the dominant form of entertainment in nightclubs." Columnist James Bacon, calling Keely and Louis "the hottest nightclub act in show business," added,

> The noise, bouncing, and general Pandemonium were there, but the musicianship was also superb. It was, in effect, well rehearsed and well-disciplined rock n' roll plus good New Orleans jazz. The act was so rehearsed that every move came across as effortless ad lib.

Butera had his own explanation for the show's success: "Louis was a showman, and everything we did with the group was entertainment," he said. "I guess that was the main reason for my not being recognized as a jazz player more often than I am. With Louie, it wasn't a laid-back show. Everything was on top. With Louis, we were always on top of the beat, pushing the beat. It's hard to play jazz when you're doing that."[27]

Somehow the antics of Louis and Keely captivated the nation. Press photos invariably caught Louis laughingly playing his trumpet on top of a table or dancing an Irish jig, while the Witnesses danced in a blur of motion about the stage, and Keely, looking both forlorn and compelling, calmly

[26]"Louis Prima—The Chief," *WYES-TV*, Byer; *Variety*, August 25, 1978.

[27]*Times-Picayune*, August 27, 1978; May 22, 1960; January 15, 1984.

gazing off into space. There seemed to be a lot of hell-raising going on, and in the complacent environment of Eisenhower America, the pulse of the late night Casbar Lounge was irresistible. How else to explain the steady stream of stars, fans, gamblers and, perhaps most interestingly of all, national reporters, who found their way to the lounge? "When the stage is alive with ridiculous farmer costumes, Keely appears in a simple stunning gown," noted the magazine *Pageant*.

> When others wear hats, she is bareheaded; when the choristers wear dresses, she wears tights. When she sings alone, her songs are sweet and low; when she sings with Louis, the tune is loud and fast. When benignly ugly Louis is making himself look short and squat in a flat hat, lovely Keely is tall and slender in spike heels. When Louis is sweaty and intense, Keely is cool and casual.[28]

Not all observers, however, were enthralled. *Time* magazine, that harbinger of American mainstream taste, seemed appalled that such an act could reach the outer boundaries of success. Claiming that Prima and Smith were "confirming the low taste," the magazine called Louis a "brassy, bulb-nosed, toupeed trumpeteer" and observed Keely scratching herself and smothering a belch. This was, they went on, a "doggedly vulgar act." The story was accompanied by an extremely unattractive photo of Smith and a quote from Prima complaining that "people in restaurants expect me to leave $50 tips." One letter writer to *Time* agreed with the magazine's appraisal: "Although you'll receive heavy abuse from their fans, and Louis will chortle 'all the way to the bank,' it's encouraging to read such a clear analysis of this gruesome two-some and their gutter-grade maneuvers," said a North Carolina woman.[29]

Time's reservations aside, Prima and Smith had few detractors in their Las Vegas domain. Part of the reason for the adulation might have been in the makeup of the nightly audiences. While it is true that a goodly portion of those who turned out to see the singer and trumpeteer were West Coast professionals and Las Vegas swingers who stayed up all night as a normal lifestyle, a large number of working-class people from the industrial

[28]*Pageant Magazine*, July 1960.

[29]*Time*, September 7, 1959; September 21, 1959.

heartland also spent their hard-earned savings in the casinos. Most hotels made it impossible for their guests to get to their rooms without encountering at least one slot machine or blackjack table, and Vegas visitors, regardless of their origins, quickly decided they wanted to spend money and have a rousing, ribald, good time. In this regard, Prima and Smith seldom failed to live up to their reputations. Other publications, too, took note of the frequent racy suggestions and blue language of the show, but were more tolerant in their reviews than *Time*. "The show is fast-paced, noisy, and funny, and not for the kiddies," *Down Beat* put it simply. In a cover story in 1959, *International Musician* said: "The Prima-Smith combination has brought broad, outrageous, often hilarious low comedy into the nation's top clubs again. Sophistication lasts about ten seconds when Prima and his crew get moving."[30]

As the months turned into years at the Casbar Lounge, and later at the Desert Inn, Prima was presented with the problem of how to best market his Las Vegas chemistry to a larger audience. Because of his long-standing fear of flying, he confined his personal appearances in the mid- and late 1950s to the continental United States, although he received a great number of invitations to appear in France, West Germany, Italy, Cuba, and Hawaii.[31]

Additionally he continued to buck the television colossus by complaining about the control TV producers wanted to exert over a possible Louis and Keely show. "If the people who run TV would just let us alone we could routine a show the way we feel," Prima angrily said. "If the ad agencies would let us do what we do in a club, the people of America would love it. I'm convinced of this." When offered a regular spot on the Milton Berle Show for thirteen weeks in the fall of 1958, Prima balked. "Milton sat down with us," Prima told columnist Earl Wilson. "We had three or four real good things planned. But we didn't want overexposure. At the end of six, seven shows, we might have been unhappy." Noting that Berle wanted Louis to conduct the show's orchestra, Prima cut short negotiations with Berle, sarcastically adding that "Uncle Miltie" should get Lawrence Welk for his show if all he wanted was an orchestra leader. But Berle, one of the most popular TV performers of the 1950s, said Prima was simply angling for a better deal: "Having Louis and Keely appear as regulars on my show was my brain child," said Berle. "I offered them a 13-week deal with a

[30]*Down Beat*, October 31, 1957; *International Musician*, November 1959.

[31]Keely Smith interview, May 1984.

13-week option period at $7,250 per show. 'You've got a deal,' Louis told me. We shook hands on it, which in this business is considered as good as a signature. When it came time to draw up the contract he reneged. He demanded a 26-week deal with their option period. He also objected to leading the large orchestra, said he just wanted to work with his small combo." Even after the Prima-Berle fight made headlines, Prima continued to fan the flames. "Milton Berle, so far as I'm concerned, is a crumb!" Prima snapped to the *New York Post*. "We will never play with Milton Berle for any amount of money." Summing up the squabble, the *New York Daily News* accused Louis of "below-the-belt blows" for maligning Berle's honesty and Welk's showmanship. But Prima remained resolute: "We don't care about TV," he said after the feud. "We don't need all that grief."[32]

Despite such incidents, Prima and Smith, when they did appear on TV, did so successfully. As guest stars on variety shows hosted by Frank Sinatra, Dean Martin, and Ed Sullivan, Louis and Keely were presented at their musical best, prompting TV columnist Kay Gardella to write in June of 1959: "Not since Elvis Presley went into the Army have any entertainers been as hot on the TV market as Louis Prima and his wife, Keely Smith." Such appearances were usually brief and lucrative for not only the Primas, but also for the host programs. Sullivan, who hosted perhaps the most popular TV variety show of the 1950s, said there were only two acts that could automatically bolster his ratings just by the announcement of their appearance. One was Elvis, and the other was the Prima-Smith duo.[33]

Even without the benefit of television's vast commercial possibilities and exposure, Louis and Keely became national hitmakers, celebrities and trendsetters as the 1950s wore on. Obviously all of America, despite the relatively inflated standard of living at the time, did not make it to a late-evening show at the Casbar Lounge. But millions of fans captured a sense of the Louis and Keely style through their successful Capital albums. And Prima rightly looked at recordings as the best and most convenient means of exporting the Casbar thrills.

Undoubtedly, critics agreed with Prima's method. In 1958, Keely was selected in a national disc jockey poll as their favorite female singer. That

---

[32]*Down Beat*, February 19, 1959; *New York Post*, July 27, 1958; *New York Daily News*, July 16, 1958. Columnist Marie Torre called up a William Morris agent for his opinion on what the Berle-Prima contract said—the agent, according to Torre, "backed Berle's story right down to the option." *New York Daily News*, July 18, 1958.

[33]*New York Daily News*, June 3, 1959; "Louis Prima—The Chief," *WYES-TV*, Byer.

was followed by a Grammy award for female vocalist the same year, a Playboy Jazz Award in 1959, and *Billboard* and *Variety*'s number one female vocalist award in both 1958 and 1959. In late 1958, Louis and Keely's restructured version of the classic popular standard "Old Black Magic" made it to the Top 40 charts and stayed there for almost two months straight. Both as a single and later as a Capitol album—"The Hits of Louis and Keely"—"Old Black Magic" proved to be a venerable and consistently popular tune for the duo and won Keely, along with Louis, yet another Grammy.[34]

But Prima wanted a greater financial piece of the action from such recordings, and not seeing what he liked when Capitol Records attempted to renew the Louis-Keely contract in 1959, he signed with Dot Records, a lable boasting such stars as Pat Boone, Debbie Reynolds, and the Mills Brothers. Although Dot's distribution potential was less than that of Capitol's, Prima benefitted from his contract with the recording company by drawing up a contract that flip-flopped the typical record company-artist arrangement of the 1950s: by the terms of the agreement, Prima would pocket the recording profits, while Dot settled for the royalties. Realizing the potential financial opportunities, Louis and Keely produced no less than eight Dot albums in a two-year period. One record, "Wonderland By Night," made it to the Top 40 in 1961. In addition, from May 1959 to July 1961, Keely and Louis released almost twenty-five single 45s, while Louis alone appeared on at least six platters and Butera and the Witnesses produced another eight sides as a separate unit. Musically, many of the Dot albums lacked the explosive quality of the Capitol releases and were less professionally produced. But Dot albums such as 1961's "On Stage" highlighting Louis and Keely's new act at the Desert Inn and "Wonderland By Night," were brisk sellers anyway, underlining the couple's commercial appeal, despite the drop-off in their creative polish.[35]

More signs of the couple's durability came when Keely and Louis ventured from the borders of Las Vegas and broke attendance at such swank clubs as the Mocambo in Hollywood, the Copacabana in New York, and the Chez Paree in Chicago. For those believing that Louis and Keely appealed primarily to the middle-age set, the *Los Angeles Times* was on hand to

[34]Joel Whitburn, *The Billboard Book of Top 40 Hits, 1955 to the Present* (n.p., 1983), p. 102.

[35]*Ibid.*

shatter illusions: "The room was packed opening night and many of those there were teenagers," said the paper of Louis and Keely's engagement at the Coconut Grove in Los Angeles. "And the mob that crammed the lobby waiting for the second show seemed to be comprised of the same age-bracket."[36]

Given such widespread acceptance of the act, Louis could be excused for interrupting Keely as she warbled "I Got It Bad . . . And That Ain't Good." Prima bopped and turned, rolling his eyes in apparent sensual heaven and interjected "I Got It Good and It Ain't Bad!" Indeed he did have it good. Fortune had shone through once again, smiling lovingly down on all things that Prima touched. Louie's "blue period" of the early 1950s had given way to probably his greatest era of professional opportunities, creative control, and personal fulfillment. When Louis and Keely rocked the entertainment world by walking out into the Nevada sun, skipping down the Strip past the El Morocco and the Desert Spa, and entering Wilbur Clark's Desert Inn in 1959, they were also walking into a binding contract that guaranteed them at least $50,000 a week.

Down Beat called the duo's success "Phenomenal," and *Variety* breathlessly added that "Probably one of the best acts in the business today, with happy musical Pandemonium for sale, is this strange, but so-effective team of Louis and his Keely." Perhaps no other husband-and-wife team had been as successful in American popular music. Productive, exhaustive, and nationally visible, the Prima-Smith marriage seemed like a Hollywood treatment of romance and happy endings. One of the imponderables of their success undoubtedly was the role their very public private lives played in their careers. Fans and friends wondered what it was like in the Prima-Smith household, were they really the good friends that they seemed onstage? Were there any tensions performing together, doing business together, and living together as husband and wife? Fan magazines speculated, but the adoring masses would have none of it. When the couple appeared on such programs as the Ed Sullivan Show and dryly joked about finding other, more stimulating, mates, everyone laughed, everyone knew it was part of the duo's *schtick.* "She's been holding out on me," Prima bellowed to audiences, while Keely explained: "I'm too young for him." They were like that other great romantic pair of the 1950s, Ralph and Alice Cramden, the creations of Jackie Gleason and Audrey Meadows on TV.

[36]*Los Angeles Times,* June 20, 1961.

Gleason almost weekly threatened to send Meadows "To the moon," with his meaty fist, but the television audience knew he'd never do it. That was the humor of it all. It wouldn't have been funny at all if Gleason actually did assault Meadows, just as Prima and Smith's incessant cutting would fall flat were there actual marital troubles between them. No, this was a beguiling union, made even more so when Keely appeared onstage pregnant and Louis seemed every bit the caring and paternal husband, although he persisted in calling her "Miss Smith."[37]

Whenever the subject came up, Louis and Keely let it be known that this was a permanent twosome, that their astounding success as evidenced by their Casbar Lounge shows and the Capitol and Dot records was not an accident, but a direct result of their personal dynamics magnified many times by their particular musical talents. The popularity of their Las Vegas shows—the very programs that brought Prima from the entertainment hinterlands in 1954 to the center of his industry's circles of success in 1959—was due almost entirely to the chemistry of the couple. In this regard, both Louis and Keely promised to maintain the status quo . . . the twosome would remain just that. "I have no single plans at all," Keely said to the world in the fall of 1959. "The act will continue as long as we're all happy." Prima concurred: "If I were to do a single," he explained, "It just wouldn't be the same at all."[38]

---

[37]*Down Beat*, February 19, 1959; *Variety*, September 13, 1957; *Time*, September 7, 1959; *Las Vegas Sun*, January 10, 1955.

[38]*International Musician*, November 1959.

CHAPTER VII

"We Are Doing Much Better Without Her"

In the spring of 1959, Louis Prima purchased several full-page ads in the largest Las Vegas newspapers to explain to his fans a recent dizzy spell he experienced while playing at the Casbar Lounge. "Dear Folks, due to all the rumors and misconceptions that have been going around, I am talking this opportunity to let everyone know the true facts," Prima began, launching into a lengthy explanation concerning his allergic reactions. He fainted onstage, he said, because of "tobacco smoke, dust, dirt, and foul air, which is the usual condition that exists in any night club where the ceiling is low and proper ventilation has not been provided." He continued: "All of this mixture accumulates and has no way of escaping and anyone who is exposed to this condition and is playing a wind instrument or singing is constantly inhaling this foul and unhealthy air." Despite such unpleasant atmospheric conditions at the Sahara, however, Prima reassured his worried fans that he would shortly return to the lounge, adding "It will be wonderful seeing all of you again."[1]

The letter may have seemed like a proper public notice from any entertainer worried about squelching unfavorable speculation that could conceivably hurt business, but Prima added a tag line that only aroused further gossip column wonder: "During my hospital stay, continual phone calls were made by certain people to the Sansum Clinic to verify my illness, my operation, and my even being there," continued Louis. "Also, rumors started that Keely and I were breaking up. This is a preposterous lie, started by some imbecile. We have a wonderful family life . . . We have two beautiful children, and Keely and I love each other very much."[2]

Prima's answer to the gossip circulating throughout Las Vegas was worthy of note. Rarely did he indulge the curious public's tastes for facts pertaining to his private life. Reporters who asked about his marital status or rumored romantic adventures were more likely to receive a stony silence than any explanation. But by 1959 and throughout 1960, speculation only

---

[1]*Las Vegas Sun*, March 27, 1959; *Variety,*April 8, 1959.

[2]*Ibid.*

increased that something was seriously wrong in the Prima household. The *New York Daily News* later observed: "Louie was pushing 50 and Keely was nearing 30 when the rumors started that their marriage was on the rocks. They either denied the rumors or refused comment when questioned by reporters . . ." Fans of Louis and Keely grew concerned when Louis was seen, with growing regularity, in pubs and at private parties *sans* Keely. Sometimes Louis would find himself in the company of attractive women who were drawn to his star status and show business power. Other times reporters talked about Louis drinking and carousing with members of his band, long after he'd sent Keely home to their two children. During the early months of Louis' Las Vegas meanderings, Keely wrote it off as "male menopause."[3]

"He was a lot older than me, and I think it got to the point where he felt he had to prove something to himself as far as other women were concerned," Keely said. "I thought it was just something he was going through, and I accepted it as that. I said that I loved him. I said, 'Well, heck, if you could give him a Rolls Royce, you'd give him a Rolls Royce, so just ignore all of this.' But it didn't stop." Keely's reluctance to demand an end to her husband's behavior was only the natural offshoot of a relationship steeped in teacher-student themes. From the moment of her signing on with Prima's big band in 1948, Keely accepted a certain status that relegated her to the dutiful, supportive partner, a status little changed by the couple's 1953 marriage. Such dynamics failed to change after the enormous success of the Keely-Louis act at the Casbar Lounge or even with the birth of their two daughters in the late 1950s. Long accustomed to receiving the attention of impressionable fans, Louis by 1959 was openly accepting love notes at the Casbar in front of Keely, as if the gestures would further prove his manhood. "He'd be flirting with the girls in the audience and he and Sam would have contests over who would make some girl first," Keely said. "It was pretty much blatant. He wouldn't talk to me about it, never said anything about it, but it happened."[4]

Prima's flirtatious ways were due, in large part, to the manners and methods he practiced all of his adult life. As a professional entertainer of no little sexual attraction, Prima was accustomed to the sometimes overt

[3]*New York Daily News*, August 6, 1965; Keely Smith interview, May 1986.

[4]Keely Smith interview, May 1986.

advances of female fans. Although he obviously did not respond to each and every pass, Louis through the years chalked up the sort of romantic conquest record that might startle those outside of such a fast-paced glitzy life. "He was a man-about-town," said Prima's longtime songwriter and general manager Barbara Belle. "I don't think any one woman could have ever satisfied him. That was just the way he was, and nothing would ever change that."[5]

His "swinging" inclinations were also an important part of Prima's act. One of Louis' greatest selling points as an entertainer was his refusal to simply play song after song onstage without providing some sort of comical narration or connecting thread. Even polished performers like Sinatra and Elvis Presley found it difficult to keep up such banter on an ongoing basis, but Prima did it regularly and with great originality. Many times his spoken words might prove to be the highlight of a show simply because Louis took his audience on a trip through his colorful stories that might ultimately lead nowhere, but included Italian scat doubletalk, a sprinkling of Yiddish slang, and continuous reference to his insatiable sexual appetite. His prelude to a song called "Coolin'," for example, had Louis flying to Tel Aviv and meeting a man named Herschel who was wearing a "continental yarmulke" and holding a "loaf of pumpernickel on the one arm and carrying a string of kosher pork sausages in the other hand and two pocketfuls of matza balls . . . all different flavors." Herschel, who was from the "Hot Club of Israel," took Prima and Butera to a private party where a sultry figure slowly shed articles of clothing as the musicians panted in anticipation. Even though, in Prima's fantasy, the joke lies in the figure turning out to be Wilbur Clark, the beefy proprietor of the Desert Inn, the suggestion that Prima was a single man on the move, constantly searching for females and cavorting with a man—Butera—nearly twenty years his junior, was clear. Prima was, to put it simply, a swinger. It was entrancing, entertaining, and the way of life Louis practiced for all of his adult years. Now at the age of 50, and in danger of falling victim to comedian Lenny Bruce's adage—"There's nothing sadder than an old hipster"—Prima was more restless than ever. Where such limitations as marital fidelity and simple propriety did little to curtail Prima's romantic escapades before, age proved to be even less effective now.[6]

[5]Barbara Belle interview, July 1986.

[6]Monologue from "Coolin'," on Dot album "On Stage," (Louis Prima and Keely Sith at the Desert Inn, 1961); Albert Goldman, *Ladies and Gentlemen—Lenny Bruce!!* (New York, 1974), p. 395.

If worries over Prima's activities weren't enough to preoccupy Keely, then the couple's hectic schedule between 1959 and 1960 was. Quite simply, they never seemed to stop working, a direct result of Louis' insatiable urge to produce and stay active professionally. Between 1954— when the Primas invaded the Casbar Lounge—into the summer of 1959, rarely did Keely or Louis stop for rest. On top of recording commitments, and their popular nightclub show, Prima and Keely were also obliged in the spring of 1959 to honor a nationwide publicity tour plugging the pleasant movie musical they filmed in 1958, *Hey Boy! Hey Girl!*, a film that was naturally promoted by the release of another Capitol record that was rushed to more than 8,000 record stores across the country. The movie, revolving around a devoted parishioner (Keely), and her attempts to persuade Prima, playing himself, to perform for a church benefit, was noteworthy for its musical quality. Prima shows extraordinary energy—jumping, twisting, and bopping on tunes like "Lazy River"—while Keely sings a handful of songs skillfully, particularly the popular "Autumn Leaves." One critic called *Hey Boy! Hey Girl!* "a pleasing experience thanks to the likeable stars." But the strain of promoting the movie added only more pressure to an already crowded agenda for Louis and Keely.[7]

A vacation cruise might have soothed out the trouble spots in the Prima marriage and given the couple a chance to relax, but even here Louis was sure to create more tension by his lack of navigational ability. Purchasing a forty-two-foot power boat for vacationing in the Atlantic Ocean and Gulf of Mexico, Prima said he loved the open air and water, and wanted to spend his later days at sea. But he frequently made it possible that neither he nor Keely would live to see such days through his erratic sailing methods. "What he doesn't know about the technical side of boats would fill a big set of books," laughed columnist Jim Bishop after he interviewed Prima and heard the musician wax eloquent on the joys of sailing. Reckoning that it took too long to sail around Florida from the Atlantic to the Gulf of Mexico, Prima wondered why he couldn't cut across the top of the state, from Jacksonville to Pensacola. Incredulous, Keely explained, "There is no water there, Louis." Nonetheless, Prima remained convinced sailing could be fun, if only it didn't take *so long* to get to certain spots. Louis forgot how he almost drowned himself and bride Tracelene in 1946 on

---

[7]*Variety*, April 15, 1959; Jay Robert Nash and Stanley Ralph Ross, *The Motion Picture Guide Book, H to K, 1927-1983* (Evanston, Ill., 1986), p. 1216.

their honeymoon through the Erie Canal. Now, in the summer of 1959, Prima wanted to sail down the Atlantic coast, but quickly grounded the boat in the Inland Waterway. There he and Keely sat. The yacht was valued at $160,000. A carpet was installed in Keely's favorite colors, orange and white, with the words "My Keely" lettered on the stern. Powered by two jet-charged Diesel engines and three generators, the yacht also included three staterooms and gold-handled bathroom fixtures. And now it was grounded because Captain Prima took a wrong turn. "The markers were supposed to be here," Louis pointed out to sea, "or over there. But somebody moved them. They send you a little thing called 'Notice to Mariners' about the changes. But they send it to your house. How was I going to get the mail out on the water?" Eventually the Coast Guard spotted the "My Keely" and pulled the Primas out of trouble. Unfazed, Louis said his newest boat reminded him of an earlier yacht he and Keely owned: "The last boat we had, Keely and I handled ourselves . . . It was nothing. We just ran aground three times." Ever the optimist, Prima announced after the Inland Waterway fiasco: "I want to make a trip to the Panama Canal this fall," as he minimized the dangers of his most recent sea-going adventures. "It was a lot of laughs . . . I guess."[8]

Such comic interludes would normally enliven any rocky marriage. Friends of Keely and Louis remembered how happy the couple seemed at home, how animated Louis became around his two daughters. Keely said that even during one of her husband's gloomiest moods, he could suddenly brighten and poke fun at himself, magically lifting the despair that earlier settled over the Prima household. It was a certain magic Louis had, a magic that both friends and family easily remembered. "You never knew what Louie was feeling or how he was feeling," said Madelyn Prima, the wife of Leon. "Sometimes it made people uncomfortable, even within his own family. If he was feeling moody, everyone was quiet then. Whatever atmosphere he created, we all went along with."[9]

Certainly to outsiders, Keely and Louis, particularly on stage, seemed a contented couple. If the use of humor within a marriage signalled a healthy sense of perspective, then the Primas appeared to have a secure union. "When she gets home, she's dead . . . Believe me," Louis said in reference to

[8]*New York Journal-American,* undated clipping, ca. 1959; *New York Post,* June 12, 1959, August 21, 1960.

[9]Madelyn Prima interview, July 1986.

Keely's amorous abilities. Keely responded: "That's the only way we can start even . . . Believe me." In other moments Keely would poke fun at Prima's large facial features, telling audiences she thought her husband looked like the American Indian image on the nickel. It was, at least on stage, a union that put a premium on self-deprecation and endless kidding. But after the laughs were over and the last note played, Keely returned home to confront a deteriorating marriage. When she asked Louis how they could repair the problems in their marriage, he'd patronize her and tell her nothing was wrong, he was tired, his schedule was too demanding, he was, still and always, happy with her. But Keely knew better. She thought she understood her husband of eight years and professional associate of more than ten years. Increasingly, Keely turned inward. Was the state of the marriage her fault? Was she too young to understand her worldly husband? The agonizing process of self-appraisal went on for days at a time. Eventually Keely began to feel tired most of the time. She lost her resolve to perform with her husband and honor the constant rehearsals Louis insisted upon for her, Butera, and the Witnesses. She was sick more often now, catching viruses, staying home frequently.[10]

Ironically, as the Keely-Louis marriage faltered, still out of the eye of national view, the couple's version of "Old Black Magic" hit and dominated the pop charts, once again displaying their commercial popularity. With another song burning up the charts, Prima accepted more TV spots and club dates. In the winter of 1960-1961, as the Primas nearly doubled their recording output on the Dot label, Louis also honored an invitation by Frank Sinatra to perform in the Inaugural Gala for President-elect John F. Kennedy in late January 1961. Prima had on occasion lent out his services to the Democratic party, particularly for political fund-raisers. But Louis was also interested in the JFK program because of his close association with Sinatra who performed with Louis onstage in Las Vegas and frequently invited him to make guest appearances on both his radio and television programs in the late 1940s and throughout the 1950s. Sinatra even endorsed a Prima record, writing "This guy's phrasing is better than anyone's in the business." Louis returned the compliment by committing himself to the presidential program.[11]

[10]"On Stage" Dot Records; Keely Smith interview, May 1986.

[11]Record notes, "Wonderland By Night," (Louis Prima, Dot Records, 1960).

Prima, Smith, and Butera concluded their Desert Inn show—a program highlighting Louie's song hits of the 1940s—on January 16. Three days later they were in the nation's capital. Waiting for the Primas to arrive at Washington's Union Station, the *Washington Star* noted "special trains carrying inaugural parties are arriving around the clock." The city was aglow in excitement. Sinatra's biographer later recalled the extraordinary infusion of entertainment imported for the inaugural, noting that Sinatra "persuaded Ella Fitzgerald to fly in from Australia to sing for five minutes, Shirley MacLaine was coming from Japan, Gene Kelly from Switzerland, Sidney Poitier from France, and Keely Smith and Louis Prima from Las Vegas . . ." The show was slated to raise $1.5 million for the Democrats, with ten thousand people paying one hundred dollars apiece for seats and ten thousand dollars for boxes. But on the night of the gala a Washington blizzard caused hundreds of empty seats at the National Guard Armory. "What had been planned as a swank affair turned into something that resembled a rummage sale," said the *New York Herald-Tribune*. "Because of the terrific snowstorm, guests were urged to come to the gala dressed as they were. A few hardy souls showed up in evening clothes, including costly French originals. But even some of those made allowances for the weather—stalking about the hall in big snowboots." Louis and Keely were introduced to the political audience by comedian Joey Bishop, who cracked that Butera's Witnesses "promised not to take the Fifth." They launched into a spirited version of "Old Black Magic"—said to be one of Kennedy's favorite songs—and glowed as Lyndon Johnson pronounced the gala a "wonderful show with the greatest array of stars ever to be found."[12]

The press agreed: "The super-benefit of all time," said *Variety*, adding that the show was "adroitly framed," and devoid of the "very bad taste that can torpedo such events." The *New York Herald-Tribune* added "with an unparalleled collection of the entertainment world's biggest stars, how could it miss?" Before the affair concluded, Sinatra presented to Louis and Keely a silver cigarette box with the inaugural invitation inlaid on top. At the end of the program the Primas were invited to Paul Young's downtown restaurant where JFK's father, Joseph Kennedy, held a sparkling dinner for all of the participating stars. It was a heady evening of pomp and glamour. Specifically noting the efforts of Louis and Keely, as well as those of the notorious "Rat Pack" of Sinatra, Sammy Davis, Jr., Dean Martin, and Peter

[12]*Washington Star*, January 18, 20, 1961; Kelly, *His Way: The Unauthorized Biography of Frank Sinatra*, pp. 308-309; *New York Herald-Tribune*, January 20, 1961.

Lawford, actress Janet Leigh later wrote "we were all for one, and he [JFK] was one for all." Sinatra's recording company, Reprise Records, taped the entire proceedings from the gala performances, including Louis and Keely's portion of the program. The album was never released publicly, however, although copies of it were distributed privately to some of the gala performers.[13]

The glow of the Kennedy inaugural, however, quickly faded for Louis and Keely as they returned to their marital disputes and an extensive tour of clubs across the country. On March 1, columnist Lee Mortimer made one of the first national disclosures of possible trouble in the Louis-Keely marriage when he reported in the *New York Daily Mirror* that the duo was considering a Screen Gems TV series slated to go into production for the 1961-62 season, but that the show depended on "whether they're still together then," adding in a photo cutline: "The true hard facts: there's money in togetherne$$." Ten days later the *Las Vegas Sun*'s Ralph Pearl wrote "Attention Louis Prima and Keely Smith: There is no secret about the rift in the Prima home." Noting that columnists were beginning to write about what had been Las Vegas speculation for more than a year, Pearl mused "Yet nothing ever comes from either of you on this subject. Why not a statement about this so-called rift?"[14]

Slated to appear at the Fountainbleau Hotel in Miami Beach in mid-March, Keely prompted more press speculation when she cancelled out of the show, forcing Louis to go on alone. Prima tried to set things straight: "I was booked here as a single act, just me and the band. I'm filling in for my friend Dean Martin who was supposed to have opened on Tuesday but he couldn't make it and so I was asked to fill in." His reason for talking to the press, Louis stressed, was to "end these untrue rumors that we're splitting up . . . Keely wasn't supposed to appear. She's sick." When Prima said he called Keely on the West Coast to report the rumors of their possible separation, she told him she'd fly to Miami as a symbolic gesture. "Maybe then these rumors will stop," Prima said, concluding "We're in harmony."[15]

[13]*Variety*, January 25, 1961; *Herald-Tribune*, January 20, 1961; Kelly, *His Way: The Unauthorized Biography of Frank Sinatra*, pp. 309-310.

[14]*New York Daily Mirror*, March 1, 1961; *Las Vegas Sun*, March 11, 1961.

[15]*New York Post*, March 19, 1961.

If not personally, Prima undoubtedly hoped that professionally he could stay "in harmony" with Keely. Quite simply he was now in danger of becoming a victim of Keely's success. The Virginia songstress that Prima molded and formed to become a major national vocal talent was, by 1961, nearly eclipsing Louis in club and record drawing power. Keely's absence from Louis' act could be, at the very least, extremely expensive. Part of his lucrative contract with the Desert Inn called for Louis and Keely to appear *together;* if either of them failed to honor the spirit of the agreement Prima stood to lose the $3 million promised by the club. The uncertainty of the marriage and the ongoing financial considerations wore on Keely. "I told him I could not handle any of this," she said. "And I said I wanted a divorce. He wanted a divorce, too, but then he turned around and said he wanted to stay together. I was so hurt and my stomach was in knots and I just didn't want to be involved with it anymore." Nonetheless, as the couple seemed headed for a personal parting of the ways, Prima prevailed upon Keely to stay in the act. "No, I really can't," Keely answered. "It just wouldn't be the same." Enraged over Keely's spark of independence as he kissed good-bye the $3 million Desert Inn contract, Prima told his wife she'd fail without him, Butera, and the Witnesses to back her up. She'd be entertainment history, Prima predicted. Besides, he added, he'd get another girl singer and call her "Kelly Smith."[16]

Incredibly, even as Prima was contemplating his act without Keely, so were some critics. *Variety* caught the Prima-Smith show at the Latin Casino in Camden, New Jersey, in late May of 1961 and mused: "The real star of the duo, of course, is Miss Smith, although Prima's clowning grows on you. In the top rank of girl singers, she has a clarity of delivery and phrasing that few can approach. Her immense singing talent, plus her own keen comedy sense, makes one wonder how far she could go on her own," a sentiment that *High Fidelity* magazine echoed in a review of a single Keely album released by Dot.[17]

By the summer of 1961, stories of the couple's impending split became commonplace. "How much longer can Keely Smith and Louis Prima keep their marriage from exploding into headlines?" asked *Photoplay.* In August, as Ralph Pearl reported that the Prima's Las Vegas golf course home, valued

---

[16]Keely Smith interview, May 1986; "The Chief—Louis Prima," *WYES-TV*, Byer.

[17]*Variety*, May 24, 1961; *High Fidelity*, August 1960.

at more than $150,000, was secretly on the market, he added that the rift between Louis and Keely, which he labeled "muchly publicized," was also "still evident." The *Las Vegas Review-Journal* followed up on Pearl's claims several weeks later with a story announcing "Rumors persist that entertainers Louis Prima and Keely Smith will break up professionally." By mid-September, the *Las Vegas Sun* said the Prima-Smith split was now about to become a reality, that all of the rumors and speculation had been true all along, and that their fall engagement at the Desert Inn "may be their last, or possibly the next to last they'll play as a team—unless, of course, they have a sudden change of heart." Continued the *Sun:* "If the insiders are right, this will put an end to one of the hottest duos in show business history."[18]

These almost-daily reports of an impending breakup carried with them one ironic note: in the same trade and Las Vegas newspapers given to speculation on the likelihood of a Prima-Smith divorce were half-page ads for the couple's final show at the Desert Inn. To judge by their photos alone, Louis and Keely never seemed happier. Taken in the summer of 1961, the Desert Inn publicity shots showed a resplendent Keely demurely coiling her thin arms around Louis' neck. Prima, who hardly ever looked handsome, does here. Wearing the type of narrow tie fashionable in the early 1960s, Prima romantically gazes up at his wife. For once, he's wearing a toupee that is convincing. It's a strangely intimate moment, and, given the emotions behind the scenes at the time, it remains particularly poignant.

For her part, Keely thought of nothing else beyond the impending split from Louis. She shunted aside suggestions to start her own career after the divorce and grew increasingly despondent as the September Desert Inn stay drew to a close. Louis had changed, Keely later said, and in their final months together she claimed to hardly know him at all: "He was not the man I married," she charged. "He started drinking, he started to smoke cigars—which I hated—and he started to gamble, which he never did before." Keely, too, exhibited unusual behavior traits. One associate recalled seeing Keely belt down "two shots of scotch for nerve medicine," before she walked onstage at the Desert Inn. Smith, the friend, said, seemed "disoriented and confused, her attention span was very short." Soon rumors began to

---

[18]*Photoplay,* August 1961; *Las Vegas Sun,* August 19, 1961; September 13, 1961; *Las Vegas Review-Journal,* September 28, 1961.

circulate on Keely's whereabouts also. *Photoplay* reported seeing actor Bob Wagner "sitting oh-so-close to Keely Smith," in a Las Vegas night club and then later observed Keely "ringsiding Paul Anka's late show at the Sands in Las Vegas. She and Louis Prima were performing down the street at the Desert Inn . . ."[19]

By the end of September, the break finally came. Prima gathered a few belongings and moved out of the large golf course residence he shared with Keely and their two daughters which was still partially under construction. His exit was front page news in Las Vegas. Paying one month's rent in advance, Prima moved into a small one-room apartment off Las Vegas' famed Strip. The *Las Vegas Sun* noted on September 30, that both Louis and Keely were avoiding reporters and were "slipping in and out of the Desert Inn," adding that none of the couple's many friends and associates would publicly comment on the impending split "other than shaking their heads sadly."[20]

With their engagement at the Desert Inn concluding on October 1, hostilities became intense. Louis and Keely refused to share the dressing room they once both used. They made a point of not speaking to one another off stage. Finally, on October 3, less than 30 hours after they happily concluded their last show, Keely walked into the Eighth Judicial Circuit Court of Nevada in Las Vegas wearing a light dress and dark sunglasses. She filed officially for divorce, charging "extreme cruelty, completely mental in nature," as her reason for the split. Reporting on the seven-minute hearing which was closed to reporters, the *Los Angeles Times* said Keely charged that Louis "stayed out nights and did not care properly for her and their two children, Toni, 6, and Louanne, 4." As she emerged from the courtroom, Keely quietly told reporters "I actually never thought it would happen." When asked if she would ever perform again with Prima professionally, Keely said she wasn't sure, although she later admitted she had actually decided to never work with Louis again. The split garnered international attention. *Newsweek*, the *Washington Post*, the *New Orleans States-Item*, and the *Los Angeles Times* were but a few papers that gave their readers coverage of the divorce. The *New York Times* called the divorce "the break-up of one of the best known teams of nightclub and

[19]Keely Smith, interview, May 1984; confidential communication; *Photoplay*, October 1961.

[20]*Las Vegas Sun*, September 30, 1961.

recording performers . . ." In Las Vegas, the *Sun* blared out in an above-the-banner headline: KEELY SMITH SHEDS PRIMA. The paper added that the divorce "left the stage status of the top-notch entertainment team uncertain," while the *New York Post* reported "although neither was available for comment on their professional future, it was learned that Prima has signed for future appearances without Miss Smith."[21]

Unfortunately for Keely, the divorce action was just the beginning of a series of suits and countersuits between her and Prima in the coming months for child custody and alimony payments. The resultant bitterness from the divorce polarized family and friends alike. Stories circulated that Prima effectively abandoned his two daughters. Gossip columnists suggested that Keely won the lion's share of Prima's earnings, forcing him to do club work in order to pay for the settlement fees. Some wondered what would happen to Prima's estates in Nevada and Louisiana, and who would become, through the legalistic maze of claims and suits, the sole owner of such lucrative properties.

Considering his enormous income in the late 1950s and early '60s, Prima got out of his divorce settlement with Keely fairly easy. The court decreed that Louis pay Keely $1,250.00 per month, plus $144.23 per week for child support. The total bill cost Prima $28,846.08 annually. But Prima maintained the ownership of Pretty Acres and kept his production company started with Keely, Keelou Productions, also in his name. But many of the legal questions were never resolved. The percentage of Pretty Acres property in Louisiana owned by Keely became a bone of contention years after the 1961 divorce, as did the ongoing battle between Keely and Louis over the regularity of her former husband's payments for alimony and child support. Inevitably, Keely neared emotional and physical collapse. Four days after the divorce she entered the Cedar's of Lebanon hospital in Hollywood where she was treated for exhaustion, resting in a room filled with flowers from her fans. Barbara Belle, who met Smith when her plane arrived in Los Angeles, told reporters: "The poor thing, when she got off the plane she just seemed to break up and fall apart."[22]

---

[21]*Las Vegas Review Journal*, October 4, 1961; *Los Angeles Times*, October 4, 1961; *Las Vegas Sun*, October 4, 1961; *New York Post*, October 5, 1961; *New York Times*, October 4, 1961.

[22]Case no. 79025, 22nd Judicial District Court, St. Tammany Parish, Division A, Volume I; *New York Post*, October 8, 1961.

To some, it seemed like the end of innocence in Las Vegas. When the dust settled, an eerie void was left in the place of one of the greatest husband-and-wife acts in modern entertainment history. The laughter, music, and quick tempo of the show-bizzy rock n' roll beat continued unabated in Las Vegas after Louis and Keely split. But somehow their separation seemed to symbolize the passing of an era for the Nevada city. By the mid-1960s, Las Vegas gained a tough, efficient image. Skyscrapers dotted the skyline.   Big business, something called "corporate entertainment" and the multi-national hotels replaced the small-time, wild frontier feeling of the town that still was in the air when Louis and Keely opened at the Sahara in 1954. Even Prima, a man with an abundance of faith in progress and change, seemed saddened by the new Las Vegas: "Vegas was great in the first years," he said later. "But it got so big that you lost contact. You used to be able to call the boss and say 'I lost a microphone.' Now you'd have to get a requisition for a replacement." Louis and Keely did not, of course, cause the spiritual destruction of the nation's most glitzy city, but their parting represented the passing of a smaller, but more colorful period, to that of a somber, business-like time.[23]

For Keely, Louis remained very much the enigma, more confusing in the years after their divorce than he was when they met in Virginia Beach. Here was the man who, in 1958, surprised Keely with a new Corvette for their anniversary, talking a group of showgirls into pushing the car into a gambling casino lobby to make the unexpected present even more exciting. Two years later, Prima staged a surprise birthday party for his wife, presenting her with $25,000 worth of furs. Yet by 1963 and 1964 Prima fell behind in his alimony payments to Keely to the tune of $5,000 and was $576 in arrears in child support payments. "He was the kindest, sweetest, gentlest man I've ever known," said Keely years later. "But he could also be one of the biggest SOBs I've ever known. He didn't like to pay his bills. He always thought the world owed him something. He could be extremely bitter and even mean." Smith added: "I never knew which was the real Louis."[24]

How much pain and regret Louis experienced over the divorce from his fourth wife is unknown. He seemed carefree and upbeat when he talked with

---

[23]*Schenectady Gazette*, July 24, 1974.

[24]*New York Post*, July 27, 1958; *New York Daily News*, August 8, 1965; Keely Smith interview, May 1986.

reporters about his career without Keely, the partner who undoubtedly gave him his greatest acclaim in a career that already spanned more than thirty years. Arriving at the Moulin Rouge in Hollywood two weeks after the divorce, Prima said he was going to begin a search for a new female vocalist for future shows with Butera and the Witnesses. "We're going to carry on like before," Prima promised, offering that it was "improbable" that he and Keely would ever perform together again. "If we get the type of girl we want, there won't be any room for Keely," Prima cooly explained. But he ran into almost instant frustration without Keely. Reported *Photoplay:* "Sign of the times, Louis Prima didn't do so well without Keely Smith at the Moulin Rouge. The show closed far ahead of its run through the Christmas holidays . . ."[25]

Prima also had immediate business demands to attend to as a result of the split from Keely. Not only did he lose the lucrative Desert Inn contract, but Prima also witnessed a series of cancelled bookings from clubs and TV shows who specifically called for appearances with Keely. He gave up hopes for the Screen Gems TV series he and Keely talked of earlier in the year, as well as a farcical portrayal on an NBC TV special of Captain John Smith and his Indian love Pochohantas, played respectively by Louis and Keely. Prima also relinquished his cherished golf course home in Las Vegas and even lost his long-time business manager Barbara Belle. "It was my choosing," Belle said later. Deciding to join Keely in an effort to promote the singer on a solo career, Belle added "Louis tried in many ways to keep me with him, but no way. I thought that, as a man, he really did not do right. He didn't do right by his children, he didn't do right by Keely . . . and I really loved Keely. She was so naive and good as a human being."[26]

Prima replaced Belle with Joseph Segreto, a long-time family friend. "Come over here right now!" Prima commanded when Segreto called him from San Francisco several weeks after the divorce from Keely. "I want to see you *right now*," Prima beckoned. Segreto, who was about to move back to Louisiana after operating a hotel in San Francisco, flew to Prima's hotel suite in Lake Tahoe and was immediately subjected to the sort of hard sell and charm routine that only Louis could get away with. "I need you," Prima told Segreto. "I want you to work as my manager, I'll show you the

[25]*Las Vegas Review Journal,* October 22, 1961; *Photoplay,* January 1962.

[26]Barbara Belle interview, July 1986.

business; you're gonna book the act, and we're gonna start up a record company, and I've got two publishing firms that I want you to get involved with." Segreto remembered being dazzled by Prima's promises to introduce him to important people and the potential for establishing crucial business connections. The next day Segreto joined Prima as his general manager, taking over a business that had lost fifty percent of its productive capacity in one fell swoop and attempting to manage a performer more accustomed to setting his own course, particularly in a time of emotional distress. When he was alone with Prima, Segreto heard the musician's frustrations, how the press was making him out to be a bad guy, how the professionals were sizing up his diminished capacity to perform and succeed without Keely, how Keely, really, had become the star attraction of the Casbar and Desert Inn shows. These people just "didn't understand," said Prima. He did not *need* Keely. He did not need anyone, for that matter. He knew the entertainment business, he knew what people were thinking when they saw him perform. In fact, if the truth be told, he said, he could *feel* what they were thinking. He knew instinctively how a show was going over, what songs were selling. He could read an audience, figure out its mood, in a manner of minutes. And he knew how to sell himself. That's why the Las Vegas act was so extraordinarily successful. He knew how to sell himself, he knew how to sell Butera and the various Witnesses, and, most importantly, he knew how to sell Keely. That's why she could be replaced. Her absence was unimportant, Prima said. The only thing that mattered was that he was there. He was the true entertainer, the veteran trouper of the outfit. With his talent he could create a great show "all alone, if I have to."[27]

Prima's obsession with proving that there was life after Keely was evident during one of his first appearances in Lake Tahoe in November of 1961. The idea, Prima told Segreto, was to clearly display that the breakup with Keely would not in any way affect his musical and entertainment abilities. Life would go on. There would be other recording hits, more packed rooms in Las Vegas, increased television appearances and even a female vocalist replacement for Keely. To underline his new-found determination, Prima concocted yet another tagline, this one clearly reflecting his post-Keely status. "This Cat's Got Nine Lives," Prima's posters and letterheads announced within one month of the divorce.

[27]Joseph Segreto interview, October 1986.

The important thing was to be seen, to appear before the public in as many forums as possible. To this end, Louis appeared in a late 1961 film designed to capitalize on Chubby Checker's "Twist" craze called *Twist All Night*. By almost unanimous consent, the critics thought the film singularly lacking in any sort of entertainment merit. Described by one writer as a movie "utterly without worth, giving its characters the most perfunctory of motivations against the framework of a highly implausible plot line," *Twist All Night* featured Prima as a club owner down on his luck. Teenagers are hanging around his club, but not spending any money. Upon investigation, Prima learns the kids are being paid to loiter by an upstairs art gallery owner who goes by the name of, naturally, "Arturo." When Prima has the man later arrested for art theft, the kids thank him and stage a "big-in-the-street twist party and the club is once again successful." Among the forgetable songs Prima plays in the film are "Oh Mama, Twist," "Trombone Staccato," "Twistin' the Blues," and "When the Saints Go Twistin' In." Said the *New Orleans States-Item*: "It's disjointed, lacks plot, and about one-third of the dialogue consists of such phrases as 'We've got to swing out from squaresville.'"[28]

The winter of 1961-62 saw Prima at his most active, conducting a large number of interviews with the press, obligingly calling up columnists to disclose his next club date or concert appearance, and announcing that he would soon begin a nationwide talent search to select a permanent replacement for Keely. It was like old times again. Prima the press agent was back in full control.

But sometimes Prima's anger, an emotion he usually hid from the public view, rose to the surface. As the winter of 1962 gave way to spring, Louis continued to field countless questions concerning Keely, offering pat observations that his wife was a talented singer who should succeed on her own as a single. He gave little indication of his private thoughts and even appeared to be an amiably divorced man. But in May of 1962, Prima's well controlled resolve finally broke. Noticing an Earl Wilson column in the *New York Post* suggesting that he wanted Keely to rejoin the act for an opening night appearance later in the month at New York's Basin Street East night club, Prima fumed. He instantly sent out a sharp, turbulent wire to Wilson, one that he may have later had second thoughts about. "I have

---

[28]Nash and Ross, *The Motion Picture Guide Book, T to V, 1927 to 1983*, p. 3528; *New Orleans States-Item*, March 17, 1962.

no desire whatsoever to have any dealings with Keely Smith under any conditions," snapped Prima. "There is nothing in the world or no one that could ever make me accept this woman in our act." For fans and the press, Prima's wire was a shocker. In one hasty statement, Prima revealed an inner self long suppressed. Here indeed was an inflamed ego, bruised by public speculation that his act would not survive without Keely, chagrined that his popular wife refused to stay on with the Las Vegas act. This was a public glimpse of a private torment, a terse exhibition of Prima's venom. Now the public would know how he truly felt. Who needs her? Prima seemed to say. In case there was any doubt concerning the drift of his remarks, Prima added a final thought in his wire to Wilson: "Furthermore, we are doing much better without her."[29]

[29]*New York Post*, May 7, 1962.

A promotional concert booklet from a 1938 concert appearance.

An advertisement announcing Louis Prima's triumphant return to New Orleans in September 1935.

A publicity shot from *Start Cheering*, a 1938 musical starring Jimmy Durante, a long-time Prima friend.

Prima accompanies singer Alice Faye in the pleasant 1937 musical *You Can't Have Everything*. Long-time Prima sideman and friend Frank Federico is on the guitar.

Throughout his life, Prima was an energetic athlete who played football, baseball, and golf with the same enthusiasm he gave to performing.

The World War II years were good years for Prima and his big band, as evidenced by this promotional piece, which appeared in 1942.

Louis Prima, crazed, in the mid-1940s. (Used by permission of the Rutgers Institute
of Jazz Studies)

A 1944 flyer for yet another return visit to New Orleans by Prima.

Prima's 1940s slogan "Be Happy" covered for a man who was driven, frequently angry, often frustrated, and certain he could be doing better.

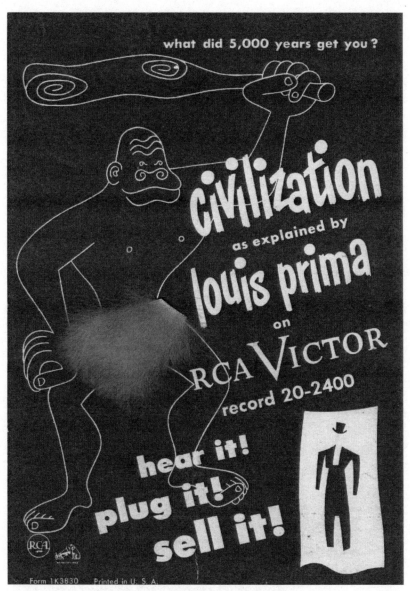

An RCA promo card advertising Prima's song hit "Civilization," his last big-band-single success. (RCA Record Label, a unit of BMG Entertainment. Used with permission.)

An advertisement for the legendary Casbar show in 1956.

Louis and Keely in June 1960. For a long time everything was perfect. (United Press International photo. Used by permission of Photofest, Inc.)

Prima, Butera, and the Witnesses blow the joint apart, while Keely contemplates the next break. (Photo by John Bryson. Used by permission of TimePix.)

Following another all-nighter, Louis and Keely calmly catch their breath at breakfast with their two daughters. (Used by permission of Photofest, Inc.)

Prima directs Smith in the 1958 film *Senior Prom,* a movie that also starred Lou Sino (seated, with trombone) and the ever-present Butera (with saxophone).

An advertisement for the 1959 Prima-Smith film *Hey Boy! Hey Girl!* (Copyright 1959 Variety Inc. Reprinted with permission.)

"I never actually thought it would happen," Keely remarks to reporters after filing for divorce from Prima in the fall of 1961. (Wide World Photos. Used by permission of Photofest, Inc.)

Sam Butera (left) watches as Prima warbles over the phone in the disastrous 1961 film *Twist All Night,* a movie designed to cash in on Chubby Checker's twist craze of the same year.

Two Italian-American icons in the fall of 1965 as Prima signed to appear at the Sands Hotel. Prima's fifth and last wife, Gia Maione, is in the center. (Courtesy of Sands Hotel Collection, Lied Library Special Collections, University of Nevada, Las Vegas)

A promo advertising a Prima personal appearance for *Twist All Night*.

Fellow trumpeter Gabriel sounds his horn above Louis Prima's tomb in the Metairie Cemetery just outside New Orleans. Carved into the marble below are the words, "When the end comes I know, they'll say, 'Just a Gigolo' as life goes on without me."

CHAPTER VIII

King Louie

The 1960s closed in on Louis Prima. Like so many other stars and entertainers who once dominated their industry, Prima in the 1960s discovered revolutionary changes in musical tastes and consumer demands. Entertainment preferences were leaving him out of the national spotlight, discarded by critics, record producers, and, finally, the fans who could always in years past be counted on to shell out for an occasional album or club appearance. Prima's problems during one of the nation's most culturally and politically explosive decades were not confined to professional concerns. During the same year of his painful divorce from Keely, Prima's father Anthony died at the age of seventy-four. Four years later, Angelina, too, passed away, leaving a void in Louis' life that would never be filled. Angelina's death in the winter of 1965 was so devastating for Louis that daughter Joyce remembered Prima's refusal to go near his mother's casket. "He wouldn't look at it, and stayed far away from it," said Joyce. "He just refused to look at her in a casket."[1]

Family emotions, so long suppressed by the dominating Angelina, reached the boiling point after her passing. Deeply grieved, Prima was haunted by the image of his mother spending her final days alone—although she remained a central figure in a close-knit matriarchal family until the end. He told one relative that "everyone deserted Angelina" and mused to another cousin that his mother died because of the stress resulting from the split with Keely. "Keely killed her," Louis said. "It was all too much for Mama." Later, Prima publicly extolled his mother's virtues, telling one interviewer that Angelina was a "warm person . . . Everybody loved my Mama, Angelina . . . If you ever saw her you would ask, 'Where did you get this woman?' " Louis also paid tribute to her by naming an album after her, writing that Angelina was "one of the greatest mothers a man ever had," and claiming that she was "solely responsible for all of the great Italian novelties" that he recorded, out of love for her, beginning in the early 1940s.[2]

---

[1] Joyce Prima interview, December 1985.

[2] *Ibid.*; *Philadelphia Inquirer*, June 20, 1974; Record notes by Louis Prima from "Angelina," (Prima One Records, Las Vegas, ca. 1973).

Whether or not, in the years after Angelina's death, Louis actually believed Keely was the cause of his mother's death, it could be argued that his former wife's absence did contribute to the slow death of his career in its final years. Throughout the 1960s, music writers and critics took pains to point out that Keely was no longer with Louis, particularly when reviewing a Prima club appearance. Their divorce became as much a part of his resume in the view of some writers as did his triumph at the Famous Door in the 1930s and his Italian novelty songs in the '40s. For Prima, there was simply no getting away from her memory, he was reminded of her almost everywhere he went. For millions of fans, Louis and Keely would forever be intertwined, living on as a couple through the yearly sales of their Capitol and Dot records produced between 1956 and 1961. Audiences never quite seemed to adjust to Keely no longer being part of the act. They asked questions about her when Louis made an appearance somewhere, sometimes someone would even shout out insults from the audience: "Hey, Louie! What happened to Keely?" or "I liked ya better when Keely was around!" Such comments underlined a painful reality: For Prima, Keely was every bit as much a factor in his career after the divorce as she was before, only this time her absence seemed to leave Louis wanting.[3]

After the divorce, Louis, when he was away from his Las Vegas power based, seemed like one of the walking dead. His "dirty old man" routine seemed more pathetic than beguiling, his romantic conquests more sad than interesting. In a few short years, *Variety* would attend a Prima concert and wonder: "Maybe he is losing some of his old touch. His physical humor seems to have an excess of grinds." The respected *New York Times* critic John Wilson noted of a Louis concert: "He is now a dour, rotund man who spends most of the evening standing around while Mr. Butera and his musicians hold the spotlight."[4]

Even Prima's continued presence in Las Vegas was suspect. Where once Vegas was portrayed as the home of the hip, to many 1960s kids the gambling mecca was viewed instead as a graveyard of misplaced values, unrealized dreams, and middle-aged juveniles. "A week in Vegas is like stumbling into a Time Warp, a regression into the late fifties," wrote the

[3]Gia Maione interview, July 1986.

[4]*Variety*, June 14, 1972; *New York Times*, June 14, 1972.

irreverent Hunter Thompson for *Rolling Stone*, who claimed that the type of people who visited Vegas were the same people "who go absolutely crazy at the sight of an old hooker stripping down to her pasties and prancing out on the runway to the big-beat sound of a dozen 50-year-old junkies kicking out the jams on 'September Song.' " Writer Joan Didion thought Las Vegas to be "the most extreme and allegorical of American settlements, bizarre and beautiful in its venality and in its devotion to immediate gratification, a place the tone of which is set by mobsters and call girls and ladies' room attendants with amyl nitrate poppers in their uniform pockets . . ."[5]

To be sure, Prima was not the only musician or entertainer of his age to be swept up in events far beyond his control. Throughout the 1960s, some of the largest recording stars and night club performers of the decade before suddenly found themselves with cancelled recording contracts, increasingly limited television appearances and a much smaller number of nightclubs from which to choose. It was not so much that the nation rejected a generation of musical values or entertainment norms so much as they embraced a new generation's artistic expressions. The beginning of the end for many of Prima's contemporaries was first signalled in the fall of 1963 when a rock n' roll song called "She Loves You" hit the pop charts like cannon fire. The song's authors, an unlikely sounding musical group named The Beatles, hailed from Great Britain, and within several months invaded the U. S. through an initial domestic appearance on the Ed Sullivan Show and then with countless song hits that dominated the charts of the nation for the duration of the decade. It was the beginning of a new epoch in music, a sound and beat as different from that of Prima's generation as was his from the John Philip Sousa strains of the age before. The sounds of the 1960s, however, went beyond music. This new sound was also the incessant clang of cash registers taking in millions of dollars annually from groups who quickly rode the Beatles wave: The Rolling Stones, the Mamas and the Papas, the Lovin' Spoonful, and the Byrds, among others.

Reacting enthusiastically to this new spirit of consumer hysteria, record companies large and small gradually discarded the vocalists and instrumentalists of the Prima era for the Top 40 kings and queens of this new uncertain decade. Performers such as Bing Crosby, Rosemary Clooney, and even Louis Armstrong—all sure-fire money-makers throughout the

---

[5]Hunter S. Thompson, *Fear and Loathing in Las Vegas* (New York, 1981), p. 156; *Saturday Evening Post,* December 16, 1967.

1950s and before—suddenly were no longer able to make a dent in the charts, let alone find a recording company to take them on. Nat King Cole, who, with Prima, sold millions of records for Capitol in the mid- and late 1950s, was one of the first to encounter the potency of this new marketing force. Sitting in his dressing room one day in early 1964 after the Beatles made their first frantic U.S. appearance, Cole called Capitol Records, heard a voice on the other end, and angrily slammed down the receiver. Singer Tony Bennett, who himself would soon be released from his long-standing contract with Columbia records, asked Cole what was bothering him. "The girl picked up and said 'Capitol Records, Home of the Beatles,' " said Cole. "Home of the Beatles. Home of the *Beatles*. What's goin' on, man? What's goin' on?" Even Prima's idol, Louis Armstrong, found it difficult to get recorded. When he made what later became a hit song called "Hello Dolly" in the spring of 1964, most of the big-name record companies refused to distribute the ditty, arguing that the song would disappear in Beatlesland. Finally Broadway producer David Merrick found a small label, Knapp Records, willing to take on the Armstrong recording, but only for a $3,000 fee.[6]

The tide turned, dramatically and ruthlessly. Left behind were a stable of singers and musicians who had by and large reigned supreme over the airwaves since the 1930s and '40s. Prima was only one of many who found refuge from the market upheaval in Las Vegas where he continued to draw big crowds and rave notices throughout the decade. On the occasions when Prima left his Vegas base, he ended up in places that seemed to reflect the status of his deflated fortunes, appearing in the fall of 1962 at a club in San Diego called The Roaring 20s which boasted the world's largest bowling alley or the Chi Chi in Palm Springs where Louis was taken to task by a *Variety* reviewer for sounding like "more noise than music."[7]

As resourceful as ever, Prima fought the good battle in the 1960s by starting his own recording company, Prima One Records, in 1962, and actively searching for a Keely Smith replacement, one who would, he hoped, help him reproduce the magic of his early Sahara Hotel days with Keely. By the spring of 1962, Prima announced he was actively auditioning female vocalists. The applicants sent Prima tapes and resumes

[6]*New York Times*, March 9, 1981.

[7]*Variety*, November 25, 1964.

by the hundreds from across the country. He was besieged by young women in Las Vegas and in a variety of cities where he appeared with Butera and the Witnesses in March, April, and May. All of the young women hoped to become the next Keely Smith, many of them took pains to duplicate his former wife's singing style and inflections. For his part, Prima naturally used the selection process itself as a means of publicity, telling one Iowa newspaper in late April he had pruned "289 aspirants for Keely's old swingin' spot down to four," but that he was "still not sure who the winner would be." The *San Francisco Examiner* reported: "Louie Prima's turning down all TV offers til' he finds a thrush to replace Keely. Auditioned 300 dolls last week, but has yet to find one to his liking."[8]

Following the newspaper coverage from Toms River, New Jersey, was twenty-year-old Gia Maione, a waitress at the local Howard Johnson's who studied voice and piano in high school. Gia collected all of Louis and Keely's recordings, learned the female parts through repeated playings, and began to dream that she, too, might audition for the role of Prima's new singing partner. When Prima appeared at the Latin Casino in Camden, New Jersey, in May 1962, Maione told her mother she was going to try to wrangle an interview with the famous musician. "I have to have a chance at it," Gia said. Her opportunity materialized through a family connection with Rolly Dee, the drummer for the Witnesses. Gia arrived at the club on a Friday afternoon, found a courteous Prima who listened to her singing without making a commitment and then asked her to return the following Sunday, Mother's Day, for an afternoon concert at the Camden B'Nai B'Rith. "I was very young and I was very naive, but I went to the luncheon anyway," said Gia. "I don't know what I was thinking. I had on a full dress with crinoline and no makeup, and, at that time, the Poodle haircut, which was very popular. I guess I was just a child."[9]

Prima, who was performing a benefit concert for the B'Nai B'Rith women, broke into his regular show to announce that he was going to select his new girl singer then and there, adding: "But the decision will be up to you. Whoever you ladies like the most, I'll go along with." After several hopefuls, Gia included, sang a few ditties, Louis walked behind them and held his hand over their heads. "Who do you like?" Prima asked, and the

[8]Gia Maione interview, July 1986; *San Francisco Examiner*, undated clipping, ca. early 1962.

[9]Gia Maione interview, July 1986.

women signalled their approval of Gia.   In retrospect, it is hard to believe
that Prima would let a gathering of the women of B'Nai B'Rith decide the
selection of such an important slot in his band.   More likely, Louis was,
on that Mother's Day, looking for the public confirmation of a decision he
made two days earlier when Gia performed for him privately. Whatever the
case, Prima wasted no time introducing his new vocalist to the press.
Checking into the prestigious Basin St. East the following week, Louis
presented Gia to an audience composed of such luminaries as Walter
Winchell, Jackie Gleason, Peggy Lee, and Ella Fitzgerald. Giving readers a
backstage glance at Gia's opening night, the *New York Post* later noted:

> She was nervous . . . showed up without a proper gown or shoes;
> she carried a bag of hair curlers and expected to set her hair herself
> before the show. Phoebe Ostrow of Basin Street shepherded Gia to
> a hairdresser, hastily bought her gowns and shoes and girdles and
> stockings (with Prima's bankroll). And on opening night the
> nervous girl, fresh from a hostessing job in a Howard Johnson's
> restaurant, was a hit.[10]

"I really do think she's better than anyone else I've ever had," said
Prima, in a pointed reference to Keely. "We didn't have much time to
rehearse, but she's done just perfectly anyway." Prima's public enthusiasm
for Gia may have gone beyond his new female singer's vocal capabilities.
Less than seven months after the angry separation from Keely, Prima
wanted to make a statement concerning his likely survival beyond the
divorce. Telling reporters he had found a new girl whom he could form,
cultivate, and gradually mold into a new Keely Smith, Prima was sending
signals to his old wife that she was, indeed, expendable, while
simultaneously beating the promotion drum like the old-time press agent he
really was.[11]
Close friends of Prima may have found the dynamics surrounding the
selection of Gia eerie. In many ways Prima's anointment of his new singer
recalled 1948 when he discovered Keely. Both women were young,
attractive, professionally inexperienced, and highly impressionable. Like

[10]*Ibid.*; *New York Post*, October 17, 1962.

[11]*New York Post*, May 15, 1962.

Keely, Gia was a fan of Louis' from a distance, having watched Louis and Keely perform at the Eden Rock Hotel in Miami Beach during the late 1950s. As with Keely, Gia soon began to collect Prima records after she saw him in person. "I fell in love with his music," said Gia.

> Just watching him, it seemed like everyone in the group was so in love with what they were doing. It seemed like the happiest music I ever heard. And, of course, his personality was unbelievable . . . From that point on everything I collected, everything I sang, everything I loved was Louie Prima.

Perhaps the most significant parallel between Keely and Gia was their willingness to defer all professional and personal matters to Prima. Gia thought Louis was "like the principal in high school," and the description was a telling one. Within a matter of months Prima began the exhaustive process of making Gia over in a manner more commercially appealing. The Poodle haircut disappeared, as did the dress with crinoline. She was taught to engage in stage banter with Louis, Butera, and the Witnesses. She wore gowns instead of dresses. By October, less than five months after she joined the band, the *New York Post* noted "auburn-haired Gia is now a brunette. She is sleekly gowned and coiffured."[12]

It was an abrupt education in entertainment for the former hostess from Howard Johnson's, but the dramatic changes for Gia were simply routine for Louis. Once again a teacher-student theme emerges in Louis' life. "He just seemed to be so smart," said Gia. "He seemed to know the business he was in. What amazed me, as far as a performance on stage goes, is that Louie knew exactly what every performer's best point was, how to sell it to the audience. He would pull out the best of each of us in a performance."[13]

It must have been enchanting. Prima gave Gia the sort of opportunity sometimes not available to most singers after years in the business. He introduced her to the powerful Broadway columnists, men like Winchell and Louis Sobol. When Prima appeared on the Ed Sullivan show, he took Gia with him. She was given top billing during his club appearances in Las Vegas, Lake Tahoe, and elsewhere. But Prima spent his greatest energies

[12]Gia Maione interview, July 1986; *New York Post*, October 17, 1962.

[13]Gia Maione interview, July 1986.

attempting to establish Gia as a recording star. By the fall of 1962, Prima's time was divided between club appearances in Las Vegas, an additional stay at Harrah's in Lake Tahoe, and the promotion of *Twist All Night*. He returned to New Orleans for a well-publicized concert appearance at the Saenger Theatre—the same hall where he played in the Lou Forbes orchestra three decades earlier. It was a sensational appearance. The Saenger was packed. Prima opened to a mighty cheer of support, then plunged into an opening medley of songs that included more than a dozen songs with which the public had identified him with for more than thirty years. After almost half-an-hour of non-stop old-time hits, Prima turned and remarked "That, folks, was our introduction," and his hometown audience roared back its approval, giving him one of several standing ovations for the evening. But beyond such sentimental trips down memory lane, Prima's market was shrinking as a result of his split from Keely and he rightly looked at recordings as a means of recapturing his lost status. He would highlight Gia as his newly discovered "singing sensation." She would be a bigger star than Keely, Prima decided. As her inaugural presentation to the public, Prima produced her first album, called "This Is . . . Gia," featuring a large pen-and-ink drawing of his discovery on the cover. Not only would Gia become a major performer, Prima hoped, but she would do so on his label, Prima One. However, given the distributional abilities of his company, establishing Gia in the nation's affections would prove difficult. Prima rented out recording studios for his Prima One cuts, sending the tapes to Hollywood to be turned into wax at Magnagroove Records. Funded entirely by Prima, the operation was only able to produce small amounts of records, sometimes as little as 20,000. This compared unfavorably with his Capitol and Dot pressings which had a minimum of 200,000 to 300,000 for each release.[14]

Sparing no expenses with the "This Is . . . Gia" album, Prima hired an orchestra of forty-eight studio musicians and took up to six months planning, arranging, and recording the album. He supervised the album's design, which featured a fold-out collage of photos showing Louis and Gia performing. Walter Winchell, George Burns, and Judy Garland wrote out endorsements of Gia's musical potential. In addition, a lengthy biography of Gia adorned the album's back cover, telling readers about the singer's childhood in New Jersey, how she played in "South Pacific" in high school,

---

[14]New Orleans *States-Item*, March 17, 1962; Bob Pepitone interview, July 1986.

won the Arian National Society Award for musical ability, and placed runner-up in the Miss Ocean County Beauty Contest. Finally, the copy read, Gia had become an "over-night sensation . . . At twenty-three years of age, Gia Maione has become the most talked-about newcomer of the last ten years." She sang standard club fare, "Tender Is the Night," "My Funny Valentine," and "How High the Moon," among other songs. But "This Is . . . Gia," as with future Prima One albums, failed to generate much critical or popular success. Gia said it was because she never had a chance in a market that was soon dominated by The Beatles and other rock groups, but some critics believed Gia's voice was the problem: "Miss Maione hasn't got much of a voice," said *Variety* later. "She starts rather cold . . ."[15]

The failure of the "This Is . . . Gia" album, as with other Prima One ventures, rankled Louis. Joseph Segreto remembered Prima's failure to make a dent in the pop charts of the 1960s as a matter of great frustration: "He hadn't had a hit since Keely left," said Segreto. "And we were desperately trying to get a new record, instead of doing old records or reprints of old records." Segreto believed that the limited distribution of Prima's records was a minimal problem. "We used to get played on the radio, but we couldn't get on the kind of stations we needed," he said. "The Top Forty people wouldn't play Louis because he had not placed in the Top Forty for several years. They didn't want to give him a chance." Said drummer Jimmy Vincent, who rejoined Prima in the mid-1960s: "He just didn't do as good without Keely."[16]

Although Prima was obsessed with the failures of his Prima One albums and was constantly searching for new record ideas, Gia may have been less concerned with professional opportunities and more interested in her increasingly close relationship with Louis. As they traveled about the country together, Gia was impressed with Prima's solicitous manner, his father-like way of protecting her in strange cities and environments. He was, she thought, a man of the world, comfortable with major entertainment names, a secure and confident businessman who made solid, definite decisions. A powerful, accomplished man with a whimsical sense of humor. "I don't remember exactly when I fell in love with him," said Gia.

[15]*Variety*, November 25, 1964.

[16]Joseph Segreto intreview, October 1986; Jimmy Vincent interview, April 1987.

"I really don't know where our friendship ended and love began. There wasn't any one moment." The relationship became official in February of 1963 when Gia and Louis were appearing at the Harrah's Club in Lake Tahoe. Between the mid- and late evening programs, Prima asked Gia to marry him and she responded affirmatively. "Let's go down the hill, then," Louis said. "I have something I want to tell you." Stepping into a limousine provided by Harrah's, Louis and Gia were driven to a justice of the peace in the town of Minden, Nevada, some 20 miles from the south shore of Lake Tahoe. The *Las Vegas Review-Journal* called the Minden wedding "the biggest event in the town's history," and went on to note that not only were the Minden townsfolk unaware of the celebrity nuptials but so were members of Prima's band. When husband and wife returned for their second show at Harrah's, Prima grabbed the microphone and announced to the stunned gambling audience "And now, ladies and gentlemen, here's Mrs. Prima."[17]

The marriage to Gia gave Louis the kind of stability he had longed for since his early days with Keely. Gia gradually abandoned her show business ambitions to mother two children to Louis: Lena Ann and Louis, Jr., who was born, fittingly enough, on Father's Day in 1965. "I had reached the epitome," Gia said. "Getting my job with Louis was the greatest. I really didn't want for anything else. Being next to him and performing was enough, let alone marrying him and giving him his first son. To me, the real importance in my life became being a good wife to Louie, giving him a wonderful family, cooking for him."[18]

As Louis and Gia settled in Las Vegas, Prima continued to cope with the predominant influence of rock music in the recording industry. He told reporters that he found many things about the new music that he admired. He even incorporated some of the more successful rock hits into his own act, playing distinctly Prima versions of such songs as "Spinning Wheel," "Mrs. Robinson," and the Beatles' "Ob-La-Di, Ob-La-Da." But Louie also took on the role of a critical veteran of live entertainment, telling the rock musicians how to excite their audiences, project their talents, and sell their strengths. In an era of cool but practiced indifference, Prima's showy exuberance may have seemed like an embarrassing echo from a long-

[17]Gia Maione interview, July 1986; *Las Vegas Review-Journal*, February 16, 1963.

[18]Gia Maione interview, July 1986.

forgotten time. But Louis' words of wisdom carried with them the experience of more than three decades in the trade. "They're gonna discover they can do with instruments what they're doing now with amplifiers," Prima said of the rock guitarists. "A lot of the kids saw the Beatles and thought all they needed was a guitar and some long hair and they could have a hit group," he explained. "Now they are finding they were wrong, and many of them are out of work." Prima used a young guitarist he hired in the late 1960s as an example: "When he does his specialty, he is sensational," said Louis. "But he can't keep up with the group because he doesn't know his changes. He's now in his fifth month of studying so that he can get into our band. And all because he didn't study his guitar in the first place."[19]

Because of the uninhibited nature of every Prima show, Louie's words of wisdom should have been particularly relevant to rock musicians. A Prima night club act or concert, like a rock concert, knew no boundaries, and had no set program, and put a high premium on instant audience reaction and participation. When Prima appeared in New Orleans for a club show, one reporter commented on his rock-like showmanship: "This was the acid rock back when," the reporter said, adding that many of the songs Prima and Butera played were "really horrible listening," but explaining, "The tunes *sound* the same as on stage, but without the sight of the organ player doing somersaults around his keyboard, without Sam Butera gyrating about, and without Louis fanning his crotch, the whole point of the form is lost."[20]

Even in his language, Prima embodied the spirit of the rock star through his use of nonsensical phrases and words understood only by Louis and a few friends. "That was real scong," Louis would say if he encountered something or someone he held a low opinion of. " 'Scong' is real new," Louis tried to explain. "Cats sometimes use 'scong' for a put-on. Like say a Wanda waitress—a Wanda's a lady who never smiles—she says to you, 'Mr. Prima, how's your steak?' And the steak's strictly nowhere. You say, 'Oh, the steak was really scong.' But the cats at your table, they know you didn't dig that steak at all." As Louis in the 1960s made the regular round of TV talk shows, via the Johnny Carson-Merv Griffin-Joey Bishop circuit,

---

[19]New Orleans *Times-Picayune*, March 11, 1974.

[20]*Figaro*, March 17, 1973.

his language would frequently confuse both host and audience alike: "That was fracturesville," Prima said on one TV program. "Until I came out here, my wheels were tired." Louis called the police "the nab," a pushy theatrical agent might be a "Bobby Business," and someone he liked was simply a "good stud." Explained Prima: "A good man is a 'stud." Like we say, 'Johnny Carson's a good stud.' "[21]

Prima also embodied the colorful ways of the decade with his flowery and unusual taste in clothing. Long before male entertainers broke away from the conventional dark business suit required for stage appearances, Prima was wearing lavender coats or yellow suits or even red, white, and blue-striped pants. Comedian Joey Bishop once told a television audience that he drove by a nightclub and "heard Louie's suit." Loud patterns, flashy colors, and the unconventional were the predominant themes in Louie's clothing. In his uninhibited and humorous style, Prima may well have been the nation's first and oldest hipster.[22]

It was the emphasis on odd language, the frenetic activity of his stage performances, and the garish taste in clothing that caught the attentions of a group of writers and producers in 1966 who were about to produce an animated version of Rudyard Kipling's classic "Mowgli Stories" for Walt Disney studio titled *The Jungle Book*. Prima was cast through his voice as the highly excitable and slightly shady "King Louie," the leader of the jungle apes who had a penchant for good jazz rhythms. Prima liked the Disney concept and was further intrigued when he learned that the Disney creators planned to develop the "King Louie" cartoon character by incorporating certain aspects of Prima's real-life personality. In 1966, the Disney studio sent for Prima, Butera and the Witnesses in an effort to study their onstage mannerisms. "The bunch of us flew in from Lake Tahoe to play for the animators so they could study the way we perform and get a feeling of us in action," Prima said. "We spent the entire afternoon in an empty sound stage laying down number after number. They kept asking us to play and wouldn't let us stop." Veteran actor George Sanders and jazz singer and comedian Phil Harris also signed up for the project.[23]

---

[21]*San Diego Union*, February 20, 1964; Gia Maione interview, July 1986.

[22]Gia Maione interview, July 1986.

[23]Leonard Maltin, *Of Mice and Magic: A History of American Animated Cartoons* (New York, 1980), p. 76; Walt Disney Archives, Burbank, California, publicity release for *The Jungle Book*, 1967.

Although the film was over a year in production, by the time *The Jungle Book* hit the screen in November 1967, viewers across the nation were treated to a rollicking, excitable "King Louie" who downed bananas by the dozen, danced and pranced with hip abandon, and sang "I'm the King of the Swingers, the Jungle V-I-P." Prima loved the "King Louie" character: "This cat really rocks the jungle," Prima said. "In fact, the whole monkey tribe in the picture really swings. And they look a lot like me and Sam Butera and the Witnesses . . ." In the unusual setting of a Disney film, old warhorses Prima and Harris presented to an entirely new generation the art of scat singing, the language of the hip cat, and the frenzy of falling under the spell of a restless jungle beat. The success of *The Jungle Book* led Prima to extoll publicly the virtues of Disney movies as an artistic form. "His movies were the best things that ever happened to kids as entertainment," Prima said. And the critics, at least as far as *The Jungle Book* went, agreed. Noted *Newsweek*: "Prima talks a great game as king of the apes." The *New York Times* thought Louie was "marvelous" as "a potentate ape (with one very amusing song)," and *Senior Scholastic* magazine added "The songs are excellent, and the vocal casting has been beautifully matched to the characters."[24]

Both Prima and Harris cut two albums as a result of their success with *The Jungle Book* movie. One was titled, appropriately, "The Jungle Book" on Disneyland Records, released during the premiere showing of the film. The sales were so strong that by 1969 Disneyland Records released a second album called "More Jungle Book" and the combined receipts from both LPs led to a gold record for Prima.

Although a variety of factors could be credited for the successful records—obviously the enormous publicity machinery of the Disney studios was not to be understated—the strong sales power exhibited by Prima and Harris gave credence to the idea that pre-Beatles stars could still place strongly in the charts, if only given a chance.

Louis did his level best to transform his popularity with *The Jungle Book* into other ventures, including his own Prima One records, but found the going rough. Tapping into the growing TV market for mail order records, Prima filmed a television commercial in the early 1970s wherein he was seen perched on a ledge overlooking Tuscan bell towers delivering what

---

[24]Walt Disney Archives, Burbank California, publicity release for *The Jungle Book*, 1967; New Orleans *Times-Picayune*, March 11, 1974; *Newsweek*, December 11, 1967; *New York Times*, December 23, 1967; *Senior Scholastic*, November 9, 1967.

Time magazine called "a husky-voiced hustle for a two-LP anthology of pop songs called 'Love Italian Style.' " Once again, though, Louis found the recording business unreceptive to his particular brand of entertainment. Long used to the dips and flows of the music business, Prima by the early 1970s had experienced his longest hiatus from the top charts of his entire career. With the exception of his musical album from *The Jungle Book*, Prima's songs had been off the best-selling lists for more than a decade, since the split with Keely.[25]

When Prima ran into his boyhood idol Louis Armstrong and suggested that they cut an album of jazz duets, Satchmo readily agreed. But the proposed venture never materialized. Armstrong's managers, ever protective of their star's commercial exposure, said such a platter would have limited popular appeal.. Prima reacted characteristically: "They're nothing! All they're interested in is percentages and profits." During this same period, Prima became increasingly interested in recording his place in history, with the accurate reading of his influences upon Swing Street in New York in the 1930s, the Big Bands of the 1940s, and the Las Vegas lounges of the 1950s. It was a noted about-face for a man with little expressed sentimentality for the "old days." Asked in 1964 if he ever missed the excitement and romanticism of 52nd Street, Prima was abrupt: "No. That was then and it was fine. But now is now and we always try to keep comin' up with somethin' new . . ." Several years later a reporter for the *Philadelphia Inquirer* noted "Louis has had many big hits through the years, but it's always the one coming up that's going to be the biggest When you talk about million-selling albums like 'Angelina' and 'Black Magic,' he doesn't want to dwell on them. It's the NEXT one that counts." Nonetheless, despite Prima's reluctance to talk about his very colorful past, he decided that he needed to preserve and honor his musical legacy, and that it could best be accomplished through a biography. Rejecting the attempts of several authors to put his story on paper, Prima decided to present his story on film. When writer Arnold Shaw interviewed Prima for his book on 52nd Street, *The Street That Never Slept*, he found a reluctant Louis hesitant to give any details of his past to an author. "He didn't want to talk very much," said Shaw. "Ant the reason was that he was working at that time, trying to get a film biography. When I'd ask him about something specifically, he'd answer 'Well, I don't want to tell you that story, I'm

[25]*Time*, November 19, 1973.

saving it for my film.' He just felt that if too much was written about him, it would hurt the chances of getting his story on screen. I tried to tell him that he was mistaken, but I couldn't convince him."[26]

Although Prima set out to collect the memorabilia and press clippings that would make up the glut of his film biography, he eventually abandoned the project when he was unable to secure financial backing for the movie. Besides his failed film project, Prima, by the early 1970s, was contending with a recording output that was largely a rehash of his former hit songs from the 1940s and '50s. In addition, his nightly Las Vegas and Lake Tahoe shows were becoming routine. To break the monotony, Prima diversified his interests, spending days on end planning, designing, and landscaping a giant golf course in Las Vegas that he whimsically dubbed "Fairway to the Stars." Gia said the golf course venture was both a means of relaxation for Louie and a possible vehicle for year-round revenue. "He wanted to make a first class golf course in the city," said Gia. "And he hoped it could generate profits and give him enough money so that he wouldn't feel guilty about not performing all of the time." Although "Fairway to the Stars" was not particularly popular among golfing enthusiasts in Las Vegas—one columnist said it was usually referred to as "Mickey Mouse, Shrapnel Alley, and just plain too easy"—the course did offer one feature of which no other green in the city could boast: the sight of Prima raking the traps, watering the greens, and sometimes wildly thwacking away at the tee in his loudly colorful sports wear.[27]

In late 1972, Prima began to entertain thoughts of returning to New Orleans, making it his home base, setting up a nightclub in the city, and living permanently on his sprawling Pretty Acres estate in Covington, across Lake Pontchartrain from the Crescent City. Appearing in a series of week-long engagements throughout the city in 1973 and 1974, Prima was initially encouraged by the enthusiastic reception he received. Boyhood friends who had followed Louie's career with adoring support since his days with the Lou Forbes Orchestra at the Saenger Theatre turned out en masse to see the native son made good. "I have a lot of friends here," said Prima after a nine-day stay at the Blue Room in the Fairmont Hotel. "Of course, I have

---

[26]*New Orleans Magazine*, March 1974; *San Diego Union*, February 20, 1964; *Philadelphia Inquirer*, March 23, 1967; Arnold Shaw interview, December 1986.

[27]Gia Maione interview, July 1986; Uncited newspaper clipping by columnist Alan Baer, "Rub o' the Green."

good friends in other cities—Las Vegas, New York, Philadelphia—but that isn't like being around the boys I grew up with."[28]

Surrounded by dozens of fans who had followed his career through the years with pride, Prima emotionally sang "Louie ain't gonna go away no more," and the crowd cheered and stamped their feet. The mayor of the city, Maurice "Moon" Landrieu, made it to the opening show to declare "Louis Prima Week in New Orleans."

Some observers couldn't help but note that somehow the always-happy Prima seemed a little somber and forlorn during his return visit to New Orleans: "The put-on, happy frivolity of the on-stage Louis Prima is surprisingly absent at other times," wrote a reporter for the *Times-Picayune*, who visited Prima in March 1974 at the Fairmont. "He laughs at jokes and smiles easily, but he is, at bottom, a serious man. He ambled into the bar without fanfare or the trappings of stardom, even eschewing the usual entourage for a single aide and good friend at his side." The reporter, Newton Renfro, added: "When he speaks, he looks into one's eyes with a compelling intentness that demands attention. He listens closely to what others say, and his responses are straight-forward and delivered in a low, relaxed voice lined at the edges by that gravelly rasp that is his trademark."[29]

City fathers took Prima on a tour of restaurants and pubs where old musical pals, fans, and relatives encouraged his return to New Orleans. "Every club he went to, people were there to tell him how much they love him," said radio disc jockey Keith Rush, who strongly urged Prima to set up permanently in New Orleans. "And Louis was so emotional about it. He'd cry at the drop of a hat. I think it really meant something to him that, after all the years, people in New Orleans still loved him and cared about him."[30]

But the tours also left Prima depressed: "It used to be more of a relaxed city, you know," he said. "It was smaller and you knew more people then. New Orleans should have stayed the way it was. We had gambling here and New Orleans always had the racing. New Orleans should have become a Las Vegas." Gone from New Orleans now were both of Prima's parents, as well as his former house on St. Peter Street, long since bulldozed over for a

[28]New Orleans *Times-Picayune*, March 11, 1974.

[29]*Ibid.*

[30]Keith Rush interview, April 1986.

public housing project. Even the remnants of Little Palermo were difficult to find—most of the Italian residents of the French Quarter had years ago moved away to other parts of the city, leaving in their place decaying shops and gaudy tourist traps.[31]

But what perhaps bothered Louis the most was a fact he was well aware of all of his adult life, but had somehow overlooked during his sentimental return to the city: New Orleans, the birthplace of jazz, was incapable of supporting its entertainers. "One of the ironic things about our town is that everybody loves jazz," said New Orleans musician Al Hirt, "but to make it big you have to go out of town." Unlike Las Vegas, a top name in New Orleans could not play a long-running engagement at a local club and expect the standing-room-only crowd Louis was long accustomed to in Las Vegas. Other than a few popular, tourist-oriented bars in the French Quarter, entertainment in New Orleans was largely a marginal industry, inhibited by poor promotional methods and suffocated by the limited economics of the city.[32]

After the initial enthusiasm greeting his reappearance in New Orleans, club receipts decreased dramatically during Prima's other engagements in the city. The return home had soured. "This town just can't support an entertainer for long," Prima sadly told Gia. "In that regard, New Orleans hasn't changed at all." Jimmy Vincent said Prima's failure to become a permanent attraction in his hometown bothered him more than he cared to admit. "He was disappointed, sure he was. He wanted to become a local favorite like Al Hirt or Pete Fountain. We ended up doing only two shows a night, down from three. The last show was never anything. There weren't that many people there. The people just didn't support us." Embittered, Prima told Vincent "I don't care who it is, what style it is, your home town never sticks up for you."[33]

By late 1974, Prima reconciled himself to staying in Las Vegas, with occasional concert and club appearances in select cities across the country. Vegas was, after all, his home base for more than two decades, perhaps two of the most financially lucrative decades of his career, despite his decreasing national profile in the 1960s. He was secure in the knowledge that his act

[31]*New Orleans Magazine*, March 1974.

[32]*Ibid.*, August 1986.

[33]Gia Maione interview, July 1986; Jimmy Vincent interview, April 1987.

would still be well-received by the thousands of people everywhere who
continued to listen to his music, the same kind of music that sparked happy
memories of Prima's days in New York, his traveling Big Band in the
1940s, the Italian novelty songs, and his hits with Keely. For proof, all
Prima had to do was go to the large cardboard boxes he kept in his Las
Vegas home which contained the many favorable reviews he continued to
generate from his personal appearances into the mid-1970s. In a time of
generally depleted professional fortunes, particularly on a national scale, the
club reviews were a source of solace. In New Orleans, the *Times-Picayune*
said Prima was a "lively vocalist" who showed "remarkable stamina for a
man who has been around as long as he has." The *States-Item* said Prima's
show was "fun from the start, and the crowd was all with it . . . It was
hilarious and it was warm." *New Orleans Magazine* called Prima's music
"swift and razzle-dazzle . . . It was nice to hear that he has not lost his
touch with his New Orleans training." The *Miami Herald* said Prima was
"simply one of a kind. He tells those awful blue jokes that nobody else
could get away with, but from Prima they are funny. His old-fashioned
finger-snapping moves are outrageously passe, but seem to belong not only
to Prima but everyone else in the room . . . His original style of singing,
which is an American institution all by itself, would be enough, but Prima
also has these funny, wiggly little moves that pre-date Elvis, and that,
intended or not, provide a funny parody of both hipsters and modern
dancers." The *Hollywood Sun-Tattler* in Hollywood, Florida, said Prima's
appearance there was a "whirlwind of a show. The pacing is fantastic, and
Louis Prima sells it with supershowmanship." In May of 1973, the
Philadelphia Inquirer caught Prima's show in that city so long supportive of
his music, and took issue with those critics who attacked Prima for his lack
of artistic integrity: "What is all this crazy talk about art? The hell with
art, whatever art is. The audience has paid to have a good time. This is the
Prima formula. Clearly it works, because the audience has a good time."
One month later the *Pittsburgh Post-Gazette* noted "A lot of people sing
better and there are plenty of more subtly crafted comedy acts. But Prima is
pure fun and demands nothing from his audience except relaxation." In one
of his final appearances in Chicago, in the summer of 1974, the *Chicago*

Tribune said Prima was a "musical clown" with a "hip-twisting style" whose audience "ate up his antics with relish."[34]

With such a mass of positive, supportive clips, Prima could easily bask in the love and affection he still generated into the mid-1970s. But it wasn't enough. Prima still wanted another chance at the national market, that one last hit song that would place high in the charts, the energy that could only be sparked from a million-selling album or chart-busting tune. Toward this end, Prima, in 1973, decided to reunite professionally with Keely. She was the last truly good thing that happened to his career, there *was* a magic when they performed together, and people everywhere still asked him about her. A reunion would bring back the entertainment explosions the duo created in Las Vegas in the 1950s. It was a public relations natural, a human interest story tinged with the kind of corny romantic endings that few Las Vegas groupies could resist. By 1971, Prima was communicating regularly with Keely, the first thaw in their divorce warfare in a decade. "We'll get together again, emphasis the comedy," Prima told Smith when he visited their two daughters. "It could be the best thing for both of us." But Keely, shell-shocked after years of legal battles with Louis and wary of his motives, rejected the offer. "I just did not trust him anymore," said Keely. "I thought he was up to something." The Prima-Smith reunion never materialized, although Keely did appear in the audience during Prima's Harrah's Club opening in Lake Tahoe in November of 1973. Singled out from the stage by Louis and coaxed to sing a song, Keely came forward, easily launched into one of their old hit standards. The audience responded with a hail of applause. People were crying. The old magic was there. Louis was right, it was *still there*. But the moment was too emotional and explosive. As the song ended Prima urged Keely to stay for another, but his former wife and singing partner instead burst into tears and quickly departed.[35]

"It could never be the same again," said Keely, who, after her divorce from Prima went on to record for a number of labels and appeared on many national television shows. Her refusal to rejoin her former husband's act was a final nail in the coffin for his dreams of a national comeback. It had

[34]New Orleans *Times-Picayune*, October 4, 1974; *New Orleans States-Item*, January 17, 1974; *New Orleans Magazine*, March 1974; *Miami Herald*, February 11, 1972; *Hollywood Sun-Tattler*, February 12, 1972; *Philadelphia Inquirer*, May 3, 1973; *Pittsburgh Post-Gazette*, June 4, 1973; *Chicago Tribune*, August 2, 1974.

[35]Keely Smith interview, May 1986; Earl Wilson clipping from Prima files in the William Hogan Ransom Archive of Jazz at Tulane University, New Orleans.

been almost fifteen years since Prima enjoyed a hit song, save the "Jungle Book" disc of 1967. It was a bitter irony that his final opportunity to regroup and attack a much-changed national market in the mid-1970s was foiled by the very singer he molded to professional acclaim in the 1950s. Once again, Louis was reminded of the painful 1961 divorce. Once again, Louis felt himself reaching for something that no longer could be, something that was there once, but had long since disappeared.

Sullen and morose, Prima exploded in a rage of emotions in a letter to long-time associated Barbara Belle in 1973. "I had given Keely *everything*," Prima began, as he complained about his former wife's refusal to give up her share of the lucrative Pretty Acres property. Calling Keely's lawyer a "miserable creep," Louis continued "That idiot really considered me a rank sucker, but then I don't blame him for thinking this after I had given up everything to Keely." Prima explained that all he wanted out of life in his final years was the complete ownership of Pretty Acres so he could

> Make this place into a palace so my children would be proud of me and so that I could, *some time in my life,* have the satisfaction of showing all the people who *put me down* that I wasn't stupid. I would now like to be able to prove to all those idiots that I wasn't a big sucker to give up everything to Keely.

But Louis admitted that Keely no longer trusted him:

> You tell me how honest Keely is and what great feeling she has for me and that she wants to do the right thing. Well, the right thing would be for her to tell me that she will turn the land over to me and let me do what I have planned for her and trust me to do the right thing. I've done the right thing for her, even though everybody put me down for it. But the trouble is, I am not trusted in spite of all this. I have a very strong feeling that Keely (in the back of her mind) thinks I am trying to pull off something.[36]

Keely never gave up the valuable parcels of land to Prima. His failure to convince Keely to rejoin him professionally was bad enough. Now his

---

[36]22nd Judicial District Court for the Parish of St. Tammany, No. 79-025, Division E, *Dorothy Keely Smith* v. *Gia Prima, executrix of the estate of Louis Prima;* letter from Prima to Belle, April 6, 1973.

formerly compliant wife was challenging his essential character, rebuking what seemed to Louis like a good business proposition. The whole thing, Louis complained—the bad feelings, Keely's skeptical behavior, his estrangement from their children—all of it had taken its toll. He was isolated now, unable to reach Keely professionally or personally. Out of reach was the success and trust of another day and time. The sense of failure experienced by a man so accustomed to success must have been daunting. "My heart is broken," was all that Louis would say, adding that "things" were "eating me up inside."[37]

---

[37]*Ibid.*

CHAPTER IX

"I'm Leaving You"

Throughout his lifetime, Louis Prima enjoyed extraordinarily good health. Although he was in a business in which many succumbed to prodigious amounts of eating, drinking, and the use of illegal and even prescribed drugs, Prima stayed far away from such temptations. The reasons for his vigor were many: he was an athlete who enjoyed a wide variety of sports and a dancer who nightly put his body through rigors that men half his age might find difficult to duplicate.

"I played football, basketball, and track at Jesuit High School," Prima once noted in explaining his general healthiness and life-long interest in sports. "And I played polo with the Riveria Club in California . . ." Even as his band travelled the country in the late 1930s and throughout the 1940s, Prima kept up a busy regimen of playing baseball and softball, golfing, and even jogging as a means of recreation. At the age of 49, Prima could boast: "We have a softball team in the band and we play golf whenever we can. I'm in the mid-80s, although I broke 80 occasionally when I was playing regularly."[1]

"He was in excellent condition," said Gia. "He had broad shoulders and a small little waist. Louie was thirty years older than me. When we got married, he was 52 and I was 21. But I never thought about it. It never occurred to me because he was so healthy. There were probably some guys at 21 who couldn't keep up with Louie. He had more spunk and energy and spirit . . . I never thought of age." Joseph Segreto: "He was like a bull. He was a big piece of man. He was athletic all of his life. He wasn't a hypochondriac, but he was extremely concerned about his health. He used to go to the clinic every year and get thoroughly examined. It was an obsession with him. He was very particular about his health."[2]

When Prima took out his famous full-page newspaper ad in the Las Vegas press in 1959 to inform his fans that he was fine after a fainting spell at the Casbar Lounge, Louis also noted that the doctors who treated him at

---

[1] *Buffalo Courier-Express*, March 3, 1950; New Orleans *Times-Picayune*, January 15, 1973.

[2] Gia Maione interview, July 1986; Joseph Segreto interview, October 1986.

the Sansum Clinic were impressed by his vitality: "You have a 100 percent health rating, and your blood pressure, heart and lungs are those of a 16 year-old," Prima said the doctors told him.[3]

Although Prima did smoke an occasional cigar, he rarely drank, leading some members of his band to think he had an aversion to alcohol. "He never drank booze," said his long-time friend and sideman Frank Federico. "I think liquor would make him sick. He stayed away from it." The only real dangers in Prima's everyday life were his continued appearances in smoky bars and clubs lacking in proper ventilation and his horn-playing, which many doctors theorize can cause an undue strain to a musician's respiratory system. To compensate for such occupational hazards, Prima spent most of his free afternoons in Las Vegas exercising, particularly on a bicycle. "I ride a racing bike," Prima said when asked what the secret of his vitality was. "I pedal around Vegas like mad. Keeps my waistline down and puts lots of fresh air into my lungs, which I can use after working in saloons until 4 or 5 a.m."[4]

Nevertheless, in the summer of 1973, Prima suffered a small heart attack while performing "When You're Smiling" at the Mill Run Theatre in Chicago. Significantly, just days before the attack, a reporter for the *Chicago Tribune* caught Prima's show and noted "He . . . seems to have added energy. He and his six instrumentalists go at a crazy pace." Although the heart attacked was characterized as "mild," Prima took it seriously. He took on a regular exercise program that included a vigorous warmup and no less than five miles of aerobic walking. "He was fine after that," Gia recalled. "Except he also, right around then, began to notice that if he would sing a high note, he'd get severe pains in his head. It started to happen more and more often. He even stopped playing the trumpet because if he had to blow, he'd end up with a headache."[5]

Between 1974 and 1975, the same years when Prima attempted to make New Orleans his home base once again, while booking himself, Butera, and the Witnesses on a never-ending tour of club stops across the country, the headaches became a regular occurrence. Prima sought out a number of doctors, but received no immediate satisfaction. Most of the physicians,

---

[3]*Las Vegas Sun*, March 27, 1959; *Variety*, April 15, 1959.

[4]Frank Federico interview, April 1985; *Los Angeles Times*, August 25, 1978.

[5]*Chicago Tribune*, August 10, 1973; Gia Maione interview, July 1986.

after giving Louis a thorough physical and listening to his complaints, found little wrong with the musician. He seemed healthy, his lungs were strong, his heartbeat steady. He practiced healthy habits, stayed away from fatty foods and regularly exercised. The only other alternative, the only remaining possibility, might be that Prima was suffering from something internally. If he was plagued by headaches, perhaps he had a brain tumor, the doctors told him.

This was, naturally enough, horrifying news for Louis. Long paralyzed by the thought of death or prolonged sickness, Prima told Gia he felt compelled to take an electroencephalogram, but dreaded what the results might show. Still, the pain was getting worse. He had headaches now even when he didn't play. "I can't stand it anymore," he told Federico in the summer of 1975. "I have to try something and I don't know what's going to happen. I'm just going to have to go in and give it a try." To brother Leon, Prima confided: "I keep getting these headaches. They are so painful."[6]

When Louis and Gia paid a visit to Leon Prima's home in Diamondhead, Mississippi, that same summer, Leon's wife Madelyn thought Louis looked tired. "He kept falling asleep all of the time," said Madelyn. "He'd sit at the dinner table and fall asleep." But even with this sudden decline in his health, Prima continued to display the carefree, magical manners that made him a national musical favorite. "One night, toward the end, we all went to a club called 'The Yacht Club,' " Madelyn recalled. "Louie got up and danced with Gia, and all of the kids were there, and he was getting his kicks again, making everybody laugh. But when he sat down and wasn't talking to anyone, he fell asleep again." Drummer Jimmy Vincent said he thought Prima's hectic booking of the band in 1974 and 1975 may have been due to his sickness. "Toward the end he was doing stupid things," said Vincent.

> He was booking the band ridiculously. He had us zig-zagging all over the United States. I thought he was crazy. He was doing any job he could get, and accepting any job he could get. I think it was because he was already very sick at that time and just didn't know what he was doing.[7]

[6]Frank Federico interview, April 1985; Leon Prima interview, May 1984.

[7]Madelyn Prima interview, July 1986; Jimmy Vincent interview, April 1987.

Even during a time when health concerns seemed to predominate, Prima was busy with his career. He recorded for Disneyland Records a fantasy album called "Louis Prima Meets Robin Hood," a record that *Footnote Magazine* in the spring of 1975 said

> Was a children's album with the ailing Louis Prima playing not one note, just talking and singing. But nonetheless a pleasant record with Louis' old hit record 'Robin Hood' being redone, the only one which really comes to life with nice playing by Sam Butera.

In April of that year, Prima made an appearance with Frank Sinatra on an Easter Seals Telethon broadcast from the Tropicana in Las Vegas. Looking gaunt and tired, Prima waved to his cheering fans and appeared to greatly enjoy himself for just being there. He also managed to do one more show at the Sands Hotel with Butera and the Witnesses as well as put the final touches on a Prima One Recording called "The Wildest '75." The album, mostly a lounge show regurgitation of familiar Prima ditties like "The Sheik of Araby," "Sing, Sing, Sing," and "That's How Much I Love You, Baby," contained one surprising difference: a teary-eyed ballad called "I'm Leaving You."[8]

The song was a radical departure from the sort of tunes Prima usually recorded. It had no clever lyrics, no silly rhymes, nothing about Italians, not even scat double-talk. Instead it was a simple song telling of a man leaving his love and the second thoughts he experienced as he considered turning back.

It was one of the few ballads Prima recorded throughout his entire career, and his last released single. Although noteworthy because of the change of pace the song afforded Prima, as well as the eerie exactness of the song's title, "I'm Leaving You" was also a sad reminder of Prima's increasingly limited abilities to produce quality recordings. Not only were the background instrumentals both uninspired and bland, but Prima's voice, by 1975, seemed to have lost that fine edge of control he so gleefully exhibited through the years with both his jazz vocals and the more

---

[8]*Footnote Magazine*, April-May, 1975.

commercial Italian novelty tunes. The vocal rasp, which in years past gave Prima a distinctive sound particularly well suited for jazz singing, now seemed to have evolved into a constant harshness of tone making some lyrics unclear and his once-fine voice more jarring than intriguing.

It was a wistful end to a sometimes brilliant recording career. But in 1975, Prima had other matters with which to concern himself, and his dominant thought never strayed from the persistent headaches. His discomfiture was due to meningitis—a tumor of the membrane around the brain. Although this tumor was later revealed to be benign, the doctors who examined Prima discovered the growth originated near the brain stem and as it continued to grow, placed increased pressure on Prima's brain. It was no wonder then why Louis was in such pain. Unfortunately, this particular tumor infiltrated itself into and around the brain stem, making it impossible for all of the growth to be removed, although certainly a portion of the tumor could be cut away. "I met with every surgeon in the UCLA area," said Gia. "And no one would operate on him after they learned what was wrong. The doctors would say 'He's 65, male, Caucasian,' and I'd say, 'And he's got two children and a young wife and everything to live for!" Finally in October of 1975, Prima entered Los Angeles' Mount Sinai Hospital, talking to Las Vegas perennial Chris Fio Rito as the two musicians drove to the hospital about his plans once the operation was over: "I drove Louis to the hospital," said Rito. "All the way there he kept telling me he wanted to come back and open up a night club in Las Vegas. He wanted me to come help him and work with him."[9]

Although doctors were successful in removing a portion of Prima's dreaded tumor, he never regained consciousness. The news stunned family and friends alike. "It was the worst thing he feared," said Gia. "He was worried about the loss of mobility. He just wanted the tumor out of there. But I don't think he had any idea that he wouldn't emerge from the hospital alive or conscious. I know he was never told he could die from such an operation." Instead Louis was hopeful that he would be fully recovered from his operation after a rest of perhaps two months. After that, he thought, life would return to normal. "He'd pre-signed eight week's worth of alimony and child support checks," Gia said. "After that he thought he'd be back to work."[10]

[9] Gia Maione interview, July 1986; *Las Vegas Review-Journal*, August 25, 1978.

[10] Gia Maione interview, July 1986.

It was the beginning of an ordeal for Gia that would last almost three years. The once invincible, always active and electric Louis was now bedridden, disabled and incapable of communication. Such a drastically altered condition naturally brought with it a sense of disbelief. Gia refused to accept Prima's condition as permanent. Friends could not imagine the coma as anything more than a temporary deep sleep.

Four months after the Los Angeles operation, in February 1976, Prima was transferred to the Ochsner Clinic in New Orleans and still later to the Touro Infirmary, also in New Orleans. Morbidly, the press began a death watch for Louis, updating readers on Prima's unchanging condition and reporting the always-upbeat hospital prognosis. "There is little hope for complete recovery," said one such release in late 1977. "But he does respond to the telephone ringing in his room, his eyes open occasionally and he seems to notice activity around him." Federico, his boyhood friend, visited Prima on a daily basis, silently sitting by his bed in the afternoon hours. "I'd play tapes of his music for him," Federico said. "If I held his hand, he might flinch or something, but other than that, there was no response." Prima's last press secretary, Dell Long, confirmed Federico's appraisal. "He's an amazing man," she told the press in the summer of 1978. "He's doing it all on his own. He's never had any life support system, never been aided by any artificial means. He looks like he walked in from the golf course and took a nap." Long also said that when Gia and their children first visited Louis in the early months of his convalescence "He'd hold their hands and squeeze real tight. But for the past six months he hasn't recognized them."[11]

Inevitably the stress on Gia began to tell as month after month wore on. She reacted angrily when columnist Earl Wilson reported Keely Smith was denied the right to visit Louis in his hospital room, and was genuinely exasperated when the *Las Vegas Review-Journal* mistakenly reported Prima's death in the fall of 1976. But the biggest burden on Gia eventually became the enormous weight of the daily financial requirements of Prima's hospital stay. Although most of the medical expenses were covered by Louie's insurance policies, a growing number of unforeseen items were not. Medication had to be purchased, with receipts required for reimbursement. Ochsner Hospital stipulated that all drugs had to be purchased from their

---

[11]Undated clipping, ca. early July 1978, Prima file, William Hogan Ransom Jazz Archive, Tulane University, New Orleans; Frank Federico interview, April 1985; New Orleans *States-Item*, July 6, 1978.

hospital supply, while the Prima family was required to underwrite the costs for three shifts of nurses. In addition, the money that may have been available through a simple liquidation of Prima's assets was out of reach due to a number of lawsuits and divorce settlements, not to mention a thoroughly confusing cast of characters and interests in most of Prima's properties. His Pretty Acres estate in Covington, for example, had parcels of land owned by Gia, Keely Smith, Tracelene Barrett, Leon Prima, and even sister Elizabeth Anne.[12]

As the expenses rose to an average of $7,000 monthly, Gia began a tour of the cafe circuit, starting in February of 1978 at Brooklyn's Copa. But even here, the maze of legal intricacies presented itself. As Gia launched her act, billed as "Gia Prima and the Witnesses," Keely Smith reunited with Sam Butera for a national tour that also included a backup group called "The Witnesses." "I bear no ill feelings toward her," Gia said of Keely. "She is a nice, talented lady. I just wish she'd stop using 'Witnesses' in her act because it's a hassle for me." Gia contended that the title "The Witnesses" belonged to something called "Louis Prima Enterprises." Said Gia: "Nobody else can use it. The name belongs to me."[13]

The fight over who bore title to the Witnesses was just one of the many explosive issues between Gia and Keely. Another struggle concerned who owned what percentage of land at Pretty Acres. Valued at more than $5 million, the Pretty Acres site became a legal battleground in a fight that would last for more than ten years. At issue was not only who owned a controlling percentage of the property, but also who owned the estate's clubhouse, small hotel, and, among other things, the 23 electric golf carts, 14 hand golf carts, 2 lawn mowers, and one tractor that came with Pretty Acres. Things were perhaps made even worse by Prima's confused will and his sometimes contradictory instructions concerning his valuables after his death. In late 1978, attorneys for Prima's four daughters by three of his wives filed suit against the Prima estate, seeking to have Louis' last will invalidated. The daughters claimed Prima was not of a "sound disposing mind and memory" in July 1975 when he wrote out a will excluding three of his six children. What went unsaid, of course, in all the legal

[12]New Orleans *Times-Picayune*, January 26, 1978; *Las Vegas Review-Journal*, October 7, 1976.

[13]Newark, N. J., *Ledger-Star*, February 9, 1978.

maneuverings was that Prima may have left such messy instructions on purpose. Habitually unable to delegate authority, Prima went his own way, slogging year after year through his tangled legal and financial affairs largely because he trusted no one else to sort out such matters for him. Even as he neared death, Prima got his way. No one seemed to know exactly what he was worth or who would get what after he departed, and Louis may have just wanted it that way.[14]

In early July 1978, Prima contracted pneumonia and what hospital officials called "an extremely high fever." Fed through a tube inserted into his mouth and receiving a battery of antibodies to combat his deteriorating condition, Louis was given the last rites from a Catholic priest, but his mighty heart struggled on for six more weeks until Thursday, August 24, when, at 5:20 p.m., Prima at long last died from complications due to his brain stem infarct. Almost thirty-five months after he entered the coma, Louis Prima was finally at rest.

He was initially buried at Greenwood Cemetery on August 26 in a private service. A line of five silver limousines led a slow procession of almost twenty-five vehicles into the burial grounds. Floral arrangements, some in the shape of a trumpet, filled both the funeral home and the plot. Gia and Keely, briefly giving their legal struggles a rest, both attended, as did most of Prima's children from his five marriages. Sam Butera and a host of New Orleans and Las Vegas musicians, along with some of Prima's boyhood pals, stood somberly by as the Rev. Msgr. Harrison A. Martin began a sermon with "Say a little prayer to Almighty God for Louis who brought so much pleasure to so many people."[15]

Prima's death was front page news with the New Orleans *Times-Picayune* and *States-Item*, as well as the *Las Vegas Sun* and the *Las Vegas Review-Journal*. The *New York Times* said Prima was a "corny, clowning entertainer with a blaring trumpet and wild, raucous antics," who, although frequently criticized by jazz purists, was also recognized for his "intricate, fast arrangements and sense of tempo." The Associated Press wire services called Louie's singing voice a "cross between Louis Armstrong and Popeye," while *Variety* said Prima would be remembered as the "Italian Satchmo." The *Los Angeles Times* praised Prima's entertainment as

---

[14]22nd Judicial District Court for the Parish of St. Tammany, No. 79-025, Division E, *Dorothy Keely Smith v. Gia Prima, executrix of the estate of Louis Prima; Las Vegas Review-Journal*, October 7, 8, 1978.

[15]New Orleans *Times-Picayune*, August 25, 1978; *Las Vegas Sun*, August 26, 1978.

"lasagna-flavored bedlam driven across the footlights with unpredictable rapidity and instinctive timing." The *London Times* took note of Prima's singing, which they said "was familiar for its hoarseness." Prima's long-time pal, New Orleans columnist Tommy Griffins, wrote "It's tough to lose a talented friend like Louis Prima, dating back to when we were in Jesuit High together in the '20s, but perhaps it was a blessing for him to die after three years in a coma . . ." The *Italian-American Digest*, in a special issue devoted to Prima, said "Prima's emotions found release in his performances which created an aura of happiness and his life was a continuous series of encores as he entertained and enraptured audiences across our nation. He made music a lot of fun and brought a new dimension to the entertainment world, mirth mixed melodies, a singular style and showmanship . . . He had magical inspirational power with his musicians and an abiding self-confidence that was reflected in the originality of his presentations."[16]

Radio stations in New York City, New Orleans, Las Vegas, and Philadelphia played day-long tributes to Prima. Reporters sought out family members, friends, and business associates who could perhaps explain the enigma of Louis Prima. Inevitably the memories were sweet and humorous, stories that recalled Prima's bizarre comedy and finger-snapping music. Benny Goodman, who played late night sessions with Prima in New York in the 1930s, noted "Gene [Krupa] wasn't the first guy to mix fine musical ability with showmanship . . . Louis was." In Las Vegas, comedian Shecky Greene called Prima "an original, no one has ever been like him, nor will anyone be like him in the future." In New Orleans, clarinetist Pete Fountain, admitting that as a youngster he idolized Prima, said "I think Louis taught a lot of people showmanship. I think he was one of the best entertainers who ever came out of New Orleans."[17]

Not all the tributes, however, came on that sad, hot summer's day in August 1978. Prima's legacy, indeed, seemed to grow in the years following his death. In 1980, the City of New Orleans named two residential streets in suburban New Orleans East after Prima. The following year, the city joined in a co-sponsorship with the Italian-American Federation of New Orleans in paying a day-long tribute to Louis

---

[16]*New York Times* autobiographical service, August 25, 1978; *Variety*, August 25, 1978; *Lost Angeles Times*, August 25, 1978; *London Times*, August 26, 1978; *Figaro*, September 6, 1978; *Italian-American Digest*, (Fall, 1978).

[17]Record notes, "Louis Prima and His Orchestra," by John L. Escalante, Sunbeam Records, Inc., Van Nuys, California, 1979; *Las Vegas Sun*, August 25, 1978; New Orleans *States-Item*, August 25, 1978.

at the city's Piazza d'Italia. The Rev. Vincent Verderame inaugurated the program by noting that Prima's life was an example of "the outpouring of love in its truest sense." In 1983, New Orleans' Public Broadcasting System affiliate, WYES-12, aired an hour-long documentary on Prima called *The Chief.* The show won high praise from critics and viewers alike with *Times-Picayune* columnist David Cuthbert summing up Prima thus: "He played the trumpet and sang. His specialty was fast, jazzed up renditions of popular songs, coupled with increasingly broad clowning. He was written off by jazz scholars as an entertainer rather than a musician and he did indeed pander to his public with a passion. He craved success and found it and lost it and reclaimed it again. He was both a savvy showman and a fool who allowed the 'hottest attraction in show business' to break up." Besides presenting one of the best film collages of Prima's career, *The Chief* also revealed publicly that Sonny and Cher, a very popular rock-singing duo in the 1960s, developed their styles by copying Louis and Keely.[18]

In 1984, the Disney studios re-released *The Jungle Book,* once again with Prima as King Louie, and watched the film garner an astonishing $15 million in box office sales in less than three months. The following year, Prima's name was summoned forth again when rock star David Lee Roth duplicated Prima's 1956 hit "Just A Gigolo" on record and video, later announcing he liked Prima's music because Prima's personality "comes out in the music. What I hear coming out in his music is a combination of maitre d', storyteller . . . the toast-master general." Roth's hit version of "Just A Gigolo," prompted a 1986 repackaging of several of the more raucous Prima, Smith, and Butera rock n' roll songs of the late 1950s, causing a whole new generational wave of critical acclaim: "Rock n' roll? Louis Prima?" music critic Art Fein asked in the summer of 1986. "Many minds boggle at this association because the Prima legacy is best described by this common response to mention of his name: 'Louis Prima? My parents bought his records.' " Fein continued: "Indeed, Prima's chosen home base of Las Vegas, and his widespread TV exposure on such family fare programs as the 'Ed Sullivan Show' caused a whole generation of 'Baby Boomers' to miss the message: Louis Prima and his band were blasting out *rock n' roll!*" Fein added that Prima's adult fans missed the message also: "They were rocking at 4 a.m. to a crazy, gravel-voice singer leading a

[18]*Polk's New Orleans City Directory, 1981* (New Orleans, 1981), p. 310; *Saluto! Louis Prima* (New Orleans, 1981), p. 3; New Orleans *Times-Picayune,* May 15, 1983; J. Randy Taraborrelli, *Cher* (New York, 1986), pp. 126-127.

howling sax, stand-up bass, crushing drum rock n' roll band *without ever knowing it . . .*" Andy Warhol's chic magazine *Interview* agreed, noting in a November 1986 issue that "Rock n' roll history has neglected to mention that Louis was one of the founding fathers. He was a New Orleans jazzman who helped shift the ears' gears from swing to jump to rock n' roll. He was an Italian guy who mixed in old-country expressions with his wild scat singing. His compositions were covered by great black R & B artists, and his wild sax section brought the honking style to swingers of all nationalities, socioeconomic profiles, and hair styles."   When Keely returned to recording for Fantasy Records in 1986, she issued a press release stating "If it weren't for Louis, there would be no Keely Smith, and even more important, he's the father of my two fantastic daughters. I'm grateful for it all." Butera, too, frequently honored Prima, perhaps most eloquently in his music. When Butera and Keely played a number of spots together, the tribute to Prima was even greater. Reporting on one such concert, *Variety* commented: "Hovering over everything is the Prima influence and both Smith and Butera frankly make obeisance to it."[19]

It may have been Gia, however, who engineered the most poignant tribute to Louis. In 1981 she moved his casket to a stately grey-marble crypt in the Metairie Cemetery just outside of New Orleans. It turned out to be a perfect, highly symbolic, location. His ethnicity is remembered because Prima's crypt is located in the same cemetery block as the grand mausoleum for members of the Societa Di Beneficenza-Contessa Entellina and the Societa Christoford Columbo. His love of horses comes to mind because the cemetery is the former site of the Metairie Race Course and Prima's tomb stands where there once was a regulation one-mile race track. But most importantly, Prima's music, indeed his very essence, lives again in the words engraved on his marble tombstone:[20]

Louis Prima
December 7, 1910-August 24, 1978
A Legend.

[19]Richard Schickel, *The Disney Version: The Life, Times, Art, and Commerce of Walt Disney* (New York, 1985), p. 374; *Rolling Stone*, April 11, 1985; *Gambit*, March 14, 1987; Record notes by Art Fein, "Zooma Zooma—The Best of Louis Prima," Rhino Records, Hollywood, California, July 1986; Interview, November 18, 1986; Fantasy press release for Keely Smith, spring 1986; *Variety*, October 22, 26, 1977; December 21, 1977.

[20]Henri Gandolfo, *Metairie Cemetery: An Historical Memoir* (New Orleans, 1978), pp. 11-15, 79; Gia Maione interview, July 1986.

When The End Comes,
I Know,
They'll Say
"Just A Gigolo,"
As Life Goes On
Without Me.

CHAPTER X

The Essence of the Gigolo

Spontaneous responses to Louis Prima among critics and fans invariably prompt widely disparate emotions. Longtime fans and concert-goers immediately smile when Prima's name is mentioned, but the serious jazz critics, perhaps envisioning Louie's unconvincing toupee, bright clothes, and Las Vegas antics, sniff and dismiss him as a minimal influence in the development of Twentieth Century jazz in America.

The respected *New York Times* music critic John Wilson has called Prima a "third-rate Louis Armstrong." Said Wilson: "He was slightly a jazz musician in his early period. He was trying to play Louie Armstrong style, but every trumpeteer in that period was trying to play like Armstrong. And they all seemed to have exactly the same throat infections. They had gravel in it somehow or other . . . the weather in New Orleans must have been terrible."[1]

Throughout his long career, as Prima grew further away from the respected jazz abilities he displayed during his Famous Door days in New York, critics increasingly pointed out that Louie's music was geared more for the masses, rather than true jazz aficionados. Prima was no longer playing swing or hot jazz, they said, but simply putting together songs that would sell well and place respectably on the popular charts. This made Prima an "entertainer," a lower form of musician and one less relevant to the history of jazz.

Throughout these criticisms lies a vein of implied sin—because Prima was no longer playing pure jazz, he had sold out; because he sold out, he was no longer a respected musician capable of integrated jazz, tricky fingering techniques, or stylistic ability.

Certainly, as one listens to some of his more successful records from the big band days of the 1940s and the Keely-Louis era of the late 1950s and early 1960s, it would be hard to argue that Prima should share the same artistic laurels bestowed on such jazz legends as Armstrong, Benny Goodman, and Duke Ellington. But one of the greatest critical oversights in examining Prima's music is a misunderstanding of Louie's motives. Many

---

[1]John Wilson interview, July 1986.

174

scholars believe Prima made a conscious decision one day to simply "sell out." It was easier, once he understood the vagaries of the national music market, for Prima to produce tunes that might sell thousands of records across the country, rather than sit down with the likes of his former sideman George Brunis, Pee Wee Russell, or Claude Thornhill and create hot jazz works that might glow for decades thereafter.

Such observations lack a fundamental insight into the essence of Prima's personality. For Louis, like his hero Louis Armstrong, music was simply a means of conveying a joyful spirit, of interpreting a comic soul.

It's important to remember Prima's New Orleans background in the evolution of his musical career. As a boy, Prima witnessed some of the finest jazz innovators, men whom historians now recognize as brilliant musicians in their artistic, yet primitive, field. He saw these musicians play on street corners, in pubs, and on the back of flat bed trailers. They were a part of everyday life in New Orleans, a fact Prima alluded to when he once commented "I think I learned to swing before I learned to talk." He added that this pervasive music heard throughout the city had no particular title: "In those days there was no such word as 'swing.' We called it 'hot jazz' or 'Dixieland' or 'gutbucket' . . . No band ever played sweet or romantic. It was strictly hot or gutbucket." Whatever it went by, this music was also a supply far exceeding demand. There were hundreds of excellent musicians playing all sorts of wonderful jazz in Prima's youth, but few found steady work as musicians. Perhaps because of this, New Orleans musicians tended to be a highly critical and judgmental lot when it came to evaluating one another. It soon became obvious to this select group that a musician needed more than just playing prowess to find work and acclaim. A truly successful musician in New Orleans was also one who could project or "reach out" to an audience long used to hearing the finest raw jazz in America. The emphasis was on "connecting" with the audience as an entertainer.[2]

The great Satchmo, who was trained and influenced by the same musical trends as Prima, embodied this same proclivity toward entertaining his audience first, damn the critics. "I don't see why I should tax myself worrying about some son of a bitch who doesn't even know one note for another, telling you how to blow your horn," Armstrong said of the critics who charged him with being too commercial and playing to his audience,

---

[2]*New York Post*, March 30, 1938.

rather than creating good jazz. For Armstrong, as well as Prima, success was not measured by the glowing adoration flowing from a critic's pen, but rather by the applause he heard from his audience. That was how it was done in New Orleans. Fulfillment for musicians like Armstrong and Prima was found in the smiles and warm responses of audience members who left their shows feeling entertained. It was no wonder then that both Armstrong and Prima were bewildered by the cool styles of Bebop and progressive jazz which seemed to disdain "entertaining."[3]

The critical disregard for Prima started almost immediately after he left the Famous Door in New York in 1935. From then on reviewers tended to pay more attention to Prima's stage antics which they criticized him for, while generally ignoring the applause that beckoned Louis to return for song after song. This haughty approach embodied by the critics bothered Prima throughout his career. But, characteristically, he seemed to go out of his way to validate such complaints, putting an even greater emphasis on entertainment, telling more off-color jokes, dancing throughout his concerts, and even requiring his sidemen to wear ridiculous costumes. Thus to Prima was given the degrading appellation of "entertainer," as though in jazz circles it were an unforgivable sin.

But it was as an entertainer that Prima perfected his form and gradually rose from the ranks of the dozens of Big Band leaders who travelled the country and simply re-created their studio sessions on stage. For recognized artists such as Goodman or Ellington, music was the only component of a concert appearance. For Prima, music was just one means of conveying his message to the audience. Between songs were the rambling folk tales, giddy footwork, and self-deprecating humor that invariably resulted in audience approval.

Prima's form in countless shows is better examined away from what is or is not legitimate jazz, and in the rich tradition of the travelling troubadours and minstrels of old. It is in this guise, finally, that Prima's contribution to the entertainment industry is clear and unmistakable. Connected to the legacy of the colorful and tireless vaudevillian, Prima encompassed all of the light entertainment art of that genre, including pantomime, dialogue, light musical drama, and comic relief. As a vaudevillian, Prima was at home in bawdy theatre shows that usually included magicians, comedians, animal acts, jugglers, singers, and dancers.

[3]Chris Albertson, *Louis Armstrong* (Alexandria, Va., 1978), p. 27.

Although official vaudeville suffered its final financial reverses in the post-World War II era of television, entertainers like Prima, Jimmy Durante, Sophie Tucker, Milton Berle, and Al Jolson kept the form alive up into the late 1950s at least. These were entertainers who mostly earned their keep by the immediate response of the audience. Unable and unwilling to seek refuge in set musical programs, these performers tailored their talents to the wiles of the paying public. In his book on American vaudeville, Albert F. McLean, Jr., writes:

> It was the essence of show business during the vaudeville era that popular taste had to be sought out and catered to, that offense be given to no one and satisfaction to the greatest number. As a ritual, vaudeville could delve beneath conscious prejudices and deal directly with the encounter of the moment, always seeking the subject matter of maximum pertinence to its audience.

The key, however, was the "encounter of the moment," something that McLean explained was comprised of the "Intimate contact between performer and his audience at the moment of presentation."[4]

By description and design, Prima was one of the last of the great vaudevillians, a talent he carried with him throughout his career, even when performing for the hip Las Vegas crowds of the 1950s and '60s. This vaudevillian emphasis on performing must first be recognized before Prima's music can be properly appreciated. Prima was a performer first and a musician second. But, conversely, it was as a performer that Louis' music emerged in its own peculiar art form.

Columnist Larry Kent once wrote in the *Chicago Tribune* that a basic artistic chasm existed between the musical talents of performers in the Beatles era, and those who sang the works of George Gershwin, Jerome Kern, and Cole Porter in the decades before the 1960s. "The problem is we're stuck with two different notions of naturalness," Kent explains, "one that takes off from human behavior as we normally experience it and one that believes there is a deeper, 'truer' nature that is at odds with the habits of human life." Kent suggested that if one followed the first path "the patterns of normal speech and singers who interpret them that way" would be found. But the second path, the path rock n' rollers took, presented "songs and

---

[4]Albert F. McLean, Jr., *American Vaudeville As Ritual* (Lexington, Ky., 1965), pp. 4-5.

singers who not only feel free to shout, mutter, swoon, and groan, but also tend to twist words this way and that to fit a rhythm or melodic design." It is interesting to note that Prima easily travelled both paths, he was that versatile. He could be a sensitive interpreter of a jazz tune, singing as a jazz male vocalist such as Armstrong might, or he could shout and groan with the best of the rock belters who dominated another age in music.[5]

Again, this musical versatility stemmed not so much from Prima's musical abilities (although they were vast) as from his intuitions as a performer. Like the vaudevillian, Prima developed a skill in rapidly alternating musical styles to suit both his audience and the feel of a show. Columnists and critics frequently expressed surprise over this talent, but it was the wise observer who even noted such an ability in the first place. For most audience members, Prima's transition between jazz innovator and rock shouter was so subtle as to be unnoticed. It was the stuff of pure entertainment, nurtured by years of toil and obsessive drive to understand the desires and demands of his audience.

Prima once explained this ability to a reporter in Las Vegas. He claimed that he could pick any member of an audience and decipher on the spot what type of music that person most enjoyed. "See that lady there?" Prima asked the journalist. "She likes waltzes." Pointing to a man wearing a sporty shirt, Prima confidently declared: "Long-hair [classical music] and maybe jazz too." The reporter refused to believe Prima. How could he know such things? But after seeking the two people out who both, amazingly, confirmed Prima's assessments, he heard Louis explain "Everybody knows their business, don't they? Why shouldn't I know mine?"[6]

Prima clearly did know his business, thus explaining why he could, all in the space of one career, play gutbucket blues for New Orleanians, hot jazz for trendy New Yorkers, silly Italian novelty tunes for big-city fans, and raucous rock n' roll for the red-eyed gamblers in Las Vegas in the 1950s and '60s. He played for the audience, wherever and whoever they may be. And this talent lasted, to a lesser degree, until his dying day. In 1968, for example, at the height of the acid rock movement in San Francisco, Prima, Butera and the Witnesses arrived in that city for a stay at a club called

[5]New Orleans *Times-Picayune*, December 6, 1985.

[6]*Pageant*, undated clipping, ca. 1960.

Bimbo's. The appearance had the makings of a disaster. This was, after all, the city that gave birth to the counter-culture movement. Drugs, revolution, and the likes of Janis Joplin and Jimi Hendrix predominated. Even worse, Ralph Gleason, the leftist musical critic for the *San Francisco Chronicle*, was planning to take in the Prima show in what promised to be a scathing indictment of Prima's Las Vegas antics and musical style. But on the night Gleason arrived at Bimbo's he was surprised to find a packed house of cool San Franciscans grooving to Butera's honking sax and Prima's Italian scat. Gleason, who could sometimes be acerbic in his reviews, saluted Prima the next day, calling him an "excellent example of a popular entertainer coming out of the jazz world." He said

> Prima looks like a headwaiter gone mad as he twists and writhes and conducts the band. But he obviously has a good time and he's a good dancer and the band is a first class professional unit with real class . . . I was surprised—though I should not have been— that they were so good musically. The comedy is straight-out night club least common denominator bad jokes and visual gags, but the people laugh. It's kind of an essay in how to make money and still be musically interesting and it succeeds because it is entertaining.[7]

Again, Prima knew his business, and the business on that fall night in 1968 San Francisco was to entertain.

What is harder to reconcile in the life of Louis Prima was his stage personae versus the private self. Like all public persons, Prima was scrutinized for clues of what he was really like on a one-to-one basis. Many times he was found wanting. A certain mean, vindictive theme emerges again and again in Prima's dealings with business associates, personal friends and lovers. Rumors concerning his ruthless ways with women, women who willingly threw themselves at him in degrading ways, are told again and again. After awhile, such tales seem less like individual incidents and more like the manifestation of a basic character flaw on the part of Prima.

How true any of these tales are can never be known. What is certain is Prima lived in a fast lane and thrived in a business known for bringing out

---

[7] *San Francisco Chronicle*, September 9, 1968.

the worst in even the most noble souls. His womanizing and frequent clashes with associates, songwriters, and theatrical agents, present us with a profile of a restless, energetic man determined to get what he wanted, damned the consequences.

Perhaps some of Prima's actions could be attributed to the sense of security he found with his mother, Angelina, who supported him in every cause and sometimes even conspired with him against his wives. "A man who has been the indisputable favorite of his mother keeps for life the feeling of a conqueror, that confidence of success that often induces real success," Freud once wrote. In Prima's case, Angelina believed her son could do no wrong. When he was involved in a business dispute or a romantic relationship that may have been ethically questionable, Louis only had to turn to his mother and other members of his family for comfort, attention, support, and solace. "He was always the center of attention at family gatherings," Leon remembered. Leon's wife Madelyn remembered how members of the Prima family spent most of their recreational hours in the basement of the large Canal Boulevard home in New Orleans Louis purchased for his parents in the late 1930s. "We were always in the basement . . . until Louie came home," said Madelyn. "Then we all went upstairs. We would go into the dining room, get out the good silver and everything . . . Louis was kind of demanding."[8]

Obviously Prima was a supreme egotist, generally accustomed to getting his way, and an extremely difficult person to be around when he did not. But what is more important is how little of an impact his private life had on his public career, with the noted exception of his divorce from Keely severely crippling his professional options after 1961. Prima had his failings, to be sure, and columnists loved to point them out, but while such negative traits may have made good copy, what ultimately endures is the public creations left by the artist.   Thus, while we may be bothered by Elvis Presley's inclination toward drug abuse or Marilyn Monroe's self-defeating and suicidal romantic involvements, what really endures is the nature of their art. Presley songs and Monroe movies will be remembered and enjoyed decades after their personality traits are forgotten. So it is that with Prima, music fans will latch onto his extraordinary abilities to make people laugh, tap their feet and feel good. In the context of entertainment, Prima fulfilled his obligation as a performer. He never shattered the art of

---

[8]Leon Prima interview, May 1984; Madelyn Prima interview, July 1986.

illusion, but presented in show after show for almost fifty years the gay troubadour who was there to help us forget our troubles and sadnesses. His 1940s slogan "Play It Pretty for the People" seems dated and ridiculous from the context of several decades later, but the message behind the theme was true to form. Prima did, in fact, play it pretty. Each song was a story, each show a separate entity, each audience member an individual with particular tastes and preferences. And because of his overwhelming drive to entertain us, to make us laugh and dance, Prima survives in many memories as a mysterious person. Everyone seems to know what he did for a living, but no one could define the *real* Prima. He was a singer, a musician, a band leader, a comedian, and a dancer. But who, really was he? In 1975, George Simon, a long-time Prima fan and former music critic for *Metronome*, tried to answer that question. "One of Prima's primary charms was that 'I'm-having-a-lot-of-fun-doing-this-crazy-stuff-but-maybe-underneath-it-all-you'll-take-my-music-a-little-seriously approach,' Simon wrote. "He made it plain that he was kidding when he sang his light, swinging versions of the ballads—some of them quite sentimental and even morbid—and yet when he was finished you had the feeling that maybe there was a bit of the 'Laugh, clown, laugh' longing welling there beneath the musical facade."[9]

Simon added that Prima's hit song "Just A Gigolo," underlined the confusion over who the real Louis was in people's minds. Historically the tune was a "wailful lament" heard from a singer trapped by his romantic lot in life. "Its melodramatic message was emoted in vaudeville houses and on radio programs throughout the English-speaking world," Simon noted. "And then the song languished . . . But along in the forties came Louis and his new approach. His band laid down a swinging, shuffle beat for its leader to tell the world how it felt to be a kept man." According to the song's tradition, the gigolo felt trapped, he hated his existence, and knew people would look down upon him long after he was gone. But Prima added a new possibility to the gigolo's life—he seemed to actually enjoy it. "He did it so delightfully that you couldn't possibly imagine that he meant it," Simon said of Prima's lament. "And yet, when it was all over, you began to wonder: Did he or didn't he."[10]

---

[9] George Simon, *The Big Band Songbooks* (New York, 1975), p. 175.

[10] *Ibid*

Prima never provided a suitable reply, so the question goes unanswered. But Simon was on target when he suggested that Prima wanted to be taken seriously. He was, after all, an entertainer with superior ability and a musician par excellence. Show after show, record after record, Prima provided America with jazz, jump, swing, and rock n' roll in its most raw uninhibited form. Within this narrow, yet diverse, genre, Prima reigned supreme, his peculiar and distinct style forever enduring in a popular culture accustomed to digesting and discarding every musical trend. In the contest of American popular music in the Twentieth Century, such songs as "Angelina," "Felicia No Capricia," and "Just A Gigolo," may never be sanctified as classic recordings equalling Armstrong's "Black and Blue," Billie Holiday's "God Bless the Child," or Duke Ellington's "Satin Doll." But they will always be remembered as a cheerful, whimsical musical form that instinctively made people smile.

"Historians in the future will congratulate us on very little other than our clowning and our jazz," writer Kurt Vonnegut has said. If Vonnegut is right, Louis Prima should be remembered as an entertainment giant.

Music in American Life

The University of Illinois Press
is a founding member of the
Association of American University Presses.

University of Illinois Press
1325 South Oak Street
Champaign, IL 61820-6903
www.press.uillinois.edu